P9-DTV-303

WITHDRAWN
UTSA Libraries

RENEWALS 458-4574

Acute Stress Disorder

Acute Stress Disorder

A HANDBOOK OF THEORY, ASSESSMENT, AND TREATMENT

Richard A. Bryant
and Allison G. Harvey

AMERICAN PSYCHOLOGICAL ASSOCIATION
WASHINGTON, DC

Copyright © 2000 by the American Psychological Association. All rights reserved. Except as permitted under the United States Copyright Act of 1976, no part of this publication may be reproduced or distributed in any form or by any means, or stored in a database or retrieval system, without the prior written permission of the publisher.

First printing November 1999
Second printing March 2002

Published by
American Psychological Association
750 First Street, NE
Washington, DC 20002

Copies may be ordered from
APA Order Department
P.O. Box 92984
Washington, DC 20090-2984

In the U.K., Europe, Africa, and the Middle East, copies may be ordered from
American Psychological Association
3 Henrietta Street
Covent Garden, London
WC2E 8LU England

Typeset in Goudy by EPS Group Inc., Easton, MD

Printer: Automated Graphic Systems, White Plains, MD
Jacket Designer: Berg Design, Albany, NY
Technical/Production Editor: Eleanor Inskip

Library of Congress Cataloging-in-Publication Data
Bryant, Richard A., 1960–
    Acute stress disorder : a handbook of theory, assessment, and treatment /
by Richard A. Bryant and Allison G. Harvey.
        p.   cm.
    Includes bibliographical references and index.
    ISBN 1-55798-612-6 (cloth)
    1. Post-traumatic stress disorder—Handbooks, manuals, etc.   2. Psychic
trauma—Handbooks, manuals, etc.   I. Harvey, Allison G., 1968.   II. Title.

RC552.P67 B79 1999
616.85'21—dc21

                                                                99-044989

British Library Cataloguing-in-Publication Data
A CIP record is available from the British Library.

Printed in the United States of America

Library
University of Texas
at San Antonio

To my loving wife, Anna
—RAB

To my parents, Janet and Ian Harvey
—AGH

CONTENTS

PREFACE

In the past 20 years, there has been an explosion of interest in the longer term effects of traumatic experiences. Since the introduction of posttraumatic stress disorder (PTSD) as a formal diagnosis in 1980, researchers and practitioners have focused unprecedented attention on the persistent psychological effects of trauma. Although our understanding of PTSD has developed impressively in recent times, there has been a relative neglect of the psychological reactions that occur in the acute trauma phase. Although many writers have recognized that acute reactions of survivors of assaults, motor vehicle accidents, and natural disasters may lay the foundation for longer term posttraumatic adjustment, researchers have largely ignored this critical period. Further, even though it is common practice for practitioners to provide a range of interventions in the initial aftermath of a trauma, this activity is typically undertaken with little empirical basis.

The introduction of acute stress disorder (ASD) as a formal diagnosis in 1994 has brought a structure to the definition of acute trauma reactions. This diagnosis now permits the scientific community to investigate acute trauma responses in a standardized way that was not previously possible. As a result, investigators are now turning their attention to theoretical and clinical features of acute trauma response and how they relate to longer term posttraumatic adjustment. In the few years that have passed since the introduction of ASD, we now have the beginnings of an empirically based understanding of how to conceptualize, assess, and treat acute trauma reactions.

We first developed a strong interest in acute stress reactions while working as clinical psychologists in a large trauma hospital. Each day we were asked to assist survivors of a range of traumatic experiences, including motor vehicle accidents, assaults, rapes, industrial accidents, and natural disasters. We were frequently struck by two issues: the minimal knowledge base on acute trauma reactions to guide our work and the difficulties in treating many patients who presented with chronic PTSD months or years after their trauma. Their complex comorbidity, pervasive avoidance behaviors, and resistance to participate in therapy impaired many of our efforts to provide effective therapy. In contrast, we noted the benefits of being able to commence therapy soon after the traumatic experience and before the traumatic response became more entrenched. Patients' motivation and willingness to overcome avoidance tendencies allowed us to work more effectively in assisting resolution of the recent traumatic experience. This stark difference between working with acutely and chronically traumatized individuals made us aware of the need to better understand the mechanisms that mediate the transition from acute stress response to trauma resolution. A key impetus in this search was to replace the folk wisdom that was commonplace among our colleagues with evidence-based strategies that would assist people who are at risk of developing PTSD.

Our awareness of the potential benefits of early intervention was highlighted by one memorable case that greatly influenced our approach. Two women, who had been savagely beaten by a gang of men 2 weeks earlier, were referred to us by nursing staff. These women were twin sisters who had been subjected to a terrifying, protracted attack that involved repeated stabbing, punching, kicking, and rape. From police reports, it appeared that they had been exposed to virtually identical threats throughout the ordeal. When both women were assessed, it appeared that they were comparably symptomatic. Both women were suffering distressing memories and nightmares, were showing dissociative responses, and were avoiding all reminders of the experience. Most notably, both were unable to recall the anal penetration to which they had been subjected. Both patients felt emotionally cutoff from the events that had transpired since the attack. Before we could commence treatment, however, one of the women left the city because she and her husband felt they needed a new start. They supposed that moving to a new city would be the best and quickest therapy. The woman who remained accepted our offer of treatment. Although she found treatment very distressing, she showed marked reductions in her distress and symptoms in the weeks following. Seven months later, we were contacted by the other twin sister. Sadly, she reported that the previous 7 months had been characterized by persistent symptoms and inability to resume daily functioning. She presented to us with severe PTSD, major depression, and a strong dependence on alcohol. Although we immediately commenced therapy, treating this woman proved to be very difficult because she had developed entrenched avoidance patterns. Any attempts to engage her with memories or reminders of the assault were thwarted by her impulse to avoid the painful memories of being assaulted. At the 2-year point, the difference between the two women in terms of functioning was stark. The woman we started treating within 2 weeks of the trauma was functioning in a very healthy manner. Unfortunately, her sister was still suffering from posttrauma symptoms and had developed a range of adjustment problems that were compounding her condition. Although this isolated case does not provide any definitive conclusions about acute interventions, it had a significant influence on our desire to understand and manage acute trauma reactions. The fact that two people who share the same genetic profile responded so differently to their traumatic experiences led us to ask the question, What would have happened if we had treated both women in the acute phase? Although we will never know the answer to that question, it is reasonable to say that much of our research has been motivated by our attempt to answer it.

This book aims to provide a comprehensive handbook of ASD, traversing the theoretical and empirical bases of the disorder and providing guidelines for its assessment and treatment. It is designed to combine the rigor of empirically based research with a strong applied focus, which we hope will provide practitioners with the skills and knowledge to confidently work with a range of acutely traumatized individuals. Throughout this book, we base our guidelines on our experiences with a range of trauma survivors, including victims of assaults, rape, motor vehicle accidents, combat, industrial accidents, and natural disasters. Part I contains a descriptive overview of ASD in terms of its historical antecedents and the assumptions underpinning its current description. Theoretical perspectives on ASD, including the dissociative, cognitive, and biological approaches, are described, and the empirical evidence for each is reviewed. Part II is devoted to the assessment of ASD and contains detailed descriptions of the means available to assess ASD. Part III begins by reviewing treatments of posttraumatic stress and outlines the treatments of choice for ASD. Practical guidelines for treating ASD are then described. In Part IV, we address clinical issues that are particularly relevant to ASD. Specifically, ASD in different trauma populations, the distinction between ASD and critical incident stress, and legal issues are discussed.

We emphasize that knowledge about ASD is in its infancy, and many of the widely held beliefs about acute trauma responses are not empirically based. Our goal is to develop more effective and appropriate assistance to those who have recently suffered trauma. To this end, as clinicians, we have a responsibility to strive for a scientifically based framework for understanding, assessing, and treating acutely traumatized individuals. It is our hope that this volume will contribute to this pursuit.

ACKNOWLEDGMENTS

We are grateful to many people who have assisted in the research program that has culminated in this volume. We thank Suzanne Dang, Tanya Sackville, Chris Basten, Gladiss Warda, Rachel Guthrie, and Michelle Moulds for their clinical assistance. Our thanks are extended to Ed Blanchard, Etzel Cardeña, Terence Keane, Roger Pitman, and David Spiegel for their expert advice in developing our assessment instruments. This book was written while Richard A. Bryant was a visiting scholar in the Department of Psychology, Harvard University. During that period, Rich McNally's enthusiasm for a science-based understanding of acute stress disorder was a refreshing source of support. Most important, we are deeply grateful to all the acutely traumatized people who shared with us their difficulties and taught us so many poignant lessons.

I

THEORETICAL AND
EMPIRICAL ISSUES

1

THE EMERGENCE OF ACUTE STRESS DISORDER

The psychological problems that arise from extreme trauma have been documented in literature since the time of Homer (Alford, 1992). The early writings have described the anguish caused by distressing memories and elevated anxiety in a wide range of trauma survivors. Despite this awareness of the psychological aftermath of trauma, our understanding of posttrauma reactions has varied considerably over the years. Interestingly, the conceptualization of trauma response has often been influenced by the social and ideological movements of the day. For example, in the 19th century, there was considerable debate over the functional or organic bases of *traumatic neurosis* or *railway spine*. In keeping with prevalent schools of thought at the time, some theorists argued that such reactions resulted from molecular changes in the central nervous system (Oppenheim, 1889), whereas others held that they were a function of anxiety (Page, 1895). Some years later, the diagnosis of shell shock became fashionable (Mott, 1919) because ascribing stress reactions to organic factors permitted an acceptable attribution for poor military performance (van der Kolk, 1996a). Similarly, we need to understand the current conceptualization of acute stress disorder (ASD) in the context of popular ideological developments in modern psychiatry.

One of the most influential developments in the current conceptualization of ASD was the work conducted at the Salpêtrière in Paris. Although this school of thought commenced 100 years ago, its powerful influence on modern psychiatry has only occurred in the last 20 years. This early theorizing represents the precursor of current proposals of trauma-induced dissociation (Nemiah, 1989; van der Kolk & van der Hart, 1989). Charcot (1887) proposed that traumatic shock could evoke responses that were phenomenologically similar to hypnotic states. Charcot held that overwhelmingly aversive experiences led to a dissociation that involved processes observed in both hysteria and hypnosis. Janet (1907) continued this perspective by arguing that trauma that was incongruent with existing cognitive schema led to dissociated awareness. Janet believed that by splitting off traumatic memories from awareness, individuals could minimize their discomfort. The price for this dissociation, however, was a loss in psychological functioning because mental resources were not available for other processes. Accordingly, Janet argued that adaptation to a traumatic event involved integrating the fragmented memories into awareness. Despite the immediate influence on his contemporaries, Janet's influence was short-lived until the renaissance of dissociation in the 1980s. Indeed, it was these early theorists who provided the basic rationale for the present diagnosis of ASD.

Increased interest in acute stress reactions developed during the 20th century as a result of both wartime and civilian traumas. In one of the earliest studies of acute stress, Lindemann (1944) documented the acute reactions of survivors of the Coconut Grove fire in Boston in 1942. He observed that the acute symptoms reported by survivors included avoidance of "the intense distress connected to the grief experience . . . , the expression of emotion . . . disturbed pictures . . . a sense of unreality . . . increased emotional distance from other people . . . and waves of discomfort" (pp. 141–143). In general, however, much of the early interest in acute traumatic stress reactions came from military sources. Acute stress reactions were reportedly common in troops from both World War I and World War II (Kardiner, 1941; Kardiner & Spiegel, 1947). The acute psychological aftermath of battle, subsequently known as *combat stress reaction* (CSR), was the most studied instance of acute stress. This is not surprising considering that CSR was observed in more than 20% of US troops in World War II (Solomon, Laor, & McFarlane, 1996). CSR is a poorly defined construct that is marked by its variability and fluctuating course (Solomon, 1993a). Its symptoms include anxiety, depression, confusion, restricted affect, irritability, somatic pain, withdrawal, listlessness, paranoia, nausea, startle reactions, and sympathetic hyperactivity (Bar-On, Solomon, Noy, & Nardi, 1986; Bartemeier, 1946; Grinker, 1945). Inherent in many of the early notions of CSR was the assumption that stress symptoms were transient reactions to an extreme stress. That is, they were not recognized as psychopathological reactions because they were observed in troops who were not regarded as having a predisposition to psychiatric disorders. These military opinions played a significant role in shaping the early diagnostic thinking of both the World Health Organization (WHO) and the American Psychiatric Association after World War II. In 1948, WHO adopted the Armed Forces' categorizations when it integrated mental disorders into the sixth revision of the *International Statistical Classification of Diseases, Injuries, and Causes of Death (ICD-6)*. Similarly, in 1952, the American Psychiatric Association developed the *Diagnostic and Statistical Manual of Mental Disorders (DSM)* on the basis of existing conceptualizations within the Veterans Administration and the Armed Forces. A major effect of this influence was that initial diagnostic categorizations regarded acute stress reactions as temporary responses in otherwise normal individuals (Brett, 1996).

Exhibit 1.1 contains a summary of the development of diagnostic categories relevant to traumatized people in both *ICD* and *DSM*. The descriptions of acute trauma reactions in *ICD–6* to *ICD–9* (World Health Organization, 1977) all shared the assumption that acute stress reactions were transient reactions in nonpathological individuals. During the same period of time, the American Psychiatric Association used variable terms to describe acute stress reactions. The first edition of *DSM* (American Psychiatric Association, 1952) classified acute posttrauma responses under *gross stress reaction*, and longer lasting reactions were subsumed under the *anxiety* or *depressive neuroses*. In *DSM–II* (American Psychiatric Association, 1968), ongoing reactions were similarly categorized, but *transient situational disturbance* was used to describe an acute posttrauma response. The major changes occurred in *DSM–III* (American Psychiatric Association, 1980), in which the diagnosis of *posttraumatic stress disorder* (PTSD) was

EXHIBIT 1.1
Diagnostic Categories for Traumatic Stress Reactions

ICD	DSM
ICD–6 (1948)	*DSM* (1952)
Acute situational maladjustment	Gross stress reactions
	Adult situational reaction
	Adjustment reaction
ICD–8 (1969)	*DSM–II* (1968)
Transient situational disturbance	Adjustment reaction
ICD–9 (1977)	*DSM–III, DSM–III–R* (1980, 1987)
Acute stress reaction	Posttraumatic stress disorder
ICD–10 (1992)	*DSM–IV* (1994)
Acute stress reaction	Acute stress disorder
Posttraumatic stress disorder	Posttraumatic stress disorder
Enduring personality change after catastrophe experience	

Note. *ICD = International Statistical Classification of Disease* (published by the World Health Organization); *DSM = Diagnostic and Statistical Manual of Mental Disorders* (published by the American Psychiatric Association).

formally introduced. Whereas *DSM–III* did not stipulate a duration for symptoms, the revised version of that edition (*DSM–III–R*; American Psychiatric Associaion, 1987) required that the symptoms be present for more than 1 month posttrauma. This stipulation precluded the inclusion of acutely traumatized individuals, who were instead diagnosed with *adjustment disorder* (Blanchard & Hickling, 1997; Pincus, Frances, Davis, First, & Widiger, 1992).

DIAGNOSIS OF ASD

In *DSM–IV* (American Psychiatric Association, 1994), there was formal recognition of the "nosologic gap" between PTSD and adjustment disorder (Pincus et al., 1992, p. 115). Specifically, some parties argued for a diagnostic means to identify traumatized people within the 1st month after a traumatic event. The major arguments put forward to justify such a diagnosis were (a) to recognize the significant levels of distress experienced in the initial month after a trauma (Koopman, Classen, Cardeña, & Spiegel, 1995), (b) to permit early identification of trauma survivors who would suffer longer term psychopathology (Koopman et al., 1995), and (c) to stimulate controlled investigation of acute posttrauma reactions (Solomon et al., 1996). Others were opposed to this new diagnosis, however, on the grounds that it would potentially pathologize a normal reaction to a traumatic event and encourage false-positive diagnoses (Pincus et al., 1992; Wakefield, 1996). Moreover, reluctance to accept this new diagnosis was reinforced by the alleged relationship between ASD and PTSD being "based more on logical arguments than on empirical research" (Koopman et al., 1995, p. 38). Whereas most diagnoses that were accepted into *DSM–IV* satisfied stringent criteria, including extensive literature reviews, statistical analyses, and field studies, ASD was included with hardly any supporting data to validate its diagnostic merits (Bryant & Harvey, 1997a).

DEFINITION OF ASD

Table 1.1 demonstrates that the criteria for ASD were closely modeled on PTSD. The structure of the ASD diagnosis follows that of PTSD in that it is described in terms of the stressor definition, reexperiencing, avoidance, arousal, duration, and exclusion criteria. There are several critical differences, however, between ASD and PTSD (see also chapter 4). The additional cluster that is unique to ASD criteria is the dissociative cluster of symptoms.

The initial requisite for a diagnosis of ASD is the experience of a precipitating stressor. This description is identical to the stressor definition

TABLE 1.1
Diagnostic Criteria for ASD and PTSD

Criterion	ASD	PTSD
Stressor	*Both* Threatening event Fear, helplessness, or horror	*Both* Threatening event Fear, helplessness, or horror
Dissociation	*Minimum three of* Numbing Reduced awareness Depersonalization Derealization Amnesia	—
Reexperienc-ing	*Minimum one of* Recurrent images/thoughts/distress Consequent distress not prescribed Intrusive nature not pre-scribed	*Minimum one of* Recurrent images/thoughts/distress Consequent distress pre-scribed Intrusive nature prescribed
Avoidance	*Marked avoidance of* Thoughts, feelings, or places	*Minimum three of* Avoid thoughts/conversa-tions Avoid people/places Amnesia Diminished interest Estrangement from others Restricted affect Sense of shortened future
Arousal	*Marked arousal, including* Restlessness, insomnia, irritability, hypervigi-lance, and concentra-tion difficulties	*Minimum two of* Insomnia Irritability Concentration deficits Hyperviligence Elevated startle response
Duration	At least 2 days and less than 1 month posttrauma Dissociative symptoms may be present only during trauma	At least 1 month posttrauma
Impairment	Impairs functioning	Impairs functioning

Note. ASD = acute stress disorder; PTSD = posttraumatic stress disorder. Dissociation symptoms were not included as PTSD criteria.
From "Acute Stress Disorder: A Critical Review of Diagnostic and Theoretical Issues," by R. A. Bryant and A. G. Harvey, 1997, *Clinical Psychology Review, 17*, p. 767. Copyright 1997 by Elsevier Science. Reprinted with permission.

of PTSD and requires that the individual has experienced or witnessed an event that has been threatening to either himself or herself or another person. Furthermore, it prescribes that the "person's response involved intense fear, helplessness, or horror" (American Psychiatric Association, 1994, p. 431). To illustrate, one of the more severe industrial accident victims we have treated clearly experienced a threatening event. Bart's arm was severely severed while operating a factory machine. During the several hours that he was trapped in the machine, Bart described extreme fright, pain, and helplessness. Bart's experience satisfactorily met the ASD stressor criteria.

The symptom cluster that distinguishes ASD from PTSD is the emphasis on dissociative symptoms. To satisfy criteria for this cluster, a person must display at least three of the following dissociative symptoms: (a) subjective sense of numbing or detachment, (b) reduced awareness of his or her surroundings, (c) derealization, (d) depersonalization, and (e) dissociative amnesia. These symptoms may occur either at the time of the trauma or in the 1st month posttrauma. *Numbing* refers to detachment from expected emotional reactions. *Reduced awareness of surroundings* involves the person being less aware than one would expect of events occurring either during the trauma or in the immediate period after it. *Derealization* is defined as the perception that one's environment is unreal, dreamlike, or occurring in a distorted time frame. *Depersonalization* is the sense that one's body is detached or one is seeing oneself from another's perspective. *Dissociative amnesia* refers to an inability to recall a critical aspect of the traumatic event. Bart met four of these five dissociative criteria. Specifically, he described that the experience seemed unreal; at the time he could not believe it was happening. During our assessment session, he said "it all seemed like a terrible dream." He reported also that during the ordeal, events seemed to move slowly, including people's speech and movements. These accounts reflect Bart's reduced awareness of his surroundings and derealization. He also reported that for a period, he felt he was watching the ordeal from the ceiling, that he was looking down on himself. This is a classic example of depersonalization because Bart was viewing himself in a detached manner. Finally, Bart reported that since the incident, he had felt detached and "emotionless" from all his daily activities, reflecting the presence of emotional numbing. Bart reported that he could recall all aspects of the trauma, and so he did not display dissociative amnesia.

The diagnosis of ASD requires also that the trauma "is reexperienced in at least one of the following ways: recurrent images, thoughts, dreams, illusions, flashback episodes, or a sense of reliving the experience; or distress on exposure to reminders of the traumatic event" (American Psychiatric Association, 1994, p. 432). By describing frequent intrusive memories of the event, especially of his bones protruding from his severed arm, Bart met the reexperiencing criterion. These images were accompanied by strong perceptions of pain in the affected arm, the smell of sawdust that was present at the time of the accident, and a sense that his arm was being torn off his shoulder. During these experiences, Bart felt that he was experiencing the event all over again. He also reported frequent nightmares in which he saw his arm being torn off his shoulder, which resulted in his waking in great fright.

The diagnostic criteria for ASD stipulate that the person must display "marked avoidance of stimuli that arouse recollections of the trauma" (American Psychiatric Association, 1994, p. 432). This avoidance may include avoidance of thoughts, feelings, activities, conversations, places, and people that may remind the person of her or his traumatic experience. In terms of avoidance, Bart displayed very marked avoidance of all thoughts, conversations, and places that reminded him of his experience. He refused to look at his arm and would not go near mirrors. He avoided proximity to any electrical or mechanical devices and refused to attend medical appointments. Bart's avoidance made talking about his experiences in therapy difficult because focusing on his accident elicited anxiety that he found difficult to tolerate.

The ASD diagnosis also requires that marked symptoms of anxiety or arousal be present after the trauma. Arousal symptoms may include restlessness, insomnia, hypervigilance, concentration difficulties, and irritability. Bart described being very aware of feeling unsafe in the world. He felt he needed to continually scan his environment for threats. In addition to this hypervigilance, he also reported marked insomnia, concentration deficits, and heightened startle response. He generalized his sense of physical vulnerability to many stimuli, even stimuli not directly related to the trauma. For example, he developed a habit of carrying a knife in his boot to protect himself from potential assailants. He also refused to turn his back on anyone and always ensured that he stood with his back to walls so that he could monitor other people's activities.

The diagnosis of ASD stipulates that the disturbance must be clinically significant in terms of interruption to social or occupational functioning and must be present for at least 2 days after the trauma, but not persist for more than 1 month. It is assumed that a diagnosis of PTSD may be suitable after this time. The diagnosis of ASD is not made if the disturbance is better accounted for by a medical condition or substance use. Bart clearly satisfied this impairment criterion for ASD because his symptoms interfered with his ability to return to any work duties, impaired his compliance with medical procedures, and prevented any meaningful interpersonal interactions.

Note that *DSM–IV*'s description of ASD is significantly different from *ICD–10*'s definition of acute stress reaction (see Table 1.2). Whereas *ASD* refers to the period after 48 hours posttrauma, *acute stress reaction* refers to the period before 48 hours. This reflects the divergence in the underlying assumptions about the course of the two disorders. Whereas ASD is conceived of as a precursor to PTSD, acute stress reactions are presented as a transient reaction. Furthermore, the symptoms required by the respective descriptions are markedly different. In particular, *DSM–IV* places consid-

TABLE 1.2
Comparison of Diagnostic Criteria for ASD (*DSM–IV*) and Acute Stress Reaction (*ICD–10*)

Criteria	ASD	Acute stress reaction
Stressor	Threat to life	Exceptional mental or
	Subjective response	physical stressor
Relationship to PTSD	Precursor	Alternative diagnosis
Time from trauma	2 days to 4 weeks	48 hours
Course	Precursor to PTSD	Transient
Symptoms	Dissociation	Generalized anxiety
	Reexperiencing	Withdrawal
	Avoidance	Narrowing of attention
	Anxiety or arousal	Apparent disorientation
		Anger or verbal aggression
		Despair or hopelessness
		Overactivity
		Excessive grief

Note. ASD = acute stress disorder; *DSM–IV = Diagnostic and Statistical Manual of Mental Disorders* (4th ed.); *ICD–10 = International Classification of Disease* (10th ed., rev.); PTSD = posttraumatic stress disorder.

erable emphasis on dissociative reactions in the acute trauma response, primarily because this reflects a strong theoretical position held in certain quarters of American psychiatry. In contrast, *ICD–10*'s description incorporates a wider range of symptoms, which include both anxiety and depression, and acknowledges the fluctuating course of acute stress reactions. This conceptualization of acute stress reflects *ICD–10*'s strong connection to military psychiatry and its attempt to provide a descriptive profile of events that occur in combat settings. Some have noted that the flexibility of the *ICD–10* diagnosis may make it more clinically useful than the more rigid *DSM–IV* definition (Solomon et al., 1996). The utility of a new diagnosis relating to acute stress reactions depends, however, on its ability to identify those individuals who will suffer chronic PTSD. The evidence for and against this critical issue is visited in chapter 3. In the next chapter, we review the various theoretical perspectives of ASD.

2

THEORETICAL PERSPECTIVES OF ACUTE STRESS DISORDER

There are numerous theoretical perspectives on trauma response, including dissociative (D. Spiegel, Koopman, Cardeña, & Classen, 1996; van der Kolk & van der Hart, 1989), biological (Kolb, 1987; Krystal, Southwick, & Charney, 1995; van der Kolk & Saporta, 1993), psychodynamic (Horowitz, 1976; Kardiner, 1941; Krystal, 1968), behavioral (Keane, Zimering, & Caddell, 1985; Kilpatrick, Veronen, & Best, 1985), cognitive (Creamer, Burgess, & Pattison, 1992; Foa, Steketee, & Rothbaum, 1989; Litz & Keane, 1989), and psychobiological (Jones & Barlow, 1990) theories. All of these approaches have made contributions to our understanding of specific aspects of PTSD. However, none has specifically and comprehensively considered the acute posttraumatic phase, and consequently, there is currently no well-developed theory of ASD. In this chapter, we review several theoretical approaches that may contribute to an understanding of ASD.

DISSOCIATIVE THEORY

Most theoretical debate about ASD has been dominated by advocates of dissociative theories (Classen, Koopman, & Spiegel, 1993; Spiegel, Koopman, & Classen, 1994; Spiegel et al., 1996). It was primarily the importance given to acute dissociation that led to the current description of ASD. Dissociation is understood to be a strategy used to reduce awareness of aversive emotions and control of cognition, which causes "disruption in the usually integrated functions of consciousness, memory, identity, or perception of the environment" (American Psychiatry Association, 1994, p. 766). Current notions of dissociation trace their historical roots to the work of Janet (1907), Prince (1905/1978), and Breuer and Freud (1895/1986). As discussed in chapter 1, this perspective proposes that people who have been exposed to a traumatic event may minimize the adverse emotional consequences of the trauma by restricting their awareness of the traumatic experience (Putnam, 1989; D. Spiegel, 1991; van der Kolk & van der Hart, 1989). Dissociative defenses may be evident in perceptual alterations, memory impairment, or emotional detachment from one's environment (Cardeña & Spiegel, 1993).

The rationale for the emphasis on dissociation in ASD has centered on the extent to which dissociation during or immediately after the trauma predicts subsequent PTSD. In considering the theoretical background for the current notion of ASD, it is useful to contemplate the evidence for a causal trauma–dissociation relationship. Support for this general proposition has come from numerous sources. First, there is evidence that those who are diagnosed with PTSD report higher levels of hypnotizability (Spiegel, Hunt, & Dondershine, 1988; Stutman & Bliss, 1985) and dissociation (Bernstein & Putnam, 1986; Branscomb, 1991; Bremner et al., 1992; Carlson & Rosser-Hogan, 1991; Coons, Bowman, Pellow, & Schneider, 1989) than other psychiatric patient groups and the general community. Second, there are numerous claims that people with dissociative disorders have higher rates of traumatic histories (Coons & Milstein, 1986; Kluft, 1987). Third, dissociative responses during traumatic experiences are reportedly common (see Bryant & Harvey, 1997a). Fourth, there are numerous reports of a link between peritraumatic dissociation and subsequent psychopathology (Bremner & Brett, 1997; Holen, 1993).

The utility of the dissociative perspective needs to be considered in the light of evidence against a causal link between trauma and dissociation. Although some of this evidence does not relate directly to ASD, it is important to understand that the reported relationship between trauma and dissociation is not as straightforward as many proponents suggest. First, much of the reported support for a relationship between trauma and dissociation comes from the alleged causal link between childhood sexual abuse and subsequent psychopathology. Recent work indicates, however, that much childhood sexual abuse does not lead to psychopathology and may not be associated with overwhelming distress (Kendall-Tackett, Williams, & Finkelhor, 1993; Rind, Tromovitch, & Bauserman, 1998). Furthermore, at least one statistical analysis of a large cohort ($n = 1,028$) showed that physical abuse, but not sexual abuse, was associated with a high rate of dissociation (Mulder, Beautrais, Joyce, & Fergusson, 1998). Second, the reported relationship between childhood trauma and dissociative disorders often neglects to consider baseline rates of childhood trauma in general psychiatric settings, which ranges from 44% to 77% (Briere & Zardi, 1989; Putnam, Guroff, Silberman, Baraban, & Post, 1986). Third, the research designs of numerous studies reporting a link between trauma and dissociation are flawed by inappropriate control groups and inadequate dependent measures (for reviews, see Kendall-Tackett et al., 1993; Tillman, Nash, & Lerner, 1994). Fourth, many studies reporting a link between childhood trauma and subsequent dissociative psychopathology have failed to consider other important contextual variables. Although Nash, Hulsey, Sexton, Harralson, and Lambert (1993) found that study participants who were sexually abused in childhood were more dissociative than those who were not abused, this influence was eliminated when family environment was used as a covariate. That is, parental or family factors appear to have a stronger influence on subsequent development than early abuse. Fifth, many retrospective reports of reported childhood abuse have not been objectively verified, including reports of significant proportions of individuals who claim to have been the victims of satanic ritual abuse (Ganaway, 1994). The acceptance of these studies should be tempered by the failure of exhaustive criminal investigations to validate these allegations. Sixth, studies of some severely traumatized populations, including Holocaust survivors (Krystal, 1991), have not found dissociation to be a prominent response in their posttraumatic adjustment. These points suggest that the proposition that trauma is directly and causally related to dissociation should not be unconditionally accepted.

In summary, the dissociative perspective reflects a general notion that trauma elicits pathological dissociation rather than representing a well-articulated model. At this stage, it is unclear whether peritraumatic dissociation may be related to subsequent PTSD because (a) it impairs resolution of traumatic memories, (b) it is elicited by more anxiety-provoking traumatic events that are likely to lead to PTSD, or (c) the symptoms of acute dissociation overlap with extreme anxiety responses (e.g., depersonalization) that can be elicited during a trauma. It has also been proposed that only those people who possess dissociative tendencies before the traumatic experience will display acute dissociation in response to a trauma (Atchison & McFarlane, 1994). This notion is consistent with evidence that those with PTSD have higher levels of hypnotizability (Spiegel et al., 1988). Hypnotizability is traditionally regarded as a trait that is very stable over time (Piccione, Hilgard, & Zimbardo, 1989). This interpretation also is consistent with Davidson and Foa's (1991) proposal that because dissociative responses are coping mechanisms, they are best regarded as secondary symptoms for some people. In this sense, acute dissociative symptoms may be regarded as one type of coping mechanism that is used by dissociative-prone individuals. The claim that acute dissociation leads to PTSD is contrary to the position that recognizes appropriate use of dissociative mechanisms as adaptive. Horowitz (1986) has argued that dissociative responses are common and potentially adaptive reactions to a trauma that can subsequently lead to adequate resolution of the traumatic experience. In chapter 3, we review the evidence for the proposal, based on dissociative theory, that acute dissociation leads to PTSD.

BIOLOGICAL THEORY

Biological theories of trauma response have been strongly influenced by apparent similarities between acute stress symptoms and various phenomena that occur under experimentally induced conditions of stress. For example, comparisons have been made between acute dissociative symptoms and the phenomenon of stress-induced analgesia, which involves a form of numbing to sensory stimuli. It has been noted that individuals with PTSD display higher levels of stress-induced analgesia (van der Kolk, Greenberg, Orr, & Pitman, 1989). This finding is consistent with Beecher's (1946) observation during World War II that 75% of severely injured soldiers on the Italian frontline did not request morphine. This response in humans has been compared with experimental findings with animals who are exposed to inescapable shock (van der Kolk, Greenberg, Boyd, & Krystal, 1985). Accordingly, stress-induced analgesia in animals (Akil, Watson, & Young, 1983) allegedly provides an animal model for the dissociative symptoms and stress-induced analgesia seen in humans with PTSD. On the basis of these similarities, it is argued that the dissociative symptoms seen in acutely traumatized humans may reflect the release of endogenous opioids (van der Kolk et al., 1989). According to one view, this reaction is conceptualized as an adaptive evolutionary response that permits management of pain during times of threat (van der Kolk, 1996a).

In recent years, there has been a proliferation of biological theories of PTSD (e.g., Kolb, 1987; Krystal et al., 1989; van der Kolk, 1996a). Most psychobiological theories of PTSD implicate the acute stress response in terms of the immediate effect of extreme stress on neuronal functions. For example, van der Kolk (1996a) has proposed that the core disturbance in PTSD lies in the inability to regulate arousal states resulting from noradrenergic dysregulation. He has argued that under conditions of acute traumatic stress, pathways between the locus coeruleus and hippocampus are activated, leading to an increase in central norepinephrine levels. This reaction leads to a greater neural uptake of norepinephrine, followed by reduced central norepinephrine levels and hypersensitivity of neurons to further norepinephrine. This view holds that repetitive intrusive reliving of the trauma is caused by the stress-induced reactivation of the locus coerulus–hippocampal pathway, which is perpetuated by repetitive stress levels associated with reexperiencing symptoms of PTSD. That is, there is a kindling process that involves the repeated stress of reexperiencing symptoms potentially leading to a long-lasting modification of limbic functions. This emphasis on neuronal changes that occur as a result of ongoing reexperiencing symptoms requires much further experimental investigation. This perspective's utility for explaining acute stress reactions is somewhat limited, however, because the focus on longer term stimulation of limbic systems does not permit detailed attention to acute physiological processes.

A major focus of psychophysiological attention, and one that has significant potential for understanding ASD, has been the role of acute arousal in the mediation of longer term trauma reactions. The earliest writings on acute stress placed considerable emphasis on acute arousal. In reference to "traumatic neuroses," Kardiner (1941) noted that "the nucleus of the neurosis is a physioneurosis" (p. 95), in which individuals display hyperreactivity to stimuli. R. R. Grinker and Spiegel (1945) observed that the acute physical changes in soldiers included tremor, gastric distress, masklike faces, and an exaggerated startle reflex. Similarly, Lindemann (1944) documented the elevated arousal displayed by civilian disaster survivors. Today there is considerable evidence that supports the notion that PTSD is marked by disordered arousal (Pitman, 1993). Individuals with PTSD demonstrate elevated autonomic arousal in response to trauma reminders, as indexed by heart rate, blood pressure, and skin conductance (Blanchard, Hickling, Buckley, et al., 1996; Blanchard, Kolb, & Gerardi, 1986; Pitman, Orr, Forgue, de Jong, & Claiborn, 1987). In keeping with this approach, recent theorists have proposed that acute physiological arousal may reflect fear conditioning that occurs after the traumatic experience, which subsequently mediates persistent intrusions and avoidance patterns (McFarlane, 1992a, 1992b; Shalev, 1992). Although the specific psychophysiological reactions are not fully understood at this stage, there is a strong theoretical view that heightened arousal in the acute trauma phase is a critical factor in the mediation of PTSD.

COGNITIVE THEORY

Most cognitive theories explain PTSD in terms of information processing and memory function (Chemtob, Roitblat, Hamada, Carlson, & Twentyman, 1988; Creamer et al., 1992; Foa & Kozak, 1986; Foa et al., 1989; Litz & Keane, 1989). These models of PTSD are based on Lang's (1977, 1979) proposal that emotions are stored in memory networks that contain information about (a) stimuli that elicit the emotional response; (b) verbal, cognitive, physical, and behavioral responses evoked by the stimuli; and (c) the meaning of the stimuli and associated response (Lang,

1977). Foa et al. (1989) have proposed that after a traumatic event, a fear network, which stores information about what is threatening, is formed. This theory holds that because trauma-related stimuli are highly represented in the fear network, they are readily activated by many internal and external cues. This aspect of the theory accounts for both the intrusive reexperiencing symptoms and hypervigilance to potentially threatening events. According to most cognitive theories, intrusive recollections will have one of two outcomes. On the one hand, reexperiencing may assist in the processing and resolution of the traumatic memories. Alternatively, the reexperiencing may prompt attempts to avoid (Creamer et al., 1992) or control (Ehlers & Steil, 1995) aversive memories of the trauma. This component of the theory accounts for the avoidance patterns associated with PTSD. This theory also holds that the predominance of threat-related cognitions in the fear network results in marked cognitive biases. Specifically, it is held that individuals with PTSD display exaggerated beliefs of vulnerability and danger (Foa et al., 1989). Cognitive theories predict that individuals with PTSD are likely to have a lower threshold for interpreting stimuli as threatening, as well as a bias toward searching for and identifying threatening information. The attentional bias to threat-related stimuli has been repeatedly demonstrated in studies that have used the modified Stroop color-naming test. This paradigm requires participants to name the color of either threat or nonthreat words, and the extent to which speed on this task is impaired reflects a bias to those stimuli. Numerous studies have found that individuals with PTSD display slower color naming of threat words after rape (Cassiday, McNally, & Zeitlin, 1992; Foa, Feske, Murdock, Kozak, & McCarthy, 1991), combat (McNally, English, & Lipke, 1993; McNally, Kaspi, Riemann, & Zeitlin, 1990), ferry disaster (Thrasher, Dalgleish, & Yule, 1994), and motor vehicle accidents (Bryant & Harvey, 1995d). Furthermore, studies that have used the masked Stroop paradigm indicate that this bias toward threat stimuli in PTSD occurs at a preattentive stage of processing (Harvey, Bryant, & Rapee, 1996; McNally, Amir, & Lipke, 1996). The attentional bias to threat also has been demonstrated in dot-probe (Bryant & Harvey, 1997b) and eye-tracking (Bryant, Harvey, Gordon, & Barry, 1995) paradigms. Moreover, information-processing theories hold that PTSD is distinguished from other anxiety disorders because its fear network is more stable and contains more threat-related representations. Accordingly, cognitive theory predicts that individuals diagnosed with PTSD will experience a stronger bias to threat than other anxiety-disordered populations. There is initial evidence that attentional bias in PTSD populations is greater than in other anxiety groups, such as those with a specific phobia (Bryant & Harvey, 1995d, 1997b).

It has been argued that resolution of the traumatic memories occurs through the activation and modification of the fear network and that this process requires two conditions. First, all elements of the memory network need to be accessed and activated because this activation weakens stimulus–response associations and reduces the magnitude and intensity of the fear network (Foa et al., 1989; Litz & Keane, 1989). Second, new information that is incompatible with the existing fear structures purportedly facilitates the formation of new cognitive schemas (Foa & Kozak, 1986).

INTEGRATIVE THEORIES

Whereas most theories have focused either on dissociation, biological processes, or information processing, some have attempted to accommodate these different mechanisms into more integrative theories. Foa and Hearst-Ikeda (1996) have attempted to integrate the role of dissociation into network theory. This proposal holds that whereas dissociative responses may be an adaptive means of managing distressing emotions, they also can be an avoidance mechanism that impedes the activation of fear structures that is required for the resolution of traumatic memories. Similarly, Ehlers and Steil (1995) have argued that cognitive strategies that attempt to control intrusions, such as dissociation and numbing, may block the successful processing of traumatic memories. Implicit in this proposal is the assumption that trauma resolution will be impeded by dissociation and avoidance strategies. Another cognitive theory that has direct relevance to dissociative mechanisms is the dual-representation theory proposed by Brewin, Dalgleish, and Joseph (1996), which recognizes both verbally accessible memories (VAMs) and situationally accessible memories (SAMs). Whereas VAMs are verbal or visual memories that can be intentionally retrieved, SAMs are subconsciously generated memories. The latter may be experienced as flashbacks, a sense of reliving a trauma, or somatic sensations that are reminiscent of the traumatic experience. This theory holds that traumatic memories can be implicitly encoded and can be reexperienced at a nonverbal level. This theory holds the advantage of being able to account for reexperiencing symptoms that are implicitly processed. Chemtob et al. (1988) have postulated a network theory that places considerable emphasis on the heightened arousal in PTSD. They have suggested that the fear network is readily activated because of the elevated arousal that occurs in PTSD. This position predicts that hypervigilance to external and internal cues is heightened by enhanced arousal.

SUMMARY

Although existing theories of PTSD offer some direction for theories of ASD, they have not specifically addressed the relationship between immediate and longer term effects of trauma. Systematic investigation of ASD requires the development of testable models that can specify theoretically driven study of the initial course of trauma recovery. Both cognitive and biological theories appear to have utility for explaining the core phenomena evident in acute stress responses. A comprehensive model of ASD needs to be able to account for the interaction among acute dissociation, reexperiencing, avoidance, and arousal and how these reactions mediate longer term PTSD. Furthermore, the test of any model of ASD depends on its ability to account for empirical findings on acute symptoms and their relationship to PTSD. In chapter 3, our goal is to comprehensively review the empirical evidence concerning acute stress reactions and to attempt to integrate this evidence into a model of ASD.

3

EMPIRICAL STATUS OF ACUTE STRESS DISORDER

Although ASD was introduced into *DSM–IV* with the claim that it would identify those trauma survivors who would subsequently develop PTSD, initial evidence indicates that this claim was premature. Studies conducted in recent years indicate that the relationship between acute and longer term posttraumatic reactions is complex and that the current conceptualization of ASD does not adequately identify people at risk for suffering chronic PTSD. More specifically, the current emphasis on acute dissociation as the primary predictor of subsequent PTSD is not supported by the evidence. In this chapter, we review the empirical evidence relating to the two rationales for introducing ASD as a new diagnosis. The first rationale was that the diagnosis recognizes the high levels of distress in the initial weeks after a trauma. The second rationale was that ASD is a precursor to the development of PTSD. We then review the empirical findings concerning the processes that mediate ASD. Finally, we synthesize this evidence by proposing an integrative model of ASD.

PTSD IN THE ACUTE POSTTRAUMA PHASE

Some of the earlier studies of acute trauma responses were conducted before the introduction of the ASD diagnosis. These studies investigated the incidence of PTSD symptoms in the initial month posttrauma (minus the duration criterion). Table 3.1 indicates that the incidence of PTSD in these studies ranged from 8% to 100%. The variable incidence of PTSD may be attributed, in part, to the type of trauma studied. The higher rates of PTSD were reported in ambushed soldiers (Feinstein, 1989) and rape victims (Rothbaum, Foa, Riggs, Murdock, & Walsh, 1992). Alternately, the variable incidence may be attributed to different assessment tools, which ranged from clinical interviews to standardized assessment instruments.

Acute Stress Symptoms

Numerous studies have used self-report or symptom checklists to index the incidence of acute stress symptoms rather than to arrive at specific diagnostic decisions. Table 3.2 contains a summary of the results of these studies, which provide further evidence of the significant levels of distress in the 1st month after a trauma. In terms of dissociative symptoms, a sense of numbing, reduction in awareness of one's environment, derealization, depersonalization, and dissociative amnesia all are common in the acute phase of a traumatic experience. Intrusive thoughts and avoidance behaviors also are common in the acute phase. Regarding acute arousal symptoms, insomnia, concentration deficits, irritability, and elevated autonomic arousal tend to be reported by most trauma survivors in the acute trauma phase. These data provide clear evidence that significant levels of distress do occur across a range of traumas within the initial month after a trauma.

Incidence of ASD

Table 3.3 summarizes the seven studies that have reported the incidence of ASD. Unfortunately, these studies have used variable procedures and assessment tools, and accordingly, their conclusions need to be interpreted cautiously. Several of the studies are limited because they used a measure of PTSD and added questions relating to the ASD dissociation symptoms. Given that this method has not been established as a valid and reliable assessment of ASD, it is difficult to know the extent to which these diagnostic decisions are valid. In addition, in one study, only half of the sample were actually present at the time of the accident, and diagnostic information was obtained in the context of a counseling session (Creamer & Manning, 1998). The rate of ASD reported ranged from 7% in a sample of typhoon survivors (Stabb, Grieger, Fullerton, & Ursano, 1996) to 33% in bystanders to a mass shooting (Classen, Koopman, Hales, & Spiegel, 1998). The latter finding was obtained by means of the Stanford Acute Stress Reaction Questionnaire (SASRQ; Cardeña, Classen, & Spiegel, 1991). As is discussed in chapter 5, the SASRQ is a self-report question-

TABLE 3.1
Studies of Incidence of PTSD (Excluding Duration Criteria) Within 1 Month Posttrauma

Study	N	Trauma type	Trauma-assessment interval	Diagnostic tool	Incidence of PTSD
Feinstein (1989)	14	Ambushed soldiers	2–24 days	Clinical interview based on *DSM–III*	100%
Patterson, Carrigan, Questad, and Robinson (1990)	54	Burn	<1 month	Clinical interview based on *DSM–III*	30%
Rothbaum, Foa, Riggs, Murdock, and Walsh (1992)	95	Rape	<1 month	Clinical interview based on *DSM–III–R*	94%
Green, McFarlane, Hunter, and Griggs (1993)	24	MVA	1 month	DIS	8%
Solomon et al. (1993)	51	War evacuees	<1 week	Clinical interview based on *DSM–III–R*	80%
North, Smith, and Spitznagel (1994)	136	Mass shooting	1 month	DIS/Disaster Supplement	Men = 20% Women = 36%
Riggs, Rothbaum, and Foa (1995)	84	Assault	<1 month	Clinical interview based on *DSM–III–R*	Women = 71% Men = 50%
Delahanty et al. (1997)	130	MVA	14–21 days	SCID	Responsible for MVA = 19% Not responsible for MVA = 29%

Note. PTSD = posttraumatic stress disorder; *DSM–III* = *Diagnostic and Statistical Manual for Mental Disorders* (3rd ed.); *DSM–III–R* = *Diagnostic and Statistical Manual for Mental Disorders* (3rd ed., rev.); DIS = Diagnostic Interview Schedule; SCID = Structured Clinical Interview for the *DSM–III–R*; DIS/Disaster Supplement = Diagnostic Interview Schedule/Disaster Supplement (Robins & Smith, 1983); MVA = motor vehicle accident.

TABLE 3.2
Studies of the Incidence of ASD Symptoms Within 1 Month Posttrauma

Symptom	% reporting symptoms	Mode of trauma	Study
Cluster B			
Numbing	9	Mass shooting	North, Smith, and Spitznagel (1994)
	23	Earthquake	Cardeña and Spiegel (1993)
Reduced awareness	66	Rescue team	Berah, Jones, and Valent (1984)
	Majority	Flood	Titchener and Kapp (1976)
	54	Airplane crash	Sloan (1988)
Derealization	18	Mixed trauma	Shalev, Peri, Canetti, and Schreiber (1996)
	40	Earthquake	Cardeña and Spiegel (1993)
Depersonalization	25	Earthquake	Cardeña and Spiegel (1993)
	54	Airplane crash	Sloan (1988)
Dissociative amnesia	6	Mixed trauma	Shalev et al. (1996)
	11	Mass shooting	North et al. (1994)
	29	Earthquake	Cardeña and Spiegel (1993)
	57	Ambush	Feinstein (1989)
Cluster C			
Intrusions	39	Earthquake	Cardeña and Spiegel (1993)
	63	Burns	Patterson et al. (1990)
	83	Mass shooting	North et al. (1994)
	71	Airplane crash	Sloan (1988)
	100	Ambush	Feinstein (1989)
Nightmares	22	Earthquake	Cardeña and Spiegel (1993)
	56	Mass shooting	North et al. (1994)
	50	Airplane crash	Sloan (1988)
	50	Ambush	Feinstein (1989)
Cluster D			
Avoidance	30	Earthquake	Cardeña and Spiegel (1993)
	50	MVA	Bryant and Harvey (1996a)
	42	Mass shooting	North et al. (1994)
Cluster E			
Insomnia	68	Airplane crash	Sloan (1988)
	50	Ambush	Feinstein (1989)
	44	Earthquake	Cardeña and Spiegel (1993)
	74	Mass shooting	North et al. (1994)
	Majority	Flood	Titchener and Kapp (1976)

Table continues

TABLE 3.2 (*Continued*)

Symptom	% reporting symptoms	Mode of trauma	Study
Cluster E (*continued*)			
Concentration	71	Earthquake	Cardeña and Spiegel (1993)
	63	Mass shooting	North et al. (1994)
	79	Airplane crash	Sloan (1988)
Irritability	71	Airplane crash	Sloan (1988)
	44	Mass shooting	North et al. (1994)
Autonomic arousal	93	Ambush	Feinstein (1989)
	67	Earthquake	Cardeña and Spiegel (1993)
Hypervigilance	93	Ambush	Feinstein (1989)
	76	Earthquake	Cardeña and Spiegel (1993)
	82	Airplane crash	Sloan (1988)

Note. ASD = acute stress disorder; MVA = motor vehicle accident.

TABLE 3.3
Studies of Incidence of ASD

Study	*N*	Trauma type	Diagnostic tool	% incidence of ASD
Stabb, Grieger, Fullerton, and Ursano (1996)	320	Typhoon	*DSM–IV* based questions	7
Creamer and Manning (1998)	47	Industrial accident	SI–PTSD + dissociative questions	6
Classen, Koopman, Hales, and Spiegel (1998)	36	Mass shooting	SASRQ	33
Brewin, Andrews, Rose, and Kirk (1999)	157	Violent assault	PSS + additional items	19
Harvey and Bryant (1998d)	92	MVA	ASDI	13
Harvey and Bryant (1998a)	79	MVA–TBI	ASDI	14
Harvey and Bryant (1999c)	70	Assault, burn, industrial	ASDI	13

Note. ASD = acute stress disorder; SI–PTSD = Structured Interview for Post-Traumatic Stress Disorder (Davidson, Smith, & Kudler, 1989); SASRQ = Stanford Acute Stress Reaction Questionnaire (Cardeña, Classen, & Spiegel, 1991); PSS = Posttraumatic Stress Disorder Symptom Scale (Foa, Riggs, Dancu, & Rothbaum, 1993); ASDI = Acute Stress Disorder Inventory (Bryant, Harvey, Dang, & Sackville, 1998); *DSM–IV = Diagnostic and Statistical Manual of Mental Disorders* (4th ed.); MVA–TBI = motor vehicle accident–traumatic brain injury.

naire that provides information about the frequency of ASD symptoms but does not provide a formal diagnosis of ASD. In our three studies on the incidence of ASD we used the Acute Stress Disorder Interview (ASDI; Bryant, Harvey, Dang, & Sackville, 1998). The ASDI is the only structured interview schedule with known psychometric properties that provides diagnostic information relating to the presence of ASD. We describe it in detail in chapter 5. Overall, the incidence of ASD is lower than previously reported rates of posttraumatic stress in the acute posttrauma phase (compare Table 3.3 with Table 3.1). The lower frequency of ASD probably can be attributed to the more stringent criteria described in the diagnosis of ASD. Nonetheless, the observed incidence of ASD supports the rationale that significant levels of distress do occur in the acute posttrauma phase.

ACUTE DISSOCIATION AND PTSD

The second reason given for the inclusion of ASD in *DSM–IV* is the purported ability of acute dissociation to predict PTSD (Koopman et al., 1995). Numerous studies have reported that dissociative reactions at the time of the trauma are highly predictive of posttraumatic stress symptoms (Bremner & Brett, 1997; Holen, 1993; Koopman, Classen, & Spiegel, 1994; Marmor et al., 1994; McFarlane, 1986; Shalev, Orr, & Pitman, 1993; Shalev, Peri, Canetti, & Schreiber, 1996; Solomon & Mikulincer, 1992; Solomon, Mikulincer, & Benbenishty, 1989). For example, in one of the first studies to investigate this issue, Holen (1993) found that peritraumatic dissociation in survivors of the 1980 North Sea oil rig disaster predicted subsequent adjustment. Similarly, Solomon et al. (1989) reported that numbing in the acute trauma phase accounted for 20% of the variance of subsequent PTSD.

There is evidence to suggest, however, that the reported relationship between acute dissociation and subsequent PTSD is more complex than has often been assumed. Furthermore, there are serious methodological problems in numerous studies offered to support the acute dissociation–PTSD relationship. This contrary evidence includes the following:

1. A number of the studies reporting a relationship between dissociation and PTSD are based on retrospective reports (Bremner & Brett, 1997; Holen, 1993; Marmor et al., 1994; McFarlane, 1986; Solomon et al., 1989).
2. Whereas early dissociative responses have been linked to persistent PTSD in nonsexual assault victims, this relationship has not been observed in rape victims (Dancu, Riggs, Hearst-Ikeda, Shoyer, & Foa, 1996).
3. One retrospective investigation of ASD after motor vehicle

accidents found that early dissociation was not indicative of poorer outcome at 6 months posttrauma (Barton, Blanchard, & Hickling, 1996).

4. Dissociation is not necessarily present in PTSD, and it has been shown to decrease over time in those who do initially display it (Davidson, Kudler, Saunders, & Smith, 1989).

5. Holen (1993) reported that whereas peritraumatic reactions were predictive of short-term outcome, they were less important in contributing to longer term adjustment.

6. Most studies of dissociative reactions after trauma are limited by their reliance on measures that have not been adequately validated. The use of questionnaires that purport to index dissociative reactions is problematic because the factors that mediate endorsement of items on dissociation questionnaires in the posttraumatic phase are unknown. For example, the use of the Dissociative Experiences Scale (DES; Bernstein & Putnam, 1986) to index dissociative psychopathology is troublesome because numerous studies have found that DES scores are associated more with gross psychopathology than with specific dissociative dysfunctions (Nash et al., 1993; Norton, Ross, & Novotny, 1990; Sandberg & Lynn, 1992).

The need for prospective study of the relationship between acute dissociation and PTSD is highlighted by evidence that memory for trauma can change over time (Foa, Molnar, & Cashman, 1995; Wagenaar & Groeneweg, 1990). Current levels of trauma symptoms can influence the recall of both trauma memories (Southwick, Morgan, Nicolaou, & Charney, 1997) and acute symptoms (Harvey & Bryant, 1999a). It is possible that highly distressed trauma survivors retrospectively report more dissociative-type reactions in the acute trauma phase because of their current mood. Accordingly, the relationship between peritraumatic dissociative reactions and subsequent PTSD must be evaluated on the basis of prospective studies.

A number of prospective studies have investigated the relationship between acute dissociative symptoms and subsequent PTSD (Dancu et al., 1996; Koopman et al., 1994). Although Koopman et al. (1994) did not diagnose ASD, acute dissociative symptoms predicted PTSD severity more accurately than initial anxiety symptoms (D. Spiegel et al., 1996). Dancu et al. (1996) found that whereas early dissociative responses were linked to persistent PTSD in nonsexual assault victims, this relationship was not observed in rape victims. This study found that initial dissociative responses after rape were related to posttraumatic psychopathology rather than PTSD. Ehlers, Mayor, and Bryant (1998) conducted a longitudinal study of patients who were admitted to an emergency room after motor vehicle accidents, and reassessed them at 3-month and 1-year follow-ups.

They found that chronic PTSD was associated with trauma severity, perceived threat, female gender, previous emotional problems, and dissociation during the trauma. Using a similar design, Shalev, Freedman, et al. (1998) assessed trauma survivors who presented at an emergency room, and reassessed them 1 week, 1 month, and 4 months posttrauma. Although they did not report predictive power of acute symptoms, they found that individuals who subsequently developed PTSD and comorbid depression reported more peritraumatic dissociation than those who subsequently developed only PTSD, who in turn reported more dissociation than those with only depression or no disorder. In summary, although there are initial indications that suggest a relationship between peritraumatic dissociation and PTSD, it appears that this relationship is not linear or uniform.

ACUTE REEXPERIENCING AND PTSD

It is recognized by most models of posttraumatic stress that emotional processing of the trauma can be facilitated by intrusive thoughts and images (Foa & Hearst-Ikeda, 1996; Horowitz, 1986). It is proposed that reexperiencing symptoms allow the person to process the trauma-related schema by allowing activation and modification of the fear network. In this sense, acute reexperiencing symptoms are potentially adaptive. In keeping with this proposal, there is evidence that intrusive recollections of the trauma are not strong predictors of ongoing PTSD (McFarlane, 1988a; Perry, Difede, Musngi, Frances, & Jacobsberg, 1992; Shalev, 1992). Accordingly, it has been postulated that persistent, rather than initial, intrusive recollections of the trauma are associated with posttraumatic psychopathology (Ehlers & Steil, 1995). There is some evidence, however, that reexperiencing symptoms in the immediate trauma phase can be predictive of persistent PTSD (Rothbaum et al., 1992). Moreover, Shalev, Freedman, et al. (1998) found that trauma survivors who subsequently developed PTSD reported higher Impact of Event Scale (IES; Horowitz, Wilner, & Alvarez, 1979) scores in the acute phase than those who developed depression.

ACUTE AVOIDANCE AND PTSD

According to network models of trauma response, initial intrusions can result in avoidance activity that impedes activation and modification of the fear network (Litz & Keane, 1989). This model suggests that the extent to which initial intrusions are predictive of later PTSD depends, in part, on the presence of avoidance during the acute trauma phase. It is held that cognitive or behavioral avoidance strategies can impair the opportunity for traumatic material to be engaged and resolved, and therefore it is theorized that avoidance is a primary predictor of chronic PTSD. Although persistent avoidance behavior in PTSD has been reported to be predictive of ongoing disturbance (Bryant & Harvey, 1995b; Schwarz & Kowalski, 1992; Solomon, Mikulincer, & Flum, 1988), the relationship between acute avoidance and intrusions appears complex. Two prospective studies used path analyses to clarify the relationship of intrusions and avoidance (Creamer et al., 1992; McFarlane, 1992a). Both studies found that avoidance did not predict disturbance 1 year later. Furthermore, although the relationship between intrusions and avoidance was strong soon after the trauma, it weakened as time elapsed (Creamer et al., 1992). Other prospective studies have indicated that whereas intrusions decline over time, avoidance behaviors can develop as time proceeds (Shalev, 1992; Solomon et al., 1993). The degree of independence between intrusions and avoidance when assessed some time after a trauma may indicate that factors other than intrusions contribute to avoidance behavior (Ehlers & Steil, 1995). In this context, note Horowitz's (1986) claim that initial avoidance may serve as a modulating defense that permits management of adverse emotions as the person copes with the experience. In this sense, initial avoidance may serve an adaptive function and assist resolution during the acute phase. Taken together, the available data suggest that the relationship between initial avoidance and later PTSD is not as critical as the role of more persistent avoidance patterns.

ACUTE AROUSAL AND PTSD

In terms of the role of acute arousal in the development of longer term psychopathology, there have been few controlled studies. McFarlane (1992a, 1992b) has noted that the emphasis on roles of intrusions and avoidance has led to a relative neglect of investigations of acute arousal. Supporting the notion that acute arousal may play a role in mediating PTSD, Weisaeth (1989a) has reported that the persistence of anxiety and sleep disturbance after the first 2 weeks posttrauma predicts subsequent PTSD. In contrast, there is evidence that acute arousal symptoms observed after trauma typically subside in the following weeks (Cardeña & Spiegel, 1993). More substantive research pertaining to arousal has focused on psychophysiological responses rather than reported symptoms. We review that research later in this chapter.

THE RELATIONSHIP BETWEEN ASD AND PTSD

The ability of the ASD diagnosis to identify acutely traumatized individuals who will subsequently develop PTSD needs to be considered in the context of current understanding of the course of PTSD development. Previous prospective studies have used PTSD criteria (minus the duration criterion) in the initial month and subsequently assessed for PTSD in the following months. For example, Riggs, Rothbaum, and Foa (1995) reported that 70% of women and 50% of men who were assaulted were diagnosed with PTSD an average of 19 days posttrauma. However, at 4 months posttrauma the rate of PTSD had dropped to 21% for women and zero for men. Rothbaum et al. (1992) reported that 94% of rape victims interviewed an average of 2 weeks posttrauma met criteria for PTSD and that 3 weeks later this proportion dropped to 64% and then to 47% at 11 weeks postassessment. Similarly, half of a sample meeting criteria for PTSD after a motor vehicle accident had remitted by 6 months, and two thirds had remitted by 1 year posttrauma (Blanchard, Hickling, Barton, et al., 1996). In slight contrast, Koren, Arnon, and Klein (1999) reported that motor vehicle accident victims who met criteria for PTSD at 1 year posttrauma had displayed more severe PTSD symptoms in the acute phase than those who did not develop PTSD. They found, however, that this difference was most apparent at 3 months posttrauma, when symptoms seemed to stabilize. Overall, prospective studies of the course of PTSD have found that most people who are symptomatic in the initial month remit in the following months. Accordingly, the merits of the ASD diagnosis need to be evaluated by comparing its ability to identify those people who will develop PTSD versus previous studies that have used existing PTSD criteria.

In an initial study that was offered to support the proposed ASD criteria, Spiegel et al. (1996) prospectively studied 154 survivors of the 1991 Oakland–Berkeley, CA, firestorm. Survivors completed an inventory of dissociative and anxiety symptoms (SASRQ; Cardeña et al., 1991) within 3 weeks of the fire and the Civilian Version of the Mississippi Scale for Posttraumatic Stress Disorder (Keane, Wolfe, & Taylor, 1987) and the IES (Horowitz et al., 1979) 7 months later. The procedure used in this study to determine the relationship between ASD and PTSD was to investigate the sensitivity and specificity of each acute symptom in predicting a group of participants who at follow-up comprised the 18 people with the highest 5% on the psychopathology measures. Using this method, Spiegel et al. (1996) observed that three dissociative symptoms combined with reexperiencing, avoidance, and arousal symptoms best predicted subsequent distress. Although this study benefited from a prospective design, its conclusions are limited by a number of procedural issues. First, this combination of symptoms was not related to a subsequent diagnosis of PTSD. Accordingly, it is impossible to determine from this data the extent to which these symptoms predicted a diagnosis of PTSD. Second, the initial sample collected by the authors represented only 21% of the population that they approached. Demonstration of the utility of acute symptoms that predict later psychopathology requires more representative samples of traumatized populations.

In the first study to investigate the relationship between ASD and PTSD, we assessed 92 successive motor vehicle accident survivors for ASD and subsequently reassessed 71 of them for PTSD 6 months posttrauma. Of those who initially met criteria for ASD, 78% were diagnosed with PTSD 6 months posttrauma (Harvey & Bryant, 1998d). In a parallel study of motor vehicle accident survivors who sustained a mild traumatic brain injury, 82% of those with ASD subsequently had PTSD 6 months posttrauma (Bryant & Harvey, 1998b). The lower remission rates in individuals with ASD relative to these previous studies suggest that the ASD diagnostic criteria performed better than the PTSD criteria in identifying those individuals who subsequently develop persistent PTSD.

In terms of participants who met criteria for a subclinical level of ASD, 60% presented with PTSD 6 months posttrauma (Harvey & Bryant, 1998d). This finding suggests that the current ASD criteria do not adequately describe all individuals who subsequently develop PTSD. Most of the subclinical participants who subsequently developed PTSD did not satisfy the dissociative criteria for ASD. It appears that although acute dissociative symptoms are important precursors of longer term PTSD, they are not sufficient to adequately identify all those who are at risk of developing chronic PTSD. This pattern is supported by the finding that the dissociative symptoms possessed high negative predictive power but only moderate-to-high positive predictive power. That is, whereas most participants who did not develop PTSD did not display acute dissociative symptoms, a significant proportion of participants who developed PTSD did not experience acute dissociative symptoms.

To further clarify the relationship between ASD and chronic PTSD, we reassessed the participants from our initial sample 2 years after their trauma. In terms of those who completed all three assessments, 75% of those who initially met criteria for ASD qualified for a diagnosis of PTSD at 2 years posttrauma (Harvey & Bryant, in press-c). Importantly, however, 70% of those who initially displayed subclinical levels of ASD also satisfied criteria for PTSD 2 years posttrauma. Considering that nearly all of the latter participants satisfied all ASD criteria except for the dissociative symptoms, this provides further evidence that acute dissociative symptoms are not necessary for the development of long-term PTSD. These findings indicate that future revisions of the ASD criteria may need to consider alternative paths by which acute stress reactions can lead to chronic PTSD. For example, whereas some individuals who develop long-term PTSD may display acute dissociative responses, others may also suffer chronic PTSD without using dissociative mechanisms in the acute phase.

Other prospective studies have added support to the predictive ability of the ASD diagnosis. Brewin, Andrews, Rose, and Kirk (1999) found that

83% of assault victims who initially satisfied ASD criteria were subsequently diagnosed with PTSD at 6 months follow-up. Classen et al. (1998) reported a study that investigated the relationship between ASD symptoms and subsequent posttraumatic stress (rather than PTSD status). This study entered demographic variables, degree of exposure to trauma, and diagnosis of ASD as three separate blocks of independent variables into a stepwise multiple regression. In keeping with the studies described above, a diagnosis of ASD within 8 days of the trauma was found to be a significant predictor of the level of posttraumatic stress symptoms at 7 to 10 months posttrauma. Although Creamer and Manning (1998) reassessed their sample 3 months posttrauma, the experience of counseling for most survivors precluded any inference concerning the predictive power of the initial ASD diagnosis.

PREDICTIVE POWER OF ASD SYMPTOMS

The longitudinal design of our studies allowed us to index the predictive power of each symptom specified by the ASD criteria. We defined *positive* predictive power as the probability of PTSD developing when an ASD symptom was present. This probability was calculated by dividing the number of participants who reported each ASD symptom and who later developed PTSD by the total number of individuals who reported each ASD symptom. We defined *negative* predictive power as the probability of not developing PTSD when an ASD symptom was absent. This probability was calculated by dividing the number of participants who did not report each ASD symptom and who later did not develop PTSD by the total number of those who did not report the symptom. The predictive power of each symptom is presented in Table 3.4. The moderate-to-strong positive and negative predictive powers found for the dissociative symptoms underscore the importance of dissociative symptoms in the acute trauma response (Koopman et al., 1995). Numbing and depersonalization had the strongest positive and negative predictive powers. The results relating to numbing were consistent with previous reports that numbing best distinguished individuals with and without PTSD after assault (Foa, Riggs, & Gershung, 1995). There was evidence in this data, however, that questioned the current emphasis on dissociation in the ASD criteria. First, the dissociative symptoms performed better at predicting the absence of PTSD rather than its presence and thus may need to be refined to maximally detect the presence of PTSD. Second, there was much overlap among the dissociative symptoms, a pattern that was observed by others (Bremner et al., 1997). This finding questioned the extent to which the dissociative symptoms specified by the ASD criteria were distinct entities. Third, 60% of those who satisfied all ASD criteria except dissociation suffered PTSD at 6 months posttrauma. This finding suggested that acute dissociation was

TABLE 3.4
Positive and Negative Predictive Power of Each ASD Symptom

ASD symptom	Positive predictive power[a]	Negative predictive power[b]
Fear	.31	.86
Helplessness	.30	.93
Numbing	.79	.88
Reduced awareness	.60	.84
Derealization	.55	.88
Depersonalization	.80	.84
Dissociative amnesia	—	—
Recurrent images and thoughts	.56	.91
Nightmares	.55	.80
Sense of reliving the experience	.86	.81
Distress on exposure	.48	.87
Avoidance of thoughts or discussions	.65	.87
Avoidance of places or people	.58	.87
Difficulty sleeping	.41	.87
Irritability	.35	.78
Poor concentration	.56	.84
Hypervigilance	.31	.85
Exaggerated startle response	.59	.85
Motor restlessness	.73	.83

Note. ASD = acute stress disorder; PTSD = posttraumatic stress disorder. Dissociative amnesia was not indexed in this study.
[a]Probability of the presence of PTSD when the symptom is present. [b]Probability of the absence of PTSD when the symptom is absent.

not necessarily a prerequisite to PTSD. Fourth, a sense of reliving the traumatic experience and motor restlessness also had strong predictive power. These findings provided support for the proposal that acute arousal and distress are also important mediators in posttraumatic adjustment (Ehlers & Steil, 1995; Shalev, 1992).

PREDICTORS OF ASD

Only a few studies have assessed predictors of ASD. This situation contrasts with the extensive body of research that exists on predictors of PTSD (Blanchard, Hickling, Taylor, et al., 1996; Blanchard, Hickling, Taylor, Loos, & Gerardi, 1994; Dunmore, Clark, & Ehlers, 1997). Although there are good reasons to suggest that similar factors will predict ASD, there is a need for further empirical study.

The first study to specifically assess the interaction between other disorders and ASD was reported by Barton et al. (1996). This study found that individuals diagnosed with ASD showed more psychiatric dysfunction (Axis I and Axis II disorders) before the trauma than a group who did not meet criteria for ASD but were later diagnosed with PTSD. In addition,

Barton et al. observed a trend suggesting that ASD participants had higher rates of prior PTSD and previous exposure to traumatic events. Although these results were limited by the retrospective diagnosis of ASD, they suggested that like PTSD, psychological vulnerability predisposes one to developing ASD.

We examined a number of predictors of severity of ASD in our initial sample. Acute stress severity was obtained from the total symptom score derived from the ASDI. The possible variables we considered were age, Beck Depression Inventory (BDI; Beck, Ward, Mendelson, Mock, & Erbaugh, 1961) score, coping style, neuroticism, objective injury severity, DES score, period of hospitalization, previous motor vehicle accidents, previous trauma, history of psychiatric treatment, history of PTSD, perceived severity of trauma, and sex. For the nontraumatically brain-injured sample, BDI, history of psychiatric treatment, history of PTSD, and previous motor vehicle accidents were the significant predictors and accounted for 61% of the variance (Harvey & Bryant, 1999d). For the traumatically brain-injured sample, BDI, PTSD history, age, and an avoidant coping style were the best predictors, accounting for 67% of the variance (Harvey & Bryant, 1998c). The percentage of variance accounted for by the multiple regressions was impressive because previous studies with motor vehicle accident populations had generated models that accounted for approximately 40% of the variance in PTSD symptoms (e.g., Blanchard, Hickling, Barton, et al., 1996; Bryant & Harvey, 1995c). It is probable that the acute trauma phase, as opposed to longer term adjustment, is dominated by specific psychological factors associated with vulnerability. In contrast, more chronic PTSD may be moderated by diverse factors relating to vocational, legal, and adjustment issues.

There is indirect evidence that people who develop ASD may have a preexisting tendency to engage in dissociative mechanisms. Hypnotizability is often regarded as a gold standard of measuring behavioral features of dissociation. Considering that hypnotizability is a reasonably stable trait over time (Piccione et al., 1989), it would be expected that people with ASD would display elevated levels of hypnotizability. To test this proposal, we administered ASD, subclinical ASD, and no-ASD participants the Stanford Hypnotic Clinical Scale (Morgan & Hilgard, 1978–1979) within several weeks of their trauma (Bryant, Guthrie, & Moulds, 1999). Interestingly, ASD participants displayed higher hypnotizability levels than subclinical ASD and no-ASD participants. ASD and subclinical ASD participants displayed comparable levels of acute stress, except that subclinical participants lacked dissociative reactions. One interpretation of this finding is that those participants who had higher dissociative skills responded to their trauma with the particular symptoms described in ASD. In contrast, those distressed participants with lower hypnotizability responded with nondissociative posttraumatic stress reactions.

A number of other studies have assessed factors associated with severity of acute dissociative, intrusive, and avoidance symptoms. For example, Koopman, Classen, and Spiegel (1996) found that early dissociative symptoms after exposure to the Oakland–Berkeley fires were associated with level of exposure to the trauma, female gender, inappropriate coping behaviors, and previous stressful events. In a study of motor vehicle accident victims, acute intrusive symptoms were predicted by fear of the motor vehicle accident, trait anxiety, and absence of traumatic brain injury, and acute avoidance symptoms were predicted by fear, trait anxiety, death of a loved one, and financial difficulty (Bryant & Harvey, 1996a). Although Solomon et al. (1993) reported no significant predictors of avoidance, severity of intrusions was predicted by the degree of threat, exposure to injury, and property loss.

Overall, the vulnerability, event-related, and response-related predictors that have emerged from these initial studies are consistent with predictors of PTSD (see Blanchard, Hickling, Taylor, et al., 1996; Blanchard et al., 1994; Dunmore et al., 1997). Considering the small number of studies that have been conducted on vulnerability to developing ASD, it is useful to consider the vast information we have concerning risk factors for developing PTSD. It is likely that a genetic predisposition plays a role in development of ASD. In a twin study of Vietnam veterans, it was found that genetics accounted for 13% to 30% of the variance of reexperiencing symptoms, 30% to 34% of avoidance symptoms, and 28% to 32% of arousal symptoms (True et al., 1993). Although twin studies have not been conducted with ASD populations, it is probable that future research will find that hereditary factors play an important contributing role.

COGNITIVE PROCESSES IN ASD

A number of studies have investigated the cognitive processes that mediate acute stress reactions. These studies have focused on the management of traumatic memories, coping strategies, cognitive biases, and attributions in the acute trauma phase.

Management of Traumatic Memories

In a qualitative investigation of the influence of dissociation on traumatic memories, we conducted an assessment of acutely traumatized individuals' narratives. We audiotaped the narrated recollections of survivors of motor vehicle accidents, who either did or did not suffer ASD. These narratives were subsequently coded in terms of dissociative content, disorganized structure, and perception of threat. In keeping with the proposal that dissociative responses characterize ASD, we found that the narratives of ASD participants included more descriptions of dissociation than did those of non-ASD participants. Furthermore, disorganization in the structure of the narrative was associated with dissociation for ASD participants (Harvey & Bryant, in press-b). This fragmented organization of trauma memories may reduce the ability to organize and retrieve traumatic memories in individuals with ASD (Spiegel, 1996; van der Kolk, 1996b). This interpretation is in keeping with findings that resolution of PTSD symptoms is associated with increased organization of traumatic memories after treatment (Foa, Molnar, & Cashman, 1995).

Recent experimental work has found that the ability to manage and recall traumatic memories is a critical factor mediating acute and longer term posttraumatic response (Harvey, Bryant, & Dang, 1998). In this study, motor vehicle accident survivors with or without ASD participated in an autobiographical memory experiment within 1 week of their trauma. Participants were provided with cue words to elicit autobiographical memories of both an unconstrained time period and also of the 12 hours after their trauma. Participants with ASD reported fewer specific memories both of the unconstrained period and of the trauma than did non-ASD participants. This finding suggests that ASD is associated with impaired access to memories of the trauma. The same participants were reassessed for PTSD 6 months later. Impaired recall of specific memories of the trauma in the acute phase accounted for 25% of the variance of PTSD severity. This finding implicates impaired retrieval of specific memories in the acute trauma phase as a mediator in the development of a chronic trauma response. Although dissociative theory would predict that individuals with ASD should have deficits in aversive memories, participants with ASD were characterized by poorer recall of positive experiences. It is possible that difficulty in accessing positive experiences in the acute phase impedes modification of fear-related beliefs because one cannot optimally compare current cognitions with previous positive experiences. This interpretation is consistent with the proposal that adaptive recovery from a trauma depends on accessing cognitive schema that can be appropriately modified (Foa et al., 1989). It is also consistent with evidence of problem-solving deficits in PTSD sufferers, who may have impaired ability to draw on past experiences to resolve current difficulties (Nezu & Carnevale, 1987).

Coping Strategies

There is considerable evidence that coping strategies play a significant role in posttraumatic adjustment. Information-processing theories hold that strategies that result in impaired activation of the fear network lead to continued dysfunction (Foa et al., 1989). Consistent with this prediction, strategies that result in avoidance of the traumatic experience tend to contribute to long-term dysfunction (Bryant & Harvey, 1995b; Solomon et al.,

1988). In an initial investigation of cognitive avoidance in ASD, Harvey and Bryant (1998b) instructed ASD and non-ASD participants to monitor the frequency of their trauma memories during three successive 5-minute periods: (a) when they were told to think about anything, (b) when they were administered suppression or nonsuppression instructions, and (c) when they were asked only to monitor their memories. Participants who were instructed to suppress their memories displayed a delayed increase in the frequency of their memories when the suppression instructions were terminated. This finding indicated that effortful cognitive avoidance could lead to increased traumatic intrusions. The inferences of this study were limited, however, because suppressing for periods of 5 minutes did not accurately reflect the prolonged cognitive avoidance typically displayed by acutely traumatized individuals.

In a replication of this design that studied the effects of attempted suppression over three 24-hour periods, Guthrie and Bryant (in press) did not find a delayed increase in intrusions. Interestingly, they observed that efforts to suppress and anxiety levels were related to participants' tendencies to use worry and punishment as coping strategies. This finding accords with reports that people with ASD use punishment and worry more often than non-ASD participants to manage their traumatic memories (Warda & Bryant, 1998b). These strategies, which attempt to control the aversive memories through maladaptive avoidance, also have been associated with other anxiety disorders (Amir, Cashman, & Foa, 1997). Furthermore, resolution of ASD after treatment is associated with a reduction in worry and punishment strategies (Bryant, Moulds, & Guthrie, 1999a). Overall, these findings raise the possibility that strategies that attempt to avoid awareness of traumatic memories may contribute to greater distress and symptomatology.

Cognitive Bias

Recent attention also has focused on the content of the cognitive responses of survivors of motor vehicle accidents diagnosed with ASD. There is evidence that people with ASD exaggerate both the probability of future negative events occurring and the adverse effects of these events more than do people without ASD (Warda & Bryant, 1998a). For example, ASD individuals may consider it more likely that they will encounter a spider than those without ASD. Furthermore, the individual diagnosed with ASD will overestimate the severity of the harm that the spider will cause him or her. These findings agree with previous reports of cognitive bias in other anxiety disorders (Butler & Mathews, 1983; Foa, Franklin, Perry, & Herbert, 1996). Interestingly, individuals with panic disorder display cognitive biases that are specific to physiological arousal and not to events that are unrelated to arousal (McNally & Foa, 1987), and social phobia individuals tend to exhibit higher probability estimates of negative social events but not of nonsocial events (Foa et al., 1996). In contrast, trauma survivors with ASD display exaggerated estimates about threats pertaining to external harm, somatic sensations, and social situations (Smith & Bryant, in press). This finding accords with theoretical propositions that posttraumatic anxiety is characterized by fear networks that are more pervasive than other anxiety disorders (Foa et al., 1989).

Attributions

The importance of cognitive responses in the acute posttrauma phase also has been underscored by findings that motor vehicle accident survivors in the acute posttrauma phase who attribute responsibility for their accident to others suffer more severe PTSD 12 months later than those who make self-attributions (Delahanty et al., 1997). A study with a similar focus assessed 157 crime victims within 1 month of the trauma and then again 6 months later (Andrews, Brewin, Rose, & Kirk, 1998). Variables assessed within 1 month posttrauma included childhood physical and sexual abuse and response to the recent trauma, including shame, blame (self and other), and anger (self and other). The major independent predictors of PTSD at 6 months posttrauma were shame and anger with others, and when baseline symptom severity was controlled for, shame alone predicted PTSD.

BIOLOGICAL PROCESSES

In recent years, there has been increasing attention to biological processes that can mediate acute stress reactions. A major line of research has implicated elevated arousal in the acute phase as a primary mediator of subsequent PTSD. One recent study reported that resting heart rates of civilian trauma survivors obtained when they arrived at a hospital emergency department and also 1 week later were higher in those who later developed PTSD than those who did not; they did not differ at 1 or 4 months follow-up (Shalev, Sahar, et al., 1998). Similarly, we found that heart rates obtained before people were discharged from a hospital after a motor vehicle accident were significantly higher in those who later developed PTSD than those who did not (Bryant, Harvey, Guthrie, & Moulds, in press). Interestingly, this study also found that participants who had acute stress reactions but no acute dissociation (i.e., subclinical ASD) had higher heart rates than those who either had ASD or did not have ASD. One interpretation of this finding is that the dissociative mechanisms displayed by ASD participants may have been associated with suppression of arousal. These results are consistent with reports that rape victims in the acute posttrauma phase who are highly dissociative are less physiologically reactive to trauma reminders than those who are not dissociative (Griffin, Resick, & Mechanic, 1997).

Another interesting development in our understanding of ASD has been findings of lowered cortisol levels in acutely traumatized people who subsequently develop PTSD. In a sample of motor vehicle accident survivors who were assessed in the acute posttrauma phase, those who subsequently developed PTSD had lower serum cortisol levels than those who did not develop PTSD and those who later developed depression (McFarlane, Atchison, & Yehuda, 1997). This finding is consistent with an earlier report that found that acute cortisol levels after rape were lower in those who had been previously traumatized (Resnick, Yehuda, Pitman, & Foy, 1995). These findings have been understood in terms of dysfunction in the feedback mechanism of the hypothalmic–pituitary–adrenal axis in PTSD populations (Yehuda, 1997). Specifically, it is proposed that cortisol functions as an antistress hormone that counters a series of biological reactions initiated by a stressful event. Consequently, reduced cortisol in the acute phase may contribute to dysfunctional elevated arousal.

A MODEL OF ASD

Figures 3.1 and 3.2 present an integrative model of ASD that addresses the available evidence concerning ASD and its relationship to PTSD (Harvey & Bryant, 1999b). Figure 3.1 depicts the processes involved in the development from acute stress reactions to PTSD. Figure 3.2 illustrates the process of acute stress reactions that result in resolution. This model recognizes that there are multiple pathways to PTSD and that acute dissociation is not a necessary precursor to PTSD. Although this model is based on network theory, it places emphasis on the interaction of acute cognitive and physiological processes in the mediation of PTSD. Our model is intended both to accommodate current findings of ASD and to generate further hypotheses, to extend our understanding of acute and longer term trauma adjustment.

The model proposes that ASD is more likely to develop in those who have predisposing characteristics, including genetic predisposition, previous psychiatric history, and avoidant coping styles. Furthermore, it is likely that future research may discover that some of the features observed to be associated with ASD, including elevated arousal, lowered cortisol, overgeneral retrieval style, and cognitive bias may be vulnerability factors rather than sequelae of ASD. The model specifies dissociative tendencies as a vulnerability factor because they appear to predispose these individuals to engage in avoidance strategies that impair processing of the traumatic memories.

In keeping with network theories, the model proposes that a fear

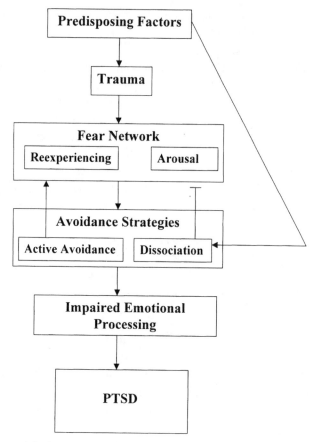

Figure 3.1. A model of acute stress reactions and posttraumatic stress disorder (PTSD).

network is established after the trauma. This network contains many representations of the traumatic experience because corrective information has not been adequately integrated. Moreover, it is held that the heightened arousal in the acute phase contributes to frequent activation of the network. The model differs from existing theories of PTSD because of the emphasis it places on the management of the fear network. Specifically, it holds that individuals who have a preexisting tendency to dissociative mechanisms will attempt to manage the fear network using dissociative responses. This activity will result in dampened arousal in the acute phase, which will be observed in lower heart rates and possibly will be mediated by reduced cortisol levels. In contrast, those who do not have dissociative tendencies will use more effortful coping skills, and these individuals will experience heightened arousal that will contribute to activation of the fear network. This aspect of the model accounts for the different arousal patterns in acutely traumatized people who dissociate and those who do not have this tendency.

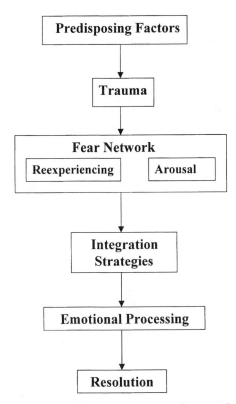

Figure 3.2. A model of acute stress reactions and resolution.

In terms of factors that mediate adjustment to the trauma, the model proposes that strategies that impede activation of the fear network, such as dissociation and avoidance, will lead to impaired emotional processing and persistent PTSD. These strategies can include dissociative responses, disorganized memory structure, impaired retrieval of trauma memories, and effortful avoidance. Individuals who continue to engage in these reactions during the acute phase will be characterized by fear networks that contribute to attentional bias to threat, reexperiencing symptoms, and catastrophic estimates of future harm. This aspect of the model accounts for findings that people can develop PTSD after suffering ASD or subclinical levels of ASD that do not involve dissociative reactions. It also recognizes that most people in the acute phase will suffer reexperiencing and, to some extent, engage in avoidance strategies. These factors are not highly predictive of subsequent PTSD, however, because only persistent avoidance strategies impede processing of traumatic material.

In contrast, those who adopt more adaptive strategies that permit sustained activation of the fear network and integration of corrective information will benefit from a resolution of a transient stress reaction (see Figure 3.2). This component of the model is consistent with treatment studies that indicate resolution of ASD through prolonged exposure and cognitive therapy (Bryant, Harvey, Dang, Sackville, & Basten, 1998; Bryant, Sackville, Dang, Moulds, & Guthrie, in press). It is also in accord with evidence suggesting that whereas most people report an array of acute stress symptoms in the initial weeks after a trauma, the majority of these people achieve resolution in the following months (Blanchard, Hickling, Barton et al., 1996; Riggs et al., 1995; Rothbaum et al., 1992).

II

ASSESSMENT

4

HOW TO DIAGNOSE ACUTE STRESS DISORDER

As noted in chapter 1, the diagnosis of ASD was introduced into *DSM–IV* with little empirical basis and without the benefits of systematic study to empirically drive its criteria. One consequence of this lack of preparation for the diagnosis is that there are a number of anomalies in the diagnostic criteria that may influence the accuracy of diagnostic decisions. In this chapter, we review the diagnostic criteria, highlight some of the problems in the current definition of ASD, and point to specific issues that need to be considered in assessing acutely traumatized people.

DIAGNOSTIC CRITERIA

Criterion A: The Stressor

The diagnostic criteria for ASD commences with the requirement that the person should have experienced or witnessed an event that has been threatening to either himself or herself or another person. Furthermore, it prescribes that the "person's response involved intense fear, helplessness, or horror" (American Psychiatric Association, 1994, p. 431). The relative contributions of the objective and subjective components of the stressor have been strongly debated in recent years. Although diagnostic reliability and homogeneity may be increased with an objective definition of the stressor, there is strong evidence that a stringent definition of the stressor severity would lead to false-negative diagnoses (Snow, Stellman, Stellman, & Sommer, 1988). There are many examples of PTSD symptoms occurring after less severe traumas (Burstein, 1985; Helzer, Robins, & McEvoy, 1987). Furthermore, there have been numerous reports that emphasize the importance of perceived threat in predicting PTSD (Bryant & Harvey, 1996a; Mikulincer & Solomon, 1988; Speed, Engdahl, Schwartz, & Eberly, 1989). Accordingly, DSM–IV adopted the position that the definition of the stressor should involve both objective and subjective dimensions (March, 1993). The use of this definition in ASD is supported by findings that acute stress responses are associated with both severe objective stressors (Marmor et al., 1994) and severe subjective perceptions of threat (Bryant & Harvey, 1996a).

The subjective component of the stressor definition is problematic, however, in the context of the dissociative cluster of symptoms. The first dissociative symptom cited in DSM–IV is "a subjective sense of numbing, detachment, or absence of emotional responsiveness" (American Psychiatric Association, 1994, p. 432). There appears to be a possible inconsistency in the juxtaposition of the requirement of a fearful perception of the event and the experience of emotional numbing. For example, a person who has survived an earthquake but reports no salient emotional response to this event would not satisfy the stressor criterion for ASD. It is possible, however, that this person's lack of emotional response may be attributed to a dissociative reaction to the trauma. Thus, a strict adherence to the DSM–IV criteria may result in false-negative diagnoses. Although this potential problem also exists in the diagnosis of PTSD, which may include emotional numbing, it appears to be a more prominent difficulty in ASD because of the requirement that diagnosed individuals must display dissociative symptoms. Modification of the description of the response to the stressor to include behavioral manifestations of distress (e.g., nonresponsiveness or detachment) may reconcile, to some extent, the anomaly of dissociative responses and the requirement that the individual responds with fear or helplessness.

Criterion B: Dissociation

The ASD criteria require the presence of three of the following dissociative symptoms: numbing, reduced awareness, derealization, depersonalization, and dissociative amnesia. In chapter 3, we reviewed evidence that in some studies (but not all), acute dissociative symptoms have been fairly good predictors of PTSD (Bryant & Harvey, 1998b; Harvey & Bryant, 1998d; Spiegel et al., 1996). It needs to be acknowledged, however, that there is significant overlap between the individual dissociative symptoms specified in the ASD criteria (Bremner et al., 1997). For example, in one study, 85% of individuals who reported lack of awareness of their surroundings also reported derealization (Harvey & Bryant, in press-a). One possible explanation for this overlap is that the constructs of derealization and reduced awareness are conceptually similar, and these allegedly distinct symptoms may be indexing a similar response to trauma. Furthermore, it may be repetitive to consider that a traumatized individual is suffering amnesia of the event if she or he did not adequately encode it because of reduced awareness during the trauma. That is, in some cases, regarding these two symptoms as separate responses may be artificially reifying two aspects of the same response.

Another potentially ambiguous aspect of the dissociative cluster is that dissociative symptoms may occur "while experiencing or after experiencing the distressing event" (American Psychiatric Association, 1994, p. 431). This flexible time frame is in contrast to the requirement that the reexperiencing, avoidance, and arousal symptoms need to be experienced as ongoing problems. It also is in contrast to the requirement that the disturbance arising from ASD must persist for a minimum of 2 days after the trauma. Much of the research that has documented a relationship between initial dissociative reactions and subsequent PTSD has not defined clearly when the dissociative response occurred (Koopman et al., 1994; Marmor et al., 1994; McFarlane, 1986; Shalev, Schreiber, & Galai, 1993; Solomon et al., 1989). Although there is evidence that peritraumatic dissociation is predictive of PTSD (Bremner et al., 1992; Marmor, Weiss, Metzler, & Delucchi, 1996; Marmor et al., 1994; Shalev et al., 1996; Weiss, Marmor, Metzler, & Ronfeldt, 1995), there are insufficient data to indicate the relative influences of short-lived and persistent dissociative reactions on subsequent PTSD. A number of writers have noted that acute dissociation can be a normal and even adaptive response to trauma (e.g., Horowitz, 1986; Ludwig, 1983). Network theories of trauma posit that dissociative responses that are only transient do not lead to psychopathology because they do not impede processing of the traumatic memories. As Hilgard (1977) has noted, dissociative experiences are commonplace and are observed at varying levels in the community (see Kihlstrom, Glisky, & Angiulo, 1994). For example, studies that have used the DES have found that some dissociative experiences are commonly reported in nonclinical populations (Frischholz et al., 1992; Ross, Joshi, & Currie, 1991). Furthermore, there is experimental evidence that responses that are similar to the ASD descriptions of dissociation can be elicited under conditions of stress in nontraumatized participants. For example, presenting experimental participants with a threatening object can lead to reduced awareness of many features of that experience (Kramer, Buckhout, & Eugenio, 1990; Maas & Kohnken, 1989). This experience clearly does not lead to long-term psychopathology and may simply reflect the allocation of attention to specific features of an event that are potentially threatening. Whereas *DSM–IV* stipulates that the intrusive, avoidance, and arousal symptoms need to be marked or persistent, there is no indication in *DSM–IV* that the dissociative symptoms need to be experienced at a significant level of severity. The potential risk of this ambiguous definition is that it may result in an overinclusive definition of dissociation.

Criterion C: Reexperiencing

The *DSM–IV* diagnosis requires that the trauma "is reexperienced in at least one of the following ways: recurrent images, thoughts, dreams, illusions, flashback episodes, or a sense of reliving the experience; or distress on exposure to reminders of the traumatic event" (American Psychiatric Association, 1994, p. 432). Although reexperiencing symptoms have been recognized as a hallmark of PTSD (Calhoun & Resick, 1993), there is little evidence (see chap. 3) to support the claim that they are predictive of long-term PTSD (Bryant & Harvey, 1998b; Harvey & Bryant, 1998d; McFarlane, 1988a; Perry et al., 1992; Shalev, 1992). Moreover, most theories of trauma response acknowledge that trauma resolution can be facilitated by intrusions (Foa & Hearst-Ikeda, 1996; Horowitz, 1986). In this sense, acute reexperiencing symptoms are conceptualized as potentially adaptive. It is for this reason that recent propositions have regarded persistent rather than initial intrusions as being associated with posttraumatic psychopathology (Ehlers & Steil, 1995). Note that the one acute reexperiencing symptom that does appear to have strong predictive power is a sense of reliving the trauma. That is, clinicians should be aware that reliving the experience in a way that involves strong engagement with the affective component appears to be an important reexperiencing symptom that may suggest a more psychopathological response.

Clinicians should also be aware that the reexperiencing criteria in the ASD diagnosis are dissimilar to their PTSD counterparts in two ways. First, whereas the PTSD diagnosis stipulates that the reexperiencing symptoms must cause the individual distress, the ASD diagnosis makes no mention of the negative emotional response to the traumatic thoughts or images. This omission seems surprising because not all intrusive thoughts are unwanted or unpleasant (Rachman & de Silva, 1978). The decision to not stipulate that reexperiencing symptoms be distressing is inconsistent also with the finding that the sense of reliving the experience (which involves a strong adverse emotional response) is the most predictive acute symptom of chronic PTSD (Harvey & Bryant, 1998d). Moreover, acutely traumatized individuals experience varying degrees of distress associated with their intrusions (Ehlers & Steil, 1995). In one study, it was found that although the frequency of intrusions was comparable across terrorist attack survivors within the 1st week, there were variable levels of distress associated with these memories (Shalev, Schreiber, & Galai, 1993). Similar variations in distress have been reported in motor vehicle accident survivors (Ehlers & Steil, 1995). The second difference between reexperiencing in the diagnoses of ASD and PTSD is that the ASD criteria do not describe the reexperiencing as unwanted or involuntary. There is strong evidence that controllability and frequency of unwanted thoughts are distinct factors (Parkinson & Rachman, 1981; Rachman & de Silva, 1978) and that poor control of posttraumatic memories is associated with elevated distress (Harvey & Bryant, 1998b). Considering that ASD was proposed as a precursor of PTSD, it is curious that ASD reexperiencing symptoms are not characterized as distressing or uncontrollable. Four weeks after a trauma, however, these same symptoms would not be considered reexperiencing in the definition of PTSD.

Criterion D: Avoidance

The diagnostic criteria for ASD stipulate that the person must display "marked avoidance of stimuli that arouse recollections of the trauma" (American Psychiatric Association, 1994, p. 432). This avoidance includes that of thoughts, feelings, activities, conversations, and people that may remind the person of his or her traumatic experience. In chapter 3, we reviewed the evidence that the relationship between acute avoidance and long-term PTSD is modest (Bryant & Harvey, 1998b; Harvey & Bryant, 1998d; McFarlane, 1992a). This situation contrasts with findings that persistent avoidance behavior is strongly associated with long-term PTSD (Bryant & Harvey, 1995b; Schwarz & Kowalski, 1992; Z. Solomon et al., 1988). Apart from the problems associated with its poor predictive power, the current definition of avoidance behavior in ASD is problematic because of its flexibiliy. Whereas the PTSD diagnosis requires that the person display at least three specified avoidance symptoms, the ASD diagnosis simply requires marked avoidance. This vague definition is troublesome because diagnosticians are not provided with any index of what constitutes marked avoidance. This ambiguity can lead to considerable variability in the context of acute stress because individuals can be exposed to a range of posttrauma events that either limit their capacity to avoid trauma reminders or restrict their opportunities to be exposed to trauma reminders. For example, the hospitalized trauma patient may not have the opportunity to demonstrate avoidance within this sheltered environment. Operationalizing marked avoidance in the acute trauma setting can be difficult and poses the likelihood of considerable variation in diagnostic decisions.

Criterion E: Arousal

The ASD diagnosis requires that arousal symptoms be present for at least 2 days after the trauma. Whereas the diagnosis of PTSD requires that at least two arousal symptoms be evident, the ASD diagnosis requires only marked arousal. Arousal symptoms may include restlessness, insomnia, hypervigilance, concentration difficulties, and irritability. The definition of marked arousal suffers from the same ambiguity as the loosely defined avoidance criterion. Considering that most trauma survivors experience arousal symptoms in the acute trauma phase (Cardeña & Spiegel, 1993; Feinstein, 1989; Sloan, 1988; Titchener & Kapp, 1976) and that there is evidence that most arousal symptoms remit in the initial weeks after a trauma (Cardeña & Spiegel, 1993), the probability of overdiagnosis of arousal is high. Moreover, the acute posttrauma phase is often marked by ongoing disturbances that may necessarily involve heightened arousal. For example, the hospitalized patient who is undergoing medical interventions or the bushfire victim who needs to relocate may be participating in activities that lead to heightened arousal. In chapter 3, we noted evidence that requiring three acute arousal symptoms provides a more accurate prediction of later PTSD (Harvey & Bryant, 1998d). Accordingly, diagnosticians should exercise some caution in considering their definition of marked arousal.

Criterion G: Duration

The diagnosis of ASD stipulates that the disturbance must be present for at least 2 days after the trauma but not persist for more than 1 month. It is assumed that a diagnosis of PTSD would be suitable after 1 month. The minimum duration of 2 days after the trauma is an arbitrary threshold because there are no empirical findings to suggest that symptoms that are present 48 hours after a trauma distinguish normal from pathological trauma reactions. On the contrary, research on civilians involved in the Gulf War indicates that many people suffered immediate stress symptoms, including dissociation and anxiety, for more than 2 days after the trauma and subsequently made satisfactory recoveries (Solomon et al., 1996). There is considerable evidence that more than half of the people who display posttraumatic stress symptoms in the initial weeks after a trauma remit in the following months (Blanchard, Hickling, Barton, et al., 1996; Rothbaum et al., 1992). It is possible that remission may be even more marked in the 1st weeks after a trauma. For example, a person may display marked ASD symptoms on the 3rd day after a trauma, process the traumatic memories in an adaptive manner in the ensuing days, and no longer meet diagnostic criteria several days later. Prospective studies are needed to determine the optimal period of time after a trauma that symptoms should be classified as predicting subsequent pathology. In the meantime, clinicians should exercise caution in making diagnostic decisions in the initial days after a trauma because it is possible that observed distress may simply reflect a transient response.

Criterion H: Exclusion

In keeping with most other *DSM–IV* diagnoses, a diagnosis of ASD is not made if the disturbance is better accounted for by a medical condition or substance use. Differentiating ASD symptoms from the effects of some medical conditions or substance abuse is particularly difficult. Traumatic brain injury, analgesic medications administered to injured patients, medical conditions that involve coma or impaired awareness, and substance abuse all may create alterations in awareness that can mimic dissociative symptoms. For example, the hospitalized patient who is receiving morphine after a traumatic physical injury may report reduced awareness, derealization, depersonalization, and amnesia as a direct result of the analgesic. Although a patient who has suffered such injuries may develop PTSD also, one cannot attribute these symptoms of altered awareness to dissociation. The presence of a medical condition or substance that can more parsimoniously explain the presenting symptoms should override any suspicion that dissociative processes may be involved. Similarly, the effects of traumatic brain injury can closely mimic a range of ASD symptoms. Depersonalization, derealization, reduced awareness, and dissociative amnesia can present similarly to the impaired consciousness that occurs after traumatic brain injury (Grigsby & Kaye, 1993; Gronwall & Wrightson, 1980). Moreover, most of the arousal symptoms described in the ASD criteria are frequently observed among the postconcussive symptoms following brain injury (Bohnen & Jolles, 1992). Considering the traumatic circumstances that surround the occurrence of many traumatic brain injuries, it is likely that many of these individuals may be vulnerable to ASD development. Although the exclusion of all patients who have sustained a traumatic brain injury may result in false-negative diagnoses, the adoption of a flexible definition of arousal and dissociative symptoms in brain-injured patients may increase the rate of false-positive diagnoses. We discuss specific issues related to the assessment and management of ASD in brain-injured populations more closely in chapter 9.

How Valid Is the ASD Diagnosis?

How valid is the new diagnosis of ASD? Robins and Guze (1970) described a set of standards for validating a new diagnostic entity, and these were used by Keane et al. (1987) to justify the initial PTSD diagnosis. Robins and Guze proposed that the first of their five criteria involve the completion of descriptive studies to provide a clear clinical picture of the diagnosis. Although a number of studies reporting the incidence of acute trauma symptoms had been reported when *DSM–IV* introduced the diagnosis of ASD, there were no studies that provided a specific and comprehensive clinical description of ASD. The second criterion involved laboratory studies that defined the physiological and psychological factors associated with the new diagnosis. At the time the *DSM–IV* was written, there were no such studies available to justify the symptom selection of ASD. Third, Robins and Guze proposed that a new diagnosis must ensure that its defining criteria distinguished it from other disorders. At the time of its introduction, there had been no work conducted that ensured the delineation of ASD from other disorders, especially depression and other anxiety disorders. Fourth, Robins and Guze proposed that prospective studies should be conducted because variable long-term outcomes might highlight problematic original diagnoses. As noted above, there had been no prospective studies conducted on ASD before its introduction. Finally, Robins and Guze proposed that family studies should be conducted to determine the presence of an increased prevalence for the particular diagnosis or other psychiatric disorders within families. Although the diagnosis of ASD did not satisfy any of these criteria at the time of its definition in *DSM–IV*, there is now initial support for a number of these criteria. Specifically, there is now evidence for the clinical description of ASD (Criterion 1), laboratory studies to define the psychological and physiological factors of associated with ASD (Criterion 2), and prospective data about the course of ASD and PTSD (Criterion 4).

It is probable that the definition of ASD will be modified in *DSM–V* as further research is conducted concerning the diagnostic parameters of ASD. This research should address a number of core issues. First, the utility of ASD as a diagnosis should be determined for a range of trauma populations. For example, the role of peritraumatic dissociation may vary across trauma populations. There is evidence that dissociative reactions are more frequently seen in more severe and prolonged traumatic events (Herman, Perry, & van der Kolk, 1989; Marmor et al., 1994; Zatzick, Marmor, Weiss, & Metzler, 1994). It is possible that the role of peritraumatic dissociative responses in more severe traumas, such as prolonged rape, may be different from the role of dissociative responses in less protracted traumas. Second, closer attention is needed to the distinction between normal and pathological responses in the acute posttrauma phase. This issue includes delineating the period of time after a trauma that best identifies those reactions that will develop into long-term psychopathology. Third, the exact definitions of each criterion needs to be specified, to reduce ambiguities that may lead to diagnostic variability. For example, the stipulation that dissociative symptoms may be either present at the time of the trauma or ongoing should be empirically validated, operational definitions of avoidance and arousal should be clarified, and uniformity between ASD and PTSD descriptions should be established. Fourth, the ASD criteria need to recognize that a significant proportion of trauma survivors can develop PTSD without displaying acute dissociation. The introduction of a new diagnosis invariably involves initial problems, and it is only through systematic research that the ASD diagnosis will be refined into a more useful tool.

CLINICAL CONSIDERATIONS IN ASSESSMENT

Assessing ASD involves a number of considerations that are specific to the acute trauma setting. One of the most distinctive features of assessing the acutely traumatized person is the situation created by the traumatic event. Assessment of longer term PTSD typically occurs in settings in which many of the individual and social effects of the trauma have settled to some degree. In contrast, the initial month after a traumatic event typically involves an upheaval of the previously existing conditions. This situation can influence assessment in a number of ways. The proximity of the assessment to the time of the traumatic event, the presence of posttrauma stressors, the distinctive symptom presentation of ASD, and the contextual problems that are often present in the acute trauma situation may pose specific problems that are not as problematic in the longer term assessment. In this section, we review the core issues that clinicians need to be aware of when assessing acutely traumatized individuals.

Motivation

It is common in the acute trauma phase for assessments of trauma survivors to be requested by people other than the actual clients. For example, assessment of emergency workers may be initiated by organizational authorities, or assessment of hospital patients may be initiated by medical staff. This practice can be problematic because the trauma survivor can perceive the assessment as a further violation of her or his tenuous control over the traumatic experience. Furthermore, trauma survivors commonly avoid mental health professionals because of the distress evoked by assessment of traumatic memory (Schwarz & Kowalski, 1992). Unwanted assessments can result in a hostile and avoidant response to the professional intervention and can jeopardize the client's willingness to participate in future therapeutic relationships. Consequently, assessments that are not initiated by the client should be conducted with particular care. Clarifying the reason for the assessment with the client is essential to ensure that he or she is aware of the clinician's role. Furthermore, to establish rapport and trust with the client, it can be useful to allow her or him to establish the ground rules for the assessment in a way that gives her or him a greater sense of control in the assessment. It may also be helpful to delay a comprehensive assessment in the initial meeting if the client appears ambivalent. Establishing rapport and creating an atmosphere for a subsequent assessment session may be more beneficial than attempting to complete the assessment at the initial meeting.

Organizational Issues

In many acute trauma settings, the mental health professional needs to be aware of his or her role within the organizational structure. After many disasters, there are established procedures determined by the relevant emergency organizations. Operating effectively in such a situation requires the mental health professional to be cognizant of both the rules of the organizations and the attitudes of the subculture in which she or he is working. For example, in many emergency organizations, there is an expectation that personnel should be able to cope with their emotional responses (O'Brien & Hughes, 1991). Assessments that question this competency can undermine an emergency worker's self-image and lead to avoidance of mental health professionals. We recently observed an incident during a major bushfire in Australia in which a psychologist was directed to assess a fire captain who was suspected of suffering excessive levels of stress during firefighting activities. The psychologist attempted to assess the captain while he was still involved in firefighting duties. The captain interpreted this assessment of his stress management as a direct threat to his competency as a captain and angrily terminated the meeting. A more sensitive appreciation of the organizational consequences of the assessment procedure may have resulted in a more favorable outcome.

Clinicians should be aware of possible conflicts of interest when the assessment is conducted within an organizational structure. The respective interests of the client and the organization can be diametrically opposed. For example, a police officer may be unwilling to participate in an assessment by a police psychologist because he or she is concerned that his or her reactions to a traumatic incident may be reported to his or her superiors and be deemed inappropriate. Clinicians should recognize possible conflicts of interest and resolve with the client any concerns about how the material elicited in the assessment will be used. This process necessarily involves clinicians being fully aware of their own roles within the organizational structure and clarifying their allegiances to both the client and the organization.

The Environment

The clinical presentation in the acute phase can be strongly influenced by environmental factors. The presence of stressors that remind the client of her or his recent traumatic experience can exacerbate her or his symptoms. For example, assessing traumatically injured patients during hospitalization may lead to heightened symptoms because of their separation from family, ongoing medical procedures, and exposure to other traumatically injured patients. Consequently, clinical presentation during hospital admission may not accurately reflect functioning after discharge. Conversely, we have observed many patients who have not reported ASD symptoms in the sheltered environment of a hospital but have become symptomatic when they return to their own environment. In particular, assessment of avoidance behaviors can often be made most accurately when individuals are in their normal surroundings because there they are exposed to the range of stimuli that will be confronted on a daily basis.

Ongoing Stressors

The acute trauma phase is marked by a range of ongoing stressful events that are secondary to the primary stressor. Pain, physical injury, legal procedures, and financial loss are some of the common burdens that the acutely traumatized person will need to manage. There is considerable evidence that posttraumatic stress is compounded by the presence of stressors occurring in the posttraumatic phase (Bryant & Harvey, 1995e; King, King, Fairbank, & Keane, 1998). A thorough assessment should include monitoring of all stressors that the client is managing in the acute phase. There are three reasons to assess continuing stressors. First, it may be premature to obtain a reliable assessment if the acutely traumatized client is still undergoing considerable stress. For example, a patient who has sustained burns during a traumatic incident will be suffering intense pain as a result of regular debridements and physiotherapy. This patient may report marked stress symptoms during the period of these procedures but report remission of this distress after the procedures have been completed. Second, the demands placed on a trauma survivor by ongoing stressors may contraindicate active intervention until the continuing stress has eased. Third, in some cases, the effects of the continuing stressors may impede optimal reporting of ASD symptoms. For example, patients who are preoccupied with severe pain may not report ASD symptoms because of the salient concern with physical pain. Reporting posttraumatic stress symptoms can be impaired by trauma survivors' poor perceptions of the role of posttraumatic stress symptoms in their current functioning (Solomon & Canino, 1990). Careful assessment of possible stressors in the acute phase can direct clients' attention to the possible interaction of current stressors and their posttraumatic adjustment.

Comorbidity

Presence of PTSD is associated with a wide range of comorbid disorders, including other anxiety disorders, depression, substance abuse, somatoform disorders, and personality disorders (Davidson & Fairbank,

1993). Initial evidence indicates that ASD is also likely to coexist with a range of Axis I and Axis II disorders (Barton et al., 1996). Depression is particularly probable in those suffering posttraumatic stress (Shore, Vollmer, & Tatum, 1989). Moreover, Shalev, Freedman, et al. (1998) have recently demonstrated that PTSD and depression can follow independent paths after exposure to a trauma. It is critical in the assessment of ASD to not focus exclusively on posttraumatic stress reactions because this narrow attention can result in neglect of other disorders. Identification of other psychiatric disorders is important because of the implications for management of the acutely traumatized person. Individuals who present with other psychiatric disorders in the acute trauma phase have often suffered these symptoms before the recent traumatic event. The presence of a psychiatric disorder at the time of the trauma predisposes these individuals to more psychopathological responses in the acute trauma phase (Barton et al., 1996; Harvey & Bryant, in press-c). Moreover, the distress caused by the recent stressor can exacerbate the previously existing disorder. Detection of any suicidal ideation is critical in this phase. Many acutely traumatized people who develop ASD in the presence of other disorders may need containment and support in the acute trauma phase. In chapter 8, we review more closely the cautions that are required in managing those traumatized people who suffer from a comorbid condition. It is sometimes difficult in the acute trauma setting to comprehensively assess all current disorders because of the limited time that is available and the competing demands that are placed on the traumatized person. This problem notwithstanding, clinicians have a responsibility to index all comorbidity and previous psychopathology before making any decisions concerning intervention.

Dissociation

Clinicians should be particularly aware of dissociative responses in acutely traumatized individuals. Sensitivity to this presentation is indicated by a number of factors. First, the absence of marked distress may suggest that a person is coping well in the acute trauma phase. The lack of emotional response may also reflect a dissociative reaction that is evoked because of the overwhelming discomfort experienced by the person. For example, we assessed a young mother who witnessed the fatal strangulation of her daughter at a local shopping center. Although a counselor who consoled this woman in the initial week after the event concluded that she was coping "bravely" with the tragedy, it became apparent that the absence of affective responses was masking intense distress and grief. During therapy, this client recalled the following:

> In the first weeks, I felt that things were very strange, like I had lost contact with reality. When people spoke to me, I found it difficult to

comprehend what they were saying, and I didn't care. Time went incredibly slowly, it was like I was walking around in a cloudy state with little grip on what was happening around me. In fact, I only had a vague awareness of the death of my little girl.

The risk of ignoring dissociative responses is that false-negative diagnoses may be made and distressed individuals may not be provided with assistance. The need to recognize acute dissociation can also have significant implications for therapy. For example, marked numbing in the acute phase may suggest that exposure therapies may not be useful because of the client's difficulty in accessing trauma-related emotions. Furthermore, dissociative responses may indicate that a client is defending against aversive emotional experiences that he or she cannot adequately manage in the acute phase. Sensitivity to this response during assessment may lead the clinician to decide that active therapy may be contraindicated for such a client.

Coping Mechanisms

Assessment also should index the person's current coping strategies. The use of an avoidant style of coping in the acute phase is predictive of severe ASD (Harvey & Bryant, 1998c, 1999d). Moreover, using cognitive strategies that distract the client from traumatic memories is associated with more severe acute symptoms (Warda & Bryant, 1998b). Other coping styles that have been identified as obstacles to resolution of traumatic memories include thought suppression (Amir et al., 1997; Clohessy & Ehlers, 1997; Ehlers, Mayor, & Bryant, 1997; Ehlers & Steil, 1995; Morgan, Matthews, & Winton, 1995) and emotion-focused coping (Morgan et al., 1995). Findings that resolution of ASD is associated with use of more adaptive cognitive strategies that facilitate reinterpretation of the traumatic experience (Bryant, Moulds, & Guthrie, 1999b) also point to the importance of coping mechanisms in the acute phase. Assessment should identify all strategies that lead to avoidance or catastrophizing of trauma-related events. Therapists should be particularly watchful for covert or subtle avoidance that may take the form of a lucky charm, anxiety medication in one's pocket, or a mantra repeated silently. Any gains that are made often are attributed to the charm, the pills, or the mantra. Such safety behaviors preclude the client from deriving full benefit from an exposure exercise (Salkovskis, 1991). Identification of these coping styles can direct therapy toward constructive modification of those strategies that are likely to impede progress.

Timing of Assessment

Although the diagnosis of ASD can be made after 2 days following a traumatic event, several issues should be considered in determining the optimal time for assessment. First, there is evidence that many acute stress symptoms may subside in the initial week after a trauma (Solomon et al., 1996). Consequently, assessing a trauma survivor 2 days after the stressor may result in diagnostic decisions that would not have been made if the assessment had been conducted a week later. Second, the clinician should determine that the traumatic event has ceased before deciding to assess for ASD. Many traumas are prolonged, and it may be premature to attempt assessment before the stressor has terminated. For example, assessing a fire-fighter before firefighting duties are completed may be unreliable because of the necessity for heightened arousal and coping skills to maintain adequate performance during the stressor. Third, many acutely traumatized people require some period of time to integrate the effects of a traumatic experience before they can adequately participate in an assessment. For example, we were asked to assess the parents of a young girl who was injured after a severe boating accident. At the time of the request, the girl was undergoing critical medical interventions in a hospital. The parents' prevailing concern for their daughter made an assessment at that point inappropriate. Although there are advantages in early assessment and intervention, it is inappropriate to believe that early assessment is necessary in every case. In many instances more effective assessment can be conducted after a delay.

The Meaning of the Trauma

One of the details that is often poorly assessed is the meaning that the traumatic experience has for the client. A traumatic event can have very idiosyncratic meaning for clients. For example, a woman that we treated for ASD after a vicious attack during a home invasion reported that the most distressing aspect of the assault was the theft of a ring that was given to her by her grandmother, who had raised her. This concern was not detected during assessment because the clinician focused attention on the savage physical assaults to the woman. It was only during therapy that the client's perception that an important reminder of her past had been stolen became evident. The initial assessment should give the client ample scope to report all his or her concerns and beliefs about the recent stressor. Comprehensive assessment of the client's interpretations of events can facilitate treatment when the meaning of the experience is ideally addressed.

Previous Traumas

The need to assess for previous trauma and prior PTSD is indicated by evidence that these factors predispose people to the development of ASD (Barton et al., 1996; Harvey & Bryant, 1999d) and PTSD (Breslau,

Davis, Andreski, & Peterson, 1991; North, Smith, & Spitznagel, 1994). There is also strong evidence that a history of childhood trauma is a predisposing factor in the development of posttraumatic stress conditions (Davidson & Fairbank, 1993). Identifying previous traumas, and the client's response to these earlier events, is especially critical in the acute phase because the recent trauma may exacerbate the effects of prior traumas. The blending of recent and prior traumatic experiences has been widely recognized. In a study on combat reactions, Feinstein (1989) observed that "for many, the ambush seemed to act as a trigger for unpleasant, intrusive thoughts concerning previous traumatic experiences, fear of mutilation and imagery of death and dying" (p. 666). We have seen many acutely traumatized clients who have suffered reexperiencing symptoms of much earlier events, as well as those pertaining to the recent stressor. For example, one man who was the victim of a bank robbery suffered distressing intrusive images of his childhood sexual abuse. The effects of this abuse had never been addressed within therapy, and the client had been able to contain his traumatic memories until the recent stressor. Management of this client was difficult because of the cumulative issues caused by the recent trauma and the childhood abuse. The extent to which the effects of early trauma have been adequately managed needs to be evaluated carefully for a number of reasons. First, the means by which the client has attempted resolution of previous traumas may inform the clinician as to how the client will respond to the recent stressor. Second, some therapeutic interventions may be problematic for clients who have not resolved previous traumas because treatment may inadvertently evoke traumatic memories that they are unprepared to confront. The management of these memories may be better attempted at a later stage. Requiring clients to deal with previous traumatic experiences when they are also managing the psychological distress of the recent stressor may be detrimental.

Social Supports

The upheaval associated with the acute trauma phase requires a close evaluation of the social supports available to the client. There is strong consensus that adaptive response to trauma is facilitated by positive social networks in the posttrauma environment (Raphael, 1986). The tendency to avoid reminders of the trauma and become socially withdrawn predisposes people to more severe stress reactions. Moreover, the extent of social support that a client has may influence therapy options. For example, a person who returns home to a supportive family after therapy sessions may be better equipped to manage exposure-based therapies than one who is isolated and without any support. The assessment should also index the nature of the social support because the client's immediate social network may also be affected by the recent trauma. In major disasters, the stressor may devastate an entire community. In more restricted traumas, such as a house fire, the immediate family may also be directly affected. The assessment needs to evaluate how the recent trauma has impacted the client's social network and the interaction between this societal effect and the client's functioning.

The Impact of Assessment

The clinician should be sensitive to the impact of the assessment on the acutely traumatized person. In the initial month after a trauma, many people are highly distressed, are functioning in a chaotic environment, and are attempting to deal with many changes. In this context, the client often presents as fragile and is striving to retain some control over her or his turbulent environment. A poorly conducted assessment has the potential to place additional stress on a person if it is perceived as a continuation of the initial traumatic experience. In extreme cases, poorly conducted assessments have contributed to suicidal attempts by fragile individuals. Accordingly, the assessment should commence with recognition by the clinician that material covered in the assessment may be distressing, and the client should be explicitly invited to communicate distress to the therapist. The clinician also should inform the client that the opportunity for respite during the assessment is available. Clinicians should be sensitive to the client's responses to the assessment, particularly to his or her capacity to relate the traumatic experience. Capacity to tolerate an assessment can be an important indicator of the client's subsequent performance in therapy. It is often useful to inform clients that they may experience an exacerbation of reexperiencing symptoms after the assessment and that this is part of the process of resolving the trauma.

SUMMARY

Clinicians need to be very sensitive to the particular problems that may exist in the acute posttrauma assessment. Most important, there needs to be recognition of the potential for the client to feel psychologically fragile and to perceive a loss of control. Awareness of these issues can help the clinician to provide the client with a safe and supportive environment in which the necessary information to make diagnostic decisions can be elicited. Alternatively, neglect of these important issues may result in compounding the client's acute stress and jeopardizing future attempts for therapeutic intervention.

5

ASSESSMENT TOOLS

Assessing the acutely traumatized person is the first important step in acute intervention. In this chapter, we outline the main techniques available to assess both ASD and its related problems. We initially describe the measures designed to assess ASD. We then review the major measures that are used to assess PTSD because these are typically required to assess the traumatized person after intervention or at follow-up. We then turn to describe some measures that index specific symptoms commonly seen in the acute phase, as well as other measures that can provide important information about the traumatized person's reaction.

MEASURES OF ASD

Clinician-Administered Measures

Two clinician-administered measures of ASD have been proposed. These measures have the advantage of using the clinicians' experience in the assessment of ASD rather than relying on trauma survivors' self-reports. They share the limitation, however, of relating to diagnostic criteria that have not yet been strongly validated.

Acute Stress Disorder Interview (ASDI). The ASDI (Bryant, Harvey, Dang, & Sackville, 1998) is the only structured clinical interview that is validated against *DSM–IV* criteria. The ASDI is reproduced in Appendix A. It contains 19 dichotomously scored items that relate to the dissociative (Cluster B, 5 items), reexperiencing (Cluster C, 4 items), avoidance (Cluster D, 4 items), and arousal (Cluster E, 6 items) symptoms of ASD. Summing the affirmative responses to each symptom provides a total score indicative of acute stress severity (ranging from 1 to 19). In addition, questions assessing the stressor (Cluster A), the impairment arising from the symptoms (Cluster F), the trauma-assessment interval (Cluster G), and the use of drugs or medication (Cluster H) are included.

Determining the clinical utility of the ASDI was hampered by the absence of any established tools to measure ASD. Accordingly, we tested the concurrent validity of the ASDI by comparing it with independent diagnostic decisions made by clinicians who were experienced in assessing PTSD and ASD. Sixty-five trauma survivors were administered the ASDI by one of three clinical psychologists between 2 and 21 days posttrauma. A clinical interview, based on *DSM–IV* criteria, was then administered by a different clinical psychologist, who was unaware of the responses on the ASDI, between 1 and 5 days later. The *sensitivity* of the ASDI, defined as the percentage of participants diagnosed with ASD by the clinical interview who also were diagnosed by the ASDI, was 91%. The rate of false-positive diagnoses was 7%. *Specificity* of the ASDI, defined as the percentage of participants not diagnosed with ASD by the clinical interview who also were not diagnosed by the ASDI, was 93%. The rate of false-negative diagnoses was 9%. Table 5.1 presents the sensitivity and specificity of each cluster of ASD symptoms. Although dissociation possessed the weakest sensitivity (79%), all symptom clusters had strong sensitivity. The arousal cluster possessed markedly weaker specificity (69%) than did the other clusters. That is, whereas the ASDI items on dissociation had the lowest power in identifying those participants who satisfied this cluster in the clinical interview, the ASDI arousal items had the lowest power in identifying those participants who did not satisfy this cluster in the clinical interview. The internal consistency of the 19 items was high ($r = .90$).

TABLE 5.1
Sensitivity and Specificity for Acute Stress Disorder
Interview (ASDI) Clusters

ASDI cluster	Sensitivity	Specificity
A: Stressor	100	100
B: Dissociation	79	90
C: Reexperiencing	100	82
D: Avoidance	96	80
E: Arousal	94	69

Note. For sensitivity, values represent the percentage of participants diagnosed with acute stress disorder (ASD) by the clinical interview and by the ASDI. For specificity, values represent the percentage of participants not diagnosed with ASD by the clinical interview or by the ASDI.

Assessing the reliability of a measure of ASD is somewhat problematic because acute stress reactions may fluctuate in a short period of time. To index test–retest reliability, we readministered the ASDI to 60 trauma survivors between 2 and 5 days after they had initially completed it. Table 5.2 contains the correlations of cluster severity scores and percentages of agreement for satisfying each cluster across the two ASDI administrations. Across the two assessments, there was strong agreement in the presence and absence of each cluster of symptoms (at least 80%) and strong correlations of each cluster severity score (at least .80).

Overall, the ASDI satisfies standard criteria for internal consistency, construct validity, and test–retest reliability. The identification of 91% of participants who were clinically diagnosed with ASD and 93% of those who had not been diagnosed suggests that it is a sound measure to identify those individuals who meet criteria for this disorder. The main advantage of the ASDI is that it is user-friendly and can be administered quickly. These qualities are often necessary when conducting an assessment in the acute trauma setting. The main disadvantage of the ASDI is that it lacks ordinal ratings of each symptom. Accordingly, it does not provide a severity or frequency index of each symptom.

Structured Clinical Interview for DSM-IV Dissociative Disorders (SCID–D). The SCID–D (Steinberg, 1993) has been offered as a structured interview for ASD (Steinberg, 1995). This interview was developed to diagnose dissociative disorders, and it has been subjected to extensive evaluation in this context (Steinberg, Cicchetti, Buchanan, Hall, & Rounsaville, 1989–1992). It provides a comprehensive assessment of five core dissociative symptoms: amnesia, depersonalization, derealization, identity confusion, and identity alteration. Although the SCID–D is an admirable tool for assessing dissociative disorders, its heavy emphasis on dissociative pathology is offset by a relative neglect of reexperiencing, avoidance, and arousal symptoms. More important, there are currently no data concerning the utility of the SCID–D in identifying people who meet criteria for ASD.

TABLE 5.2
Test–Retest Agreement for Acute Stress Disorder Interview Clusters

ASDI cluster	Presence of cluster	Absence of cluster	Cluster severity correlation
A: Stressor	100	100	
B: Dissociation	81	94	.85
C: Reexperiencing	87	100	.86
D: Avoidance	80	100	.80
E: Arousal	96	80	.87

Note. Items in Columns 1 and 2 are percentages of agreement. No correlation is given for Cluster A because the three items are not scored.

Self-Report Measures

Stanford Acute Stress Reaction Questionnaire (SASRQ). The original version of the SASRQ (Cardeña et al., 1991) was a self-report inventory that indexed dissociative (33 items), intrusive (11 items), somatic anxiety (17 items), hyperarousal (2 items), attention disturbance (3 items), and sleep disturbance (1 item) symptoms. Each item asks respondents to indicate the frequency of each symptom that can occur during and immediately after a trauma on a 6-point Likert scale ranging from 0 (*not experienced*) to 5 (*very often experienced*). The SASRQ possesses high internal consistency (Cronbach's α = .90 and .91 for dissociative and anxiety symptoms, respectively) and concurrent validity with scores on the IES (r = .52–.69; Koopman et al., 1994). Different versions of the SASRQ have been used in a number of studies conducted by the authors (Cardeña & Spiegel, 1993; Classen et al., 1998; Freinkel, Koopman, & Spiegel, 1994; Koopman et al., 1994). The SASRQ recently has been modified to a 30-item inventory that indexes the specific ASD symptoms (see Stam, 1996). The advantages of the SASRQ include the ordinal ratings that provide frequency indexes of each symptom, a wide coverage of acute stress symptoms, and reasonable ability to predict subsequent posttraumatic stress in acutely traumatized individuals (Classen et al., 1998). The major disadvantage of the SASRQ is that it has not yet been validated against clinician diagnoses of ASD. Accordingly, it is uncertain at this stage how accurately this measure can identify those people who meet criteria for ASD.

Acute Stress Disorder Scale (ASDS). The ASDS (Bryant, Moulds, & Guthrie, in press) is a self-report measure that is based on the same 19 ASD symptoms contained in the ASDI. The ASDS is reproduced in Appendix B. Respondents are asked to rate the intensity of each symptom on a 5-point Likert scale ranging from 1 (*not at all*) to 5 (*very much*). Table 5.3 contains the correlation coefficients of the ASDS cluster scores and scores on the IES, Beck Anxiety Inventory (Beck & Steer, 1990), DES-Taxon (Waller, Putnam, & Carlson, 1996), and BDI. The content validity of the ASDS is strong, in that the reexperiencing, avoidance, and arousal cluster scores correlate highly with scores on the IES–Intrusion, IES–Avoidance, and Beck Anxiety Inventory, respectively. Moreover, each of the symptom cluster scores correlate strongly with the respective scores on the ASDI.

To determine a decision rule for identifying people with ASD on the basis of the ASDS, we compared the ASDS against the only established measure of ASD, the ASDI. We administered the ASDS and ASDI to 99 survivors of motor vehicle accidents, industrial accidents, or nonsexual assaults. Twenty-eight (28%) of the sample met criteria for ASD on the basis of their ASDI responses. Sensitivity and specificity were calculated for different scores on the ASDS relative to the diagnosis of ASD. We found

TABLE 5.3
Intercorrelations of the Acute Stress Disorder Scale (ASDS) With
Validity Measures

| | ASDS scale | | | | |
Scale	Total	Dissociation	Reexperiencing	Avoidance	Arousal
ASDI Total	.86*	.70*	.82*	.77*	.84*
ASDI Dissociation	.65*	.69*	.59*	.54*	.61*
ASDI Reexperi-encing	.78*	.59*	.81*	.71*	.75*
ASDI Avoidance	.80*	.64*	.74*	.79*	.76*
ASDI Arousal	.76*	.55*	.72*	.66*	.80*
DES–T	.18	.11	.19	.12	.19
IES–Intrusion	.81*	.60*	.83*	.71*	.81*
IES–Avoidance	.87*	.71*	.76*	.88*	.83*
BAI	.78*	.66*	.79*	.64*	.80*
BDI	.80*	.66*	.79*	.66*	.79*

Note. ASDI = Acute Stress Disorder Interview; DES–T = Dissociative Experiences Scale—Taxon; IES = Impact of Event Scale; BAI = Beck Anxiety Inventory; BDI = Beck Depression Inventory.
*$p < .001$.

that the optimal formula for scoring the ASDS relative to the ASD diagnosis was to consider the dissociative and other clusters separately. By using a cutoff for the dissociative cluster of ≥ 9 combined with a cutoff of ≥ 28 for the cumulative scores on the reexperiencing, avoidance, and arousal clusters, we achieved sensitivity of .95, specificity of .83, positive predictive power (of the ASDS cutoff identifying ASD) of .80, negative predictive power (of the ASDS cutoff identifying no ASD) of .96, and efficiency (the percentage correctly identified as meeting or not meeting ASD criteria) of .87.

In terms of test–retest reliability, we administered the ASDS to 107 survivors of bushfires within 3 weeks of the trauma. All participants were recontacted between 2 and 7 days after initial completion of the ASDS and were asked to complete the ASDS a second time. The internal consistency of the ASDS was strong, with alpha coefficients being .96 for the ASDS total score, .84 for dissociation, .87 for reexperiencing, .92 for avoidance, and .93 for arousal. Adopting the cutoff criteria described above, 30 participants (28%) received a diagnosis of ASD on the initial ASDS administration. At the second administration, 28 (26%) received a diagnosis. In terms of reliability, 83% of participants who received a diagnosis at the first administration also received a diagnosis at the second administration. Furthermore, 100% of participants who did not receive a diagnosis at the first assessment also did not receive a diagnosis at the second assessment. The ASDS total scores correlated .94 between the two assessments.

To index the utility of the ASDS in predicting subsequent PTSD, we reassessed 82 of the 107 bushfire survivors who initially completed the ASDS. At follow-up, 11 (13%) met criteria for PTSD according to assessments based on the Clinician Administered PTSD Scale (CAPS; Blake et al., 1990). We calculated the optimal predictive formula for predicting PTSD on the basis of ASDS scores. Consistent with evidence that acute dissociation is not necessary for subsequent development of PTSD (Harvey & Bryant, 1998d), we found that better predictive ability was obtained by a total severity score on the ASDS rather than by requiring a minimum score on the dissociation cluster. Specifically, a cutoff of ≥ 56 on the ASDS resulted in 91% of those who later met criteria for PTSD being identified (sensitivity) and 93% of those who did not develop PTSD being correctly identified (specificity). The main flaw with this cutoff was that 33% of individuals who scored above this score did not subsequently develop PTSD. This result is consistent with evidence that many people who have high levels of acute stress will remit in the following months. Accordingly, we caution that the ASDS requires further validation in a variety of trauma populations. Nonetheless, at the current time, it possesses the strongest psychometric properties among those self-report instruments that attempt to screen acute stress reactions that may subsequently develop into PTSD.

MEASURES OF PTSD

After treating clients with ASD, or in follow-up assessments of traumatized individuals, the clinician often must apply PTSD criteria because the assessment occurs more than a month after the traumatic event. We review below some of the major assessment tools available to assess for PTSD. This review (by no means comprehensive) briefly describes some of the measures that can be of use to clinicians for assessing PTSD.

Clinician-Administered Measures

Structured Clinical Interview for DSM–IV (SCID–IV). The PTSD module of the SCID (Spitzer, Gibbon, & Williams, 1996) is the most widely used clinical interview across a range of trauma populations. One of its advantages is that it provides a comprehensive assessment of the comorbid disorders that can be present in trauma populations. The SCID–IV has good reliability across clinicians and possesses sound sensitivity and specificity for diagnostic decisions (Kulka et al., 1990). The SCID–IV is limited, however, because it indexes the presence, absence, or subthreshold presence of each symptom. Accordingly, it does not permit measurement of changing severity of PTSD. This limits the utility of the SCID–IV in measuring trauma adjustment after treatment.

Clinician Administered PTSD Scale (CAPS). The CAPS (Blake et al., 1990; Weathers, 1993) was designed to index the frequency and severity of each symptom and was intended to be used by clinicians and nonclinicians. It indexes both the 17 primary symptoms of PTSD, as well as 8 additional items that index associated features (including guilt, depression, and hopelessness). Each scale has clear anchors for both the frequency and severity ratings. The CAPS has credible psychometric properties (Weathers et al., 1992). It has strong test–retest reliability for the 17 items (range = .90–.98), high internal consistency (.94), and good convergent validity with other measures, such as the Mississippi Scale for Combat-Related PTSD (r = .91) and the SCID (r = .89). Overall, the CAPS enjoys a very good reputation among clinicians and researchers. Its main flaws are that it has yet to be strongly validated in civilian populations and that it requires considerable time to administer.

PTSD Symptom Scale Interview (PSS–I). The PSS–I was developed to assess the severity of PTSD symptoms over the preceding 2 weeks (Foa, Riggs, Dancu, & Rothbaum, 1993). The 17 items from this scale are rated on a 0–3 scale of frequency and severity. The items are based on the symptoms listed in *DSM–III–R*. In terms of the psychometric properties of this interview schedule, internal consistency (Cronbach's α = .85) and test–retest reliability (1 month; Pearson product–moment correlation = .80) are acceptable. Furthermore, the interrater reliability for diagnosis (κ = .91) and symptom severity (r = .97) are good (Dancu et al., 1996). The disadvantages of this scale include its validation being limited to female assault victims, the absence of clear anchors, and the unavailability of lifetime diagnoses (Newman, Kaloupek, & Keane, 1996).

Posttraumatic Stress Disorder Interview (PTSD–I). The PTSD–I (Watson, Juba, Manifold, Kucala, & Anderson, 1991) comprises 17 items that describe the three diagnostic sections of the *DSM–III–R* description of PTSD. The respondent scores the severity of each symptom on a 1–7 Likert scale, so that an overall symptom severity score can be calculated. Watson et al. has argued that a rating of 4 (described as "somewhat" or "commonly") can be regarded as indicating the presence of the symptom. In comparison with the Diagnostic Interview Schedule (DIS; Robins & Helzer, 1985), the PTSD–I has been shown to have good specificity and sensitivity and excellent test–retest reliability. The main limitation of the PTSD–I is that it has not been validated with civilian trauma populations.

Diagnostic Interview Schedule (DIS). The PTSD section of the DIS (Robins, Helzer, Croughan, & Ratliff, 1981) has been primarily applied in epidemiological studies. The DIS was developed to be administered by trained technicians, as opposed to mental health professionals. Accordingly, it is simple to administer. The main disadvantages of the DIS are that it uses a dichotomous scoring system, requires the respondent to link each symptom to a specified traumatic event, and has questionable psychometric support. Several studies have indicated that the DIS has less-than-adequate specificity and sensitivity in making diagnostic decisions (e.g., Anthony et al., 1985; Keane & Penk, 1988).

Self-Report Measures

Posttraumatic Diagnostic Scale (PTDS). The PTDS (Foa, Cashman, Jay-cox, & Perry, 1997) is a 17-item checklist that corresponds to each of the *DSM–IV* criteria for PTSD. Each symptom is rated on a 4-point scale in terms of its frequency over the past month. It also includes useful measures of the traumatic event and impairment level. The PTDS provides both a diagnostic decision concerning PTSD and a PTSD severity score. It possesses very good psychometric properties, including high internal consistency and test–retest reliability and sound sensitivity and specificity. The major advantages of the PTDS are its correspondence to *DSM–IV* criteria, its validation with a range of trauma populations, and its rating format for each symptom.

Davidson Trauma Scale (DTS). The DTS (Davidson et al., 1997) is a 17-item scale that measures each *DSM–IV* symptom. Items are completed on 5-point scales that index both frequency and severity of each symptom. This scale was validated with a range of combat and civilian trauma populations and has very sound psychometric properties. One disadvantage of the DTS is that whereas it asks about intrusive and avoidance symptoms with reference to the traumatic event, numbing, withdrawal, and hyper-arousal items are rated without linking these responses to the traumatic event. This procedure precludes definitive diagnostic decisions based on *DSM–IV* criteria. This limitation notwithstanding, the DTS possesses good diagnostic accuracy (83%), using a cutoff score of 40. Overall, the DTS is a very useful self-report instrument to index change in PTSD severity.

Mississippi Scale for Combat-Related PTSD. The Mississippi Scale for Combat-Related PTSD (Keane, Caddell, & Taylor, 1988) was conceptually based on *DSM–III–R* and consists of 35 items that are scored on 5-point scales. It possesses sound psychometric properties, has very good sensitivity and specificity relative to SCID diagnoses, and is one of the most commonly used self-report measures of PTSD. Shortened forms of this scale have been developed that also show promising psychometric properties (Fontana & Rosenheck, 1994). This scale does not include all the diagnostic items, however; and this represents one disadvantage in using it to make diagnostic decisions.

Civilian Mississippi Scale. Vreven, Gudanowski, King, and King (1995) modified the Mississippi Scale for Combat-Related PTSD to apply to civilian populations. Unfortunately, this scale did not perform well in that its convergent validity was poor and it correlated more strongly with general psychopathology measures than with PTSD (Vrana & Lauterbach,

1994). Accordingly, the Revised Civilian Mississippi Scale (Norris & Perilla, 1996) was developed to contain 30 items that were more focused on PTSD. The first 18 items are anchored to the traumatic event, and the last 12 are not related to the event. Initial data indicate that this scale has good psychometric properties. The major weakness of this scale is that its convergent validity has yet to be determined.

MEASURES OF ACUTE STRESS SYMPTOMS

As well as assessing for diagnostic status, clinicians also may wish to index specific acute stress symptoms. We review here the scales most commonly used to measure the symptoms observed in the acute trauma phase.

Dissociative Experiences Scale (DES). The DES (Bernstein & Putnam, 1986) is the most popular measure of dissociative experiences and has been used very widely in studies of trauma-related dissociation (Branscomb, 1991; Bremner et al., 1992; Dancu et al., 1996; Orr et al., 1990). The DES is a 28-item measure of dissociative experiences and contains a subscale that indexes pathological dissociation (DES–T; Waller et al., 1996). This scale has been shown to have good test–retest, internal, and interrater reliability and good concurrent and criterion-related validity (Carlson & Putnam, 1993). Note, however, that critical reviews of the DES have suggested that the extent to which it indexes dissociation is influenced by respondents' perceptions of the purpose of the questionnaire (Silva & Kirsch, 1992) and their level of general psychopathology (Nash et al., 1993; Norton et al., 1990; Sandberg & Lynn, 1992). Moreover, because there are no general population norms of the DES, it is difficult to interpret the meaning of elevated scores (Briere, 1997).

Peritraumatic Dissociative Experiences Questionnaire (PDEQ). The PDEQ (Marmor et al., 1994) was developed to index dissociative responses during and immediately after a trauma. It consists of nine items that index depersonalization, derealization, and amnesia. In reviewing the studies that have used the PDEQ, Marmor (1997) concluded that the scale has acceptable internal consistency, reliability, and validity. Furthermore, the scale was found to be positively associated with posttraumatic stress measures and dissociative coping style but not correlated with general psychopathology. Most impressively, in a prospective study Shalev et al. (1996) found that PDEQ scores 1 week after the trauma predicted symptomatology 5 months later.

Clinician-Administered Dissociative States Scale (CADSS). The CADSS has been recently developed to provide a structured interview for trauma-related dissociation (Bremner et al., 1997). The CADSS has been shown to have good interrater reliability and sound construct and discriminant validity. The CADSS has much potential to assess posttraumatic dissociative symptoms because it provides the clinician with a structured interview to assess both the individual's subjective experience of dissociation and the observer's perceptions of behavior that is indicative of dissociation. It is a 27-item scale; Items 1 to 23 are subjective items read out by the interviewer, and Items 24 to 27 are objective items that measure the interviewers' observations of the client.

Impact of Event Scale (IES). The IES (Horowitz et al., 1979) has been used to index intrusive and avoidance symptoms in the acute posttraumatic phase (Bryant & Harvey, 1995b, 1996a; Dancu et al., 1996; Shalev, 1992). The IES is a 15-item inventory that comprises intrusion and avoidance scales, has been shown to correlate with PTSD, and possesses sound psychometric properties (Zilberg, Weiss, & Horowitz, 1982). The IES is probably the most popular index of the intrusive and avoidance symptoms of PTSD. Caution is required in using it for diagnostic purposes, however, because Blanchard and Hickling (1997) have demonstrated the inadequacy of the IES as a diagnostic instrument. To address the omission of arousal symptoms, Weiss and Marmor (1997) developed the IES–Revised (IES–R), which added seven items pertaining to hyperarousal. Studies to date indicate that the IES–R possesses sound internal consistency and test–retest reliability.

Beck Depression Inventory–2 (BDI–2). The second edition of the BDI (BDI–2; Beck, Steer, & Brown, 1996) is a 21-item self-report measure of depressive symptoms. Its items are based on *DSM–IV* descriptions of depressive disorders, and each item is scored on a 4-point scale. The BDI–2 possesses very strong psychometric properties. Its scoring criteria permit respondents to be classified as reporting minimal, mild, moderate, or severe depression.

Spielberger State–Trait Anxiety Inventory (STAI). The STAI (Spielberger, Gorsuch, Lushene, Vagg, & Jacobs, 1983) indexes both state and trait anxiety. This instrument contains 40 items and measures levels of anxiety experienced "at the moment" (state) and "generally" (trait). It possesses good internal consistency and test–retest reliability (Anastasi, 1988).

COMORBIDITY AND PREVIOUS PSYCHOPATHOLOGY

As noted in chapter 3, it is common for acutely traumatized clients to present with either preexisting or coexisting disorders. Consequently, it is wise to assess for previous and current psychopathology. A number of structured clinical interviews allow comprehensive assessment of Axis I and Axis II disorders. For example, the SCID–IV (Spitzer et al., 1996) provides a well-validated measure of previous and current psychopathology. In the acute posttrauma phase, there is often limited time to conduct a comprehensive assessment. In such cases, the clinician can select specific modules that address the presenting comorbidity.

COPING STYLE

Albert Einstein College of Medicine Coping Styles Questionnaire. This questionnaire, developed by Plutchik (1989), contains 87 items that are rated on a 4-point scale. Subscales include Suppression, Help-Seeking, Replacement (finding alternative solutions), Blame (blaming others), Substitution (engaging in alternative activities to reduce tension), Mapping (collecting information about the problem), Reversal (trying to act or feel the opposite of the way in which the individual would really want to act or feel), and Minimization. Individual scales have acceptable internal reliability and predictive validity (Buckley, Conte, Plutchik, Wild, & Karasu, 1984). This scale has identified PTSD patients as being more likely to use suppression and less likely to use replacement (Amir et al., 1997).

Ways of Coping Checklist (WOC). The WOC (Folkman & Lazarus, 1980) is a 68-item measure of emotion-focused and problem-focused coping strategies. The inventory yields 5 subscales: Problem-Focused, Blames Self, Avoidance, Wishful Thinking, and Seeking Social Support. Using this scale, Delahanty et al. (1997) found that motor vehicle accident victims who felt they were responsible for the accident used more self-blame coping than individuals who felt another was responsible. Furthermore, self-blame was associated with more distress.

Coping Style Questionnaire (CSQ). The CSQ (Billings & Moos, 1981) is a 19-item, dichotomously scored measure that indexes active cognitive, active behavioral, avoidance, problem-focused, and emotion-focused strategies. The Avoidance subscale has proved to be effective in predicting both ASD (Harvey & Bryant, 1998c) and PTSD (Bryant & Harvey, 1995b).

Thought Control Questionnaire (TCQ). The TCQ (Wells & Davies, 1994) is a 30-item questionnaire that indexes five different strategies that may be used to control unwanted thoughts: distraction, punishment, reappraisal, social control, and worry. This measure has been useful in identifying the greater use of punishment and worry in ASD populations (Warda & Bryant, 1998b) and in indexing the enhancement of adaptive cognitive strategies after therapy (Bryant, Moulds, & Guthrie, 1999).

TRAUMATIC COGNITION SCALES

Post-Traumatic Cognitions Inventory (PTCI). The PTCI (Foa, Ehlers, Clark, Tolin, & Orsillo, 1998) is a 36-item self-report inventory that requires the respondent to indicate on a 7-point scale the extent to which she or he ascribes to trauma-related cognitive beliefs. This scale indexes negative cognitions about oneself and the world and self-blame. It possesses sound psychometric properties, discriminates between people with and without PTSD, and correlates strongly with PTSD severity. This new measure is a very promising tool to index the typical cognitions that traumatized clients report and in this sense represents a useful measure for assessing ASD clients.

Personal Beliefs and Reactions Scale (PBRS). The PBRS (Resick, Schnicke, & Markway, 1991) is a 60-item scale that requires respondents to indicate on a 7-point scale the extent to which they hold cognitions about safety, trust, power, esteem, intimacy, self-blame, undoing, and rape. This scale has good test–retest reliability and internal consistency; it is used primarily with rape victims (Resick & Schnicke, 1993).

World Assumption Scale (WAS). The WAS (Janoff-Bulman, 1992) is a 33-item measure that respondents answer on 6-point scales. The WAS indexes the extent to which respondents believe cognitions about benevolence of the world, self-worth, benevolence of other people, justice, controllability, randomness, self-controllability, and luck. It possesses sound psychometric properties.

PSYCHOPHYSIOLOGICAL ASSESSMENT

There is increasing attention being given to psychophysiological measures to complement clinical interviews and psychometric tools in the assessment of traumatized populations. The major psychophysiological indexes are heart rate, blood pressure, skin conductance level and response, muscle tension, and peripheral temperature (Newman et al., 1996). This approach to assessment has the advantage of being less vulnerable to response bias and being able to detect processes that may not be identifiable through other means. Bryant, Harvey, et al. (in press) have reported that meeting criteria for ASD or having a resting heart rate of > 90 beats per minute in the acute phase had strong sensitivity (88%) and specificity (85%) in predicting PTSD 6 months later. This pattern suggests that measuring heart rate may usefully supplement the ASD diagnosis in predicting people who will suffer PTSD. Most studies of PTSD have indexed multiple psychophysiological activity in response to trauma cues, and there is convergent opinion that these responses can discriminate people with and without PTSD (Blanchard et al., 1986; Pitman et al., 1987). Although only a few studies have been conducted on psychophysiological responses of acutely traumatized populations (Bryant, Harvey, et al., in press; Griffin et al., 1997; Shalev, Sahar, et al., 1998), it is likely that this approach will be developed in the future.

SUMMARY

Considering the recent development of the ASD diagnosis, it is not surprising that few measures of the diagnosis have been published. The relatively recent development of standardized measures for the assessment of ASD will allow an acceleration of attention to this disorder that was not previously possible. Clinicians need to be cognizant of the limitations of measurement tools for ASD because empirical investigations in this area have only just begun. Using multiple approaches to assessing ASD is indicated because the convergent information obtained from clinical interviews, self-report measures, and psychophysiological measures will improve the accuracy of the clinician's assessment.

III

TREATMENT

6

EMPIRICAL BASIS FOR TREATMENT

One of the most exciting developments associated with the ASD diagnosis is the opportunity to provide early intervention for those individuals who are likely to suffer long-term PTSD. The notion of treating all people who are symptomatic in the acute trauma phase is unjustified because of evidence that most of these people recover without formal intervention (Barton et al., 1996; Rothbaum et al., 1992). In identifying those select individuals who are at risk of chronic PTSD, the ASD diagnosis paves the way for treating individuals who do require intervention. Treatment of PTSD can be hindered by a number of factors: Chronic avoidance behaviors can reduce motivation to seek therapy (Weisaeth, 1989b), complex avoidance behaviors are also often resistant to many treatment interventions (Solomon, Gerrity, & Muff, 1992), and furthermore, longer term PTSD is often associated with comorbid disorders that interfere with therapeutic success (Frueh, Turner, & Beidel, 1995). The treatment of posttraumatic stress in the acute phase may avoid some of these problems because it addresses the presenting symptoms before some of the more complicated forms of posttraumatic adjustment develop.

RATIONALE FOR COGNITIVE–BEHAVIORAL THERAPY

As we noted in chapter 2, network theories propose that resolution of a traumatic experience requires two processes (Foa et al., 1989; Litz &

Keane, 1989). First, all elements of the fear network must be accessed and activated. Second, new information that is incompatible with the existing fear-related schema must be integrated to facilitate the formation of new cognitive schema. The primary technique used to activate the fear network is exposure. The main rationale for exposure-based therapies is that maintenance of anxiety during proximity to the feared stimuli eventually results in habituation. In the context of traumatic stress, it has been proposed that exposure to traumatic memories leads to symptom reduction because (a) the individual learns that reminders of the trauma do not actually cause harm, (b) recalling the trauma does not involve reliving the threat, (c) there is habituation of the anxiety while the individual remains in proximity to the feared memories, and (d) the experience of anxiety does not result in the feared loss of control (Jaycox & Foa, 1996). That is, it is held that exposure leads to improvement because of two associated, but distinct, processes. First, there is habituation of anxiety, and second, there is learning that the exposure does not lead to renewed threat.

EFFICACY OF COGNITIVE–BEHAVIORAL THERAPY IN TREATING PTSD

Although there is an increasing number of treatment-outcome studies with longer term PTSD (see Bryant, 1999; Foa & Meadows, 1997), one cannot generalize these findings to the treatment of acute stress reactions. It is useful to consider the findings of PTSD treatment studies, however, because there are few controlled studies of ASD treatment. Accordingly, we review the major findings of treatments of PTSD in this section, to assist in the understanding of treatment of ASD.

Systematic Desensitization

The earliest studies to apply behavioral principles to trauma victims used systematic desensitization. This procedure pairs imagination of the feared stimulus with relaxation and typically requires the individual to master feared scenes in a hierarchically graded regime (Wolpe, 1958). Although two studies that compared systematic desensitization to a no-treatment control condition with war veterans indicated that systematic desensitization was effective (Bowen & Lambert, 1986; Peniston, 1986), many sessions were required, and change in PTSD symptoms was not directly assessed. Brom, Kleber, and Defares (1989) compared the effectiveness of systematic desensitization, hypnotherapy, and brief psychodynamic therapy with a wait-list control condition in a mixed group of trauma survivors. After an average number of 15 treatment sessions, individuals in the active treatment groups displayed better improvement than did the controls. The systematic desensitization group displayed marginally superior improvement, but this was not statistically significant. Frank and Stewart (1983, 1984) investigated the efficacy of systematic desensitization in a series of studies with female rape victims. In these studies, systematic desensitization involved imagination of the traumatic scenarios combined with positive scenes. Although these authors concluded that treatment led to reduced fear and improved social adjustment, these conclusions were limited because there was no control group, PTSD measures were not used, and in 75% of cases, the individuals initiated *in vivo* exposure exercises. Furthermore, some improvement may have been a result of natural adjustment because a proportion of participants were treated in the acute trauma phase. Overall, although systematic desensitization shows some beneficial results, methodological flaws in the available studies preclude any firm conclusions concerning its efficacy. At this stage, systematic desensitization does not appear to provide a promising technique for treating ASD.

Exposure Therapies

Exposure therapies may take the form of either imaginal or *in vivo* exposure. Whereas *in vivo* exposure requires the individual to remain in close proximity to the actual stimuli, imaginal exposure involves the individual imagining feared events or memories of the trauma. Exposure therapies of PTSD have focused on imaginal exposure because of the need to target traumatic memories. In most imaginal exposure protocols, the individual is asked to focus attention on her or his traumatic memories in a way that encourages full engagement with the distress associated with these memories. This form of prolonged exposure typically requires the individual to maintain this focus for at least 50 minutes, by which time it is assumed that habituation will have commenced.

In one of the first controlled studies, Keane, Fairbank, Caddell, and Zimering (1989) randomly allocated Vietnam veterans either to flooding (imaginal exposure) or to a wait-list control group. This study reported marked improvements for the exposure treatment, including greater reductions in reported fear, depression, and reexperiencing symptoms compared with the control group. In another study, Cooper and Clum (1989) provided veterans with PTSD with either a standard treatment program (psychological–pharmacological) or the standard treatment combined with imaginal flooding. Imaginal flooding resulted in greater reductions in nightmares and anxiety. Boudewyns and colleagues reported two studies of veterans who, in addition to an inpatient treatment program, received either direct therapeutic exposure or traditional individual counseling (Boudewyns & Hyer, 1990; Boudewyns, Hyer, Woods, Harrison, & McCrame, 1990). Although both studies reported greater improvement on general psychological functioning, PTSD symptoms were not reported. A common flaw with all these studies was the lack of blind posttreatment assessments. The absence of independent posttreatment assessments raises significant concerns over the extent to which posttreatment measures may reflect expectancy bias.

More rigorous investigation of the efficacy of exposure was conducted by Foa, Rothbaum, Riggs, and Murdock (1991). This study randomly assigned female victims of sexual or nonsexual assault to either prolonged exposure (PE), stress inoculation training (SIT), supportive counseling (SC), or a wait-list control group. The treatment involved nine twice-weekly sessions and included blind assessments at posttreatment and at 3 months follow-up. Whereas SIT resulted in greater gains than SC or wait-list control at posttreatment, the PE condition led to greater reduction in PTSD symptoms at follow-up. Foa, Rothbaum, et al. (1991) suggested that whereas SIT led to short-term symptom reduction, PE resulted in longer term benefits because the fear networks were activated and modified. Although PE was relatively superior, Foa, Rothbaum, et al. (1991) reported that at follow-up, 45% of clients treated with exposure still satisfied criteria for PTSD, and 44% did not achieve clinically significant gains. Despite the proven utility of PE, it appears that a significant proportion of individuals with PTSD do not respond to this intervention.

The role of *in vivo* exposure has been poorly investigated in treatment of posttraumatic stress. Treatment studies have typically included *in vivo* exposure as a secondary amendment to imaginal exposure (Foa, Rothbaum, et al., 1991) or as an unexpected addition to imaginal exposure that is initiated by participants (Frank et al., 1988). That is, treatment studies have not rigorously implemented *in vivo* exposure by systematically accompanying clients and monitoring performance as they habituate to feared stimuli. The relative lack of emphasis placed on *in vivo* exposure is curious considering that imaginal exposure treatments typically perform poorly in reducing avoidance symptoms of PTSD (Frueh et al., 1995; Solomon et al., 1992). Keane et al. (1989) reported that whereas imaginal exposure resulted in decreased intrusive and arousal symptoms, it did not lead to reductions in avoidance or numbing. In contrast, studies that have systematically used *in vivo* exposure have reported marked reductions in avoidance behavior (Brom et al., 1989). In the only study to date to compare *in vivo* and imaginal exposure, Richards, Lovell, and Marks (1994) found that *in vivo* exposure was more effective than imaginal exposure in reducing avoidance. Although this study lacked a control group, it supports the proposition that *in vivo* exposure is the most effective means of reducing avoidance behavior (Marks, 1987). Overall, these findings suggest that PE has considerable potential for treating ASD and that *in vivo* exposure may constructively address avoidance patterns.

Cognitive Therapy

One of the cornerstones of network theories is that people develop exaggerated beliefs about their vulnerability to future harm (Foa & Riggs, 1993). In terms of acute trauma reactions, there is evidence that people with ASD exaggerate the likelihood of further negative events occurring and the adverse consequence of those events (Smith & Bryant, in press; Warda & Bryant, 1998a). Despite the importance of cognitive patterns in trauma response, there has been surprisingly little investigation of the role of cognitive therapy in facilitating trauma resolution. This is particularly curious considering that cognitive therapy aims to identify maladaptive cognitions and modify them with more realistic appraisals (Beck, 1972). One reason for this development is that information-processing theories have proposed that PE permits cognitive restructuring because during exposure one learns that fear-based beliefs are not reality based (Jaycox & Foa, 1996). For example, Foa, Hearst-Ikeda, and Perry (1995) have suggested that coping with exposure to traumatic memories may lead rape victims to modify their beliefs about themselves as inadequate. The assumption that exposure leads to cognitive restructuring can be questioned, however, because many posttraumatic beliefs may not be necessarily challenged through exposure to traumatic memories. For example, entrenched beliefs relating to guilt or anger may not necessarily be modified through a habituation paradigm.

The extent to which cognitive therapy is an effective treatment of posttraumatic stress has not been adequately tested because studies tend to integrate cognitive therapy with PE (Foa, Feske et al., 1991; Foa, Rothbaum, et al., 1991; Resick & Schnicke, 1992a). This tendency is most strongly reflected in Resick and Schnicke's (1992b) cognitive-processing therapy, which explicitly combines PE with cognitive therapy that is based on five major beliefs that are purportedly central to rape victims' cognitive schema. In an initial study, these authors reported that cognitive-processing therapy resulted in symptom reduction of 40% compared with only 1.5% for wait-list controls (Resick & Schnicke, 1992a). These findings need to be interpreted cautiously, however, because their outcome measures lacked blind assessment and did not index PTSD symptoms. Resick and Schnicke (1992b) subsequently increased their initial sample size so that it included 54 rape victims and found that whereas 96% of the sample initially met criteria for PTSD, 88% of those who received cognitive-processing therapy did not meet criteria after treatment. Frank et al. (1988) provided rape victims with either systematic desensitization or cognitive therapy, which included self-monitoring, graded task assignments that reduced avoidance, and cognitive restructuring. This study concluded that there were no differences in outcome between the treatments and that both led to clinical gains. This study's conclusions are limited, however, because there were no control groups and the cognitive therapy condition included various behavioral components.

There are several studies in progress that have attempted to clarify the relative contributions of PE and cognitive therapy to the treatment of PTSD. Foa, Feeny, Zoellner, Fitzgibbons, and Hembree (1998) have reported that combining PE and cognitive therapy results in benefits that are comparable to PE alone. Similarly, Resick, Nishith, Weaver, and Astin (1998) have reported comparable reductions in PTSD symptoms for rape victims who receive cognitive-processing therapy and those who receive only PE. Marks, Lovell, Norshirvani, Livanou, and Thrasher (1998) compared PE alone, cognitive restructuring alone, combined cognitive restructuring and PE, or relaxation alone. They found that PE alone, cognitive restructuring alone, and the combined treatment produced similar outcomes that were superior to relaxation. Similarly, Tarrier et al. (1999) reported that PE and cognitive therapy resulted in comparable reduction of PTSD symptoms. Although these data indicate that PE and cognitive therapy are instrumental in alleviating PTSD symptoms, there is insufficient evidence concerning the interaction of PE and cognitive therapy. At this time, it appears useful to integrate both PE and cognitive therapy in the management of ASD.

Eye Movement Desensitization and Reprocessing

One popular variant of imaginal exposure is eye movement desensitization and reprocessing (EMDR). This procedure requires the individual to focus her or his attention on a traumatic memory while simultaneously visually tracking the therapist's finger as it is moved across their visual field (Shapiro, 1995). Although there are many case studies attesting to the efficacy of this technique (see Lohr, Kleinknecht, Tolin, & Barrett, 1996), this approach is the subject of much methodological and ethical criticism (Lohr et al., 1996; Lohr, Lilienfeld, Tolin, & Herbert, 1999; McNally, 1999; Rosen, 1999; Singer & Lalich, 1996; Tolin, Montgomery, Kleinknecht, & Lohr, 1996). There are now a number of controlled outcome studies, and although the methodological merits of these studies are mixed, the evidence for EMDR is poor.

In terms of favorable evidence, several outcome studies have reported that participants treated with EMDR perform better than control participants on a wait list (Rothbaum, 1997; Wilson, Becker, & Tinker, 1995, 1997), participants treated with nondirective counseling (Scheck, Schaeffer, & Gillette, 1998), or participants treated with relaxation training and biofeedback (Carlson, Chemtob, Rusnak, Hedlund, & Muraoka, 1998). The methodological problems with these studies preclude acceptance of any firm conclusions, however (see Foa & Meadows, 1997; Lohr et al., 1999; McNally, 1999). For example, conclusions are limited by the use of wait-list controls that do not index placebo effects (Rothbaum, 1997; Wilson et al., 1995, 1997), the lack of blind assessments (Carslon et al., 1998), reliance on self-report data (Wilson et al., 1995), and ambiguity about pretreatment PTSD severity (Wilson et al., 1995).

Although eye movements are the defining feature that discriminates EMDR from other exposure techniques, there are serious concerns about the role of eye movements in this approach. In recent years, a series of sophisticated studies have delineated the effects of eye movements by comparing EMDR with variations of EMDR that modify the eye movement component by requiring participants to perform a different task, such as finger tapping (Bauman & Melnyk, 1994; Boudewyns & Hyer, 1996; Devilly, Spence, & Rapee, 1998; Dunn, Schwartz, Hatfield, & Wiegele, 1996; Foley & Spates, 1995; Gosselin & Matthews, 1995; Pitman, Orr, et al., 1996; Renfrey & Spates, 1994; Sanderson & Carpenter, 1992; Wilson, Silver, Covi, & Foster, 1996). Apart from that of D. L. Wilson et al., all these studies found that EMDR was not more effective than the various control techniques. Considering that the methodology of the D. L. Wilson et al. study has been solidly criticized (Lohr et al., 1999), there is convergent evidence that eye movements themselves do not play a beneficial role in trauma recovery.

Overall, there is no evidence that EMDR provides any additional therapeutic benefits relative to standard exposure treatments. Moreover, Devilly and Spence (1999) found that although cognitive–behavioral therapy (CBT) and EMDR significantly reduced PTSD symptoms, CBT was more effective in terms of both clinical gains and tolerance of treatment. Importantly, whereas the CBT participants continued to improve at follow-up, the EMDR participants tended to relapse. On the basis of available data, there is no reason to consider that EMDR can provide any additional benefits in the treatment of ASD that are not provided by established exposure techniques. Moreover, there is preliminary evidence that standard CBT approaches may serve people with ASD more effectively than EMDR. This issue remains to be empirically addressed because no randomized outcome studies have yet been conducted on EMDR with ASD populations.

Anxiety-Management Techniques

Numerous studies have evaluated the utility of anxiety-management interventions to reduce the anxiety symptoms of posttraumatic stress. The most common form of anxiety management has been SIT (Meichenbaum, 1975), which involves psychoeducation, relaxation skills, thought stopping, and self-talk. Several early studies indicated the utility of this approach in treating PTSD. Veronen and Kilpatrick (1982) provided female rape victims with persistent anxiety and avoidance with 20 sessions of SIT. Although this study lacked a control condition and did not index PTSD symptoms, it demonstrated marked remission of fear, avoidance, and depression 3 months after treatment. In a later study, the same authors provided rape victims with either SIT, peer counseling, or systematic desensitization (Veronen & Kilpatrick, 1983). Interestingly, most women declined therapy, and of the 15 who accepted, 70% chose SIT, 30% chose peer counseling, and none chose desensitization. Posttreatment results indicated that SIT led to a reduction in rape-related anxiety. Resick, Jordan, Girelli, Hutter, and Marhoefer-Dvorak (1988) provided rape victims with either SIT, assertiveness training, SC, or a wait-list control conditon. All treatments led to comparably effective treatment gains at 6-month follow-up. The inferences of this study for SIT are uncertain, however, because SIT included *in vivo* exposure. Foa, Rothbaum, et al. (1991) compared PE, SIT, SC, and a wait-list control condition in the treatment of sexual and nonsexual assault victims. SIT included education, breathing control, muscle relaxation, thought stopping, cognitive restructuring, modeling, and role-playing. Whereas SIT was the most effective treatment at posttreatment, it was not as effective as PE at follow-up.

Combined Treatments

There have also been attempts to evaluate the efficacy of combining components of CBT in the treatment of PTSD. Hickling and Blanchard (1997) have reported a case series that piloted a treatment program that included education, relaxation training, exposure, cognitive therapy, and pleasant-event scheduling. Although this package was effective in treating all participants, their evaluation lacked a control condition. In a well-controlled study, Foa et al. (1999) compared PE, SIT, PE combined with SIT, and a wait-list control condition. They found that at follow-up, PTSD severity and depression reduced more after PE than SIT or PE combined with SIT. The relatively lower improvement by the combined treatment was attributed to the reduced amount of exposure provided to participants who received the combined treatments. Overall, these findings suggest that anxiety-management techniques may have utility for treating ASD. This proposal is supported by evidence that acute arousal plays a role in the development of PTSD (Bryant, Harvey, et al., in press; Shalev, Sahar, et al., 1998).

TREATMENT STUDIES OF ACUTE POSTTRAUMATIC STRESS

A number of treatment studies conducted before the introduction of the ASD diagnosis have direct relevance to treating ASD. Kilpatrick and

Veronen (1983) conducted a brief behavioral intervention with rape victims immediately after the assault. Fifteen victims were randomly assigned to either repeated assessments, delayed assessment, or an active intervention. This treatment involved 4 to 6 hours of education, imaginal exposure, cognitive restructuring, and anxiety management. It did not result in greater symptom reduction than the control conditions. The lack of any significant results in this study may be attributed to the small sample sizes, variable degrees of psychopathology after the rape, and the lack of rigorous application of exposure procedures (Kilpatrick & Calhoun, 1988).

Brom, Kleber, and Hofman (1993) randomly allocated motor vehicle accident victims to either a monitoring group or an active treatment group. This treatment included three to six sessions of education, supportive counseling, reality testing, and exposure. This study concluded that the early intervention did not lead to greater improvement than natural adaptation. This conclusion should be considered in the context of a number of methodological problems. First, the sample was self-selective because participants were recruited from letters sent to motor vehicle accident survivors identified by police records. Second, all respondents were included in the study regardless of their clinical presentation. Third, the study did not report any information concerning diagnostic status. Fourth, the monitoring and treatment groups differed on a number of pretreatment variables. Foa, Hearst-Ikeda, and Perry (1995) have reported on a brief early-intervention program for victims of sexual and nonsexual assault. Participants were provided with either four sessions of CBT or repeated assessments. The CBT program comprised PE, anxiety management, *in vivo* exposure, and cognitive therapy. Participants were independently assessed after treatment and 5 months later. Ten percent of the CBT participants met criteria for PTSD posttreatment compared with 70% of the control group. At 5-month follow-up, however, the incidence of PTSD was comparable across groups. Despite this diagnostic similarity, the CBT participants reported less depressive and reexperiencing symptoms than did the control participants. Although this study highlights the potential for preventing PTSD symptoms, its conclusions are limited by the possibility that a proportion of participants improved as a result of natural adaptation in the acute phase. The documented remission of many acute posttraumatic stress symptoms in the initial months after a trauma (Blanchard, Hickling, Barton, et al., 1996) highlights the importance of research relating to early intervention to use rigorous inclusion criteria to minimize confusion of treatment effects and natural recovery.

TREATMENT STUDIES OF ASD

The diagnosis of ASD provides more stringent criteria for identifying those individuals in the acute phase who are less likely to recover without formal intervention. There is now convergent evidence that approximately 80% of individuals who are initially diagnosed with ASD subsequently suffer chronic PTSD (Brewin et al., 1999; Bryant & Harvey, 1998b; Harvey & Bryant, 1998d). The success of any treatment of ASD should be measured in terms of its capacity to reduce chronic PTSD below the documented rate of 80%. We have now completed two treatment studies of ASD that have been based on CBT principles.

In our first study, we randomly allocated survivors of motor vehicle accidents or industrial accidents who met criteria for ASD to either a brief CBT program or SC (Bryant, Harvey, Dang, Sackville, & Basten, 1998). Participants were offered five 1½-hour individual sessions within 2 weeks of their trauma. The CBT program was similar to that described by Foa, Hearst-Ikeda, and Perry (1995) in that it included education, PE, anxiety management, in vivo exposure, and cognitive therapy. The SC condition involved education, nondirective support, and general problem solving. Participants were independently assessed at posttreatment and at 6-month follow-up. Fewer participants in CBT (8%) than SC (83%) met criteria for PTSD at posttreatment. More impressively, there were also fewer cases of PTSD in the CBT (17%) than SC (67%) conditions 6 months posttrauma. There were also greater statistically and clinically significant reductions in intrusive, avoidance, and depressive symptoms in the CBT group than the control group at follow-up. In the context of findings that 80% of individuals with ASD suffer chronic PTSD, this finding points to the utility of early CBT in preventing PTSD.

We conducted a second treatment study to identify the elements of CBT that are most effective in treating ASD (Bryant, Sackville, et al., in press). Forty-five civilian trauma survivors (either motor vehicle accident or nonsexual assault) with ASD were given five sessions of either (a) PE and cognitive therapy (CT), (b) a combination of PE and CT plus anxiety management (PE–CT + AM), or (c) SC within 2 weeks of their trauma. Fewer participants allocated to the PE and CT (14%) and PE and CT plus AM (20%) conditions than the SC (56%) condition met criteria for PTSD at posttreatment. At 6-month follow-up, there were fewer cases of PTSD in the PE and CT (15%) and PE and CT plus AM (23%) than SC (67%) conditions. These findings suggest that the combination of PE and cognitive therapy may be the critical ingredients in the reduction of ASD symptoms. This study's design did not permit inferences concerning the relative efficacies of PE and cognitive therapy because both active treatment conditions included these components. Note, however, that early intervention is not a panacea for all acutely traumatized people. In our second treatment study, we found that 20% of our sample dropped out of treatment and that the dropouts were characterized by more severe ASD than the completers.

SUMMARY

These initial studies point to the utility of treating ASD with CBT. It is important to recognize a number of limitations in our understanding of ASD treatment. First, our studies have been applied to victims of motor vehicle accidents, industrial accidents, and nonsexual assault. Prospective studies indicate that the recovery process is not identical across trauma populations. For example, there are different recovery processes in victims of sexual and nonsexual assault (Riggs et al., 1995; Rothbaum et al., 1992). The efficacy of early intervention needs to be established with a range of trauma populations. Second, there is currently no information concerning the influence of early intervention on comorbid conditions. Although our first study indicated that early intervention led to reduced depression at follow-up (Bryant, Harvey, Dang, Sackville, & Basten, 1998), we did not index comorbid diagnoses. There is evidence that acute depression and posttraumatic stress are independent sequelae of a traumatic event but can interact and compound the adjustment process (Shalev, Freedman, et al., 1998). There is a need for future treatment studies to index the influence of early intervention on longer term depression, substance abuse, and other anxiety conditions. Third, the finding that the 20% of participants who dropped out of our second treatment study were more symptomatic than those who completed treatment suggests that early intervention may be less useful for more severely distressed people. There is increasing understanding that exposure therapies are not appropriate for all trauma survivors (Pitman et al., 1991), and our data suggest that extremely disturbed individuals may not cope with active treatments in the acute phase. Identifying those individuals who can cope with early intervention is a challenge for future treatment studies. Fourth, existing treatment studies have been conducted with relatively small sample sizes. Larger numbers would increase the statistical power and allow analysis of factors that predict responses to treatment. Fifth, most treatment studies have used follow-up periods of approximately 6 months (e.g., Bryant, Harvey, Dang, Sackville, & Basten, 1998; Foa, Rothbaum, et al., 1991). Considering Foa, Rothbaum, et al.'s (1991) finding that treatment efficacy altered markedly from posttreatment to follow-up assessments, it would be useful for future studies to assess participants 1 and 2 years after treatment. The influence of ongoing stress on posttraumatic adjustment (King et al., 1998; Solomon et al., 1988) reinforces the need to index functioning for prolonged periods after treatment of ASD. Specific therapeutic interventions in the acute phase may differentially mediate management of posttrauma stressors. Finally, there is a need to index the processes that mediate response to treatment. Integrating cognitive, behavioral, and psychophysiological measures would permit fuller understanding of the processes that result in positive outcomes after specific treatments.

7

TREATING ACUTE STRESS DISORDER

In this chapter, we outline the techniques that can be used to treat ASD. We emphasize that although this outline is based on our work that has demonstrated efficacy in treating ASD, the information contained in the chapter cannot be applied in a cookbook style to the management of acutely traumatized people. Instead, therapeutic interventions must be tailored to the particular needs of the client. Whereas many people with ASD may benefit from all the techniques we describe, others may benefit from only some of them. Moreover, there are a proportion of people for whom any early intervention may be inappropriate. We review the reasons for withholding early intervention in chapter 8. The review of treatment studies in chapter 6 indicated that the techniques that may be usefully applied to ASD include education, anxiety management, cognitive therapy, PE, *in vivo* exposure, and relapse prevention. Accordingly, our treatment programs include each of these components. Depending on the client's clinical presentation, other approaches also may be indicated. Acutely traumatized individuals with severe depression may require antidepressant medication, those with marked family disruption may benefit from family therapy, and those with significant substance abuse may need drug and alcohol intervention. The techniques we describe here are intended to reduce ASD symptoms. Therapists should ensure that other suitable interventions are provided to address the range of problems that may be present.

WHEN SHOULD TREATMENT COMMENCE?

Although the diagnosis of ASD can be made 2 days after the traumatic experience, as we have noted in chapter 4, there is no sound evidence for the selection of this period of time. The practice of diagnosing ASD after 2 days has been criticized because many people can be symptomatic in the initial days after a trauma and report remission a week later (Solomon et al., 1996). Despite this evidence, those who adhere to crisis-intervention approaches suggest that treatment should commence immediately after a trauma. For example, Spiegel and Classen (1995) have advocated treating the person with ASD "as soon after the trauma as possible" (p. 1526). This view is based on some evidence that trauma survivors, who have been treated early after a trauma, display better adjustment than those who have delayed intervention (Bordow & Porritt, 1979; Solomon & Benbenishty, 1986). We are reluctant to commence treatment within a week of a trauma and usually provide treatment 2 weeks after a trauma. We have adopted this policy because it (a) allows the client additional time to gather his or her resources before treatment, (b) decreases the likelihood of presenting symptoms being transient reactions to the trauma, and (c) increases the opportunity for the immediate problems associated with the traumatic event to have settled.

HOW LONG SHOULD TREATMENT LAST?

Our treatment studies have been conducted using five sessions that each lasts 1½ hours. These programs have resulted in significant clinical gains for most participants. Therapists should allow 1½ to 2 hours for each session, to ensure that all necessary material is covered. The number of sessions provided to any trauma survivor should be determined, however, by the symptom presentation. We have seen a significant number of clients who have required additional therapy and have displayed clinical gains after receiving further sessions. We typically offer the client further therapy if she or he has satisfied one of the following criteria:

1. She or he has demonstrated some gains after having complied with the techniques that have been attempted but is still suffering symptoms that impede functioning.
2. There has been a marked decrease in reexperiencing symptoms, but the client is still showing persistent avoidance behaviors. In these cases, the client should be started on a graded *in vivo* exposure program to ensure that persistent avoidance will not impede recovery.
3. Significant stresses are evident in the acute trauma phase that

are contributing to posttraumatic adjustment. The client's response to therapy may be enhanced if he or she is given additional sessions to learn techniques (often anxiety management and cognitive therapy) to cope with the ongoing problems.

We tend not to offer additional sessions when the client displays the following signs:

1. The client has not responded to the techniques offered, and there is little indication that future attempts will result in therapy gains.
2. The client has not adequately complied with therapy, and there is little evidence that future sessions will lead to enhanced compliance.
3. The client's ASD symptoms have diminished, but the client is presenting with other problems that relate to previous psychopathology. These issues are often better addressed within another context to reduce the likelihood of the client attributing these longer term problems to the recent stressor.
4. The client is starting to become entrenched in criminal or civil litigation procedures that can contaminate her or his motivation for participating in therapy.

We also have seen a small proportion of clients who have displayed full remission after only a few sessions of exposure and have expressed a desire to cease therapy before completion of the contracted number of sessions. In these cases, it is wise to provide cognitive therapy to increase the likelihood that future appraisals of posttraumatic events will be interpreted adaptively. It is also important to ensure that relapse-prevention exercises are included, to aid the client in coping with subsequent problems. Finally, it is especially important in these cases to conduct follow-up assessments to ensure that these clients do not relapse.

HOW OFTEN SHOULD TREATMENT HAPPEN?

Our treatment is based on weekly sessions. There are a number of exceptions to this rule, however. First, if a client has not habituated to exposure during the initial exposure session, an additional therapy session should be arranged within several days to permit further exposure to the traumatic memories. Second, if a client is extremely distressed by the recent trauma or by the exposure exercise, it is useful to commence therapy with biweekly sessions. Third, if a client displays extreme avoidance or ambiv-

TABLE 7.1
Summary of Treatment Plan

	Session				
	1	2	3	4	5
Education	X				
Anxiety management	X	X			
Cognitive therapy		X	X	X	X
Prolonged exposure (imaginal)		X	X	X	X
In vivo exposure			X	X	X
Relapse prevention				X	X

alence toward the therapy exercises, more frequent therapy sessions can facilitate the building of rapport with the therapist and enhance compliance with the procedures. Fourth, some clients have restricted access to therapy in the acute phase and may require more frequent therapy to ensure completion of treatment. For example, we often provide biweekly therapy to clients who are treated during hospital admission if therapy will not be possible after discharge. In all cases, the therapist and client should agree on the frequency of sessions before commencement. Table 7.1 contains a summary of the treatment components that typically occur in each session. Therapists should consider the content of each treatment session, however, on the basis of each client's specific needs.

COMMENCING TREATMENT

Feedback and Psychoeducation

The first session begins by providing the client with a formulation of the information gathered during the assessment. The aims of this education are to give the client a framework in which she or he can understand current symptoms and develop some mastery over her or his reactions and to lay the foundations for participating in CBT. We provide education by presenting the following information to the client.

> After a trauma, people often experience the sorts of problems you have told me about. We call this *posttraumatic stress*. It means that after you have been through a traumatic experience, you tend to feel very scared, on edge, and uncertain about things. This happens because when you go through a trauma, you can learn that things around you can be harmful and you tend to be on the lookout for other things that might hurt you again. It is common for people to have upsetting memories of their trauma, to dream about it, and to feel very distressed when they are reminded of it. People can get very upset after a trauma because they are on the alert for harmful things to happen again. These

are all common and understandable responses to an event that has taught you to be wary of things around you. I want you to understand that all the sorts of problems that you are having are very common considering what you have been through.

First, intrusive thoughts or feelings may come in the form of flashbacks, dreams, or memories of the trauma popping into your mind when you do not want them. They can be very upsetting. It is important to be aware that these sorts of memories serve the purpose of allowing the mind to process the trauma by playing it over repeatedly. Because the experience you have had is so important to you, your mind has a need to keep thinking about it, so that it can understand and resolve it. This may seem strange to you, but these sorts of memories and feelings can be useful because they give us plenty of occasions to learn about our experiences and to sort through them.

It is very common after a traumatic experience to avoid all thoughts and reminders of the trauma. People often do this because thinking about it is so distressing that it seems much better to simply put it all aside. In fact, doing this often makes people feel a little better for that moment because they can distract themselves from the distress associated with the experience. What we need to be aware of here, however, is that this sort of avoidance can actually prevent you from getting over the experience.

One of the ways that people try to avoid the distress associated with the trauma is to block the feelings that they have about it. Often people can feel emotionally flat or detached from things. Sometimes people feel like everything seems strange or dreamlike. Other people report feeling that they are not their normal selves. All these reactions might be happening because people are distancing themselves from what has happened. In a sense, it is a way of turning your back on the whole experience. Although this form of avoidance can reduce the distress in the short term, it eventually gets in the way of resolving this experience because it does not allow people to connect with and resolve what they have been through.

Finally, many people who have suffered a traumatic experience report problems with sleeping, concentration, feeling restless and irritable, or being very sensitive to what is going to happen next. These problems occur because after the trauma, the body is in a state of heightened physical arousal. Physical arousal is a sign that even though the trauma is over, the body is still in the "alert" mode and is still prepared to deal with the threat. This elevated arousal can be very distressing for people because it leads to all these problems that can interfere with daily functioning. What we need to do is learn some ways to reduce this arousal. That is, we need to teach the body that the trauma is now over and it can relax a bit more. When we do this, some of these problems caused by the arousal will ease off.

During this initial discussion, it is important to illustrate each point with examples from the client's own experience. This will increase the relevance of the information for the client and his or her confidence that the therapist has heard and understood his or her experience. It is very important to allow opportunities for the client to ask questions and clarify the ideas presented because this initial information forms the basis for the subsequent treatment rationale. After hearing the therapist's account of trauma reactions, we ask clients to explain to us their new understanding of how their trauma has affected them. This practice can be useful because it highlights to the therapist educational issues that need to be clarified before proceeding to therapy.

Description and Rationale for Treatment

Understanding the rationale of treatment is critical for therapeutic success. Clients require a thorough understanding of the treatment rationale if they are to overcome the ambivalence that they feel about approaching traumatic material that they have previously avoided. Providing a written summary of the rationale can be useful because many clients have difficulty absorbing information in the weeks after the trauma. An overview of the treatment rationale can be presented in the following way:

> As we discussed before, a major problem at the moment is that although we do not really need these stress reactions anymore, your body and mind think that we do still need them. We discussed before how you have responded to this experience in a number of ways that are contributing to your current problems. First, your body has responded with elevated arousal because it is still expecting to have to deal with a threatening event. Second, you are frequently thinking about the trauma and feeling distressed because your mind is still trying to process what you have been through. Third, you are often avoiding thoughts or feelings about the trauma because you want to reduce the distress you feel about it. As we discussed earlier, this response brings short-term benefits, but in the long run, it prevents you from really dealing with the experience. I would like to introduce you to the components of our treatment so you can understand why we are going to do each one. Each part of the treatment is going to target one of these problems. That means our goal is to reduce all the symptoms that you have told me about here.
>
> This treatment will take five sessions, and each session will last about 90 minutes. We will meet once a week, although sometimes we may meet more often if it suits us. Everyone responds uniquely to this treatment, so let's keep an open mind about how long we will work together on this. It may happen that at the end of five sessions you might require a bit more time. If that happens, then we can discuss having another

couple of sessions. The overall aim of this program is to tackle these problems before they become entrenched. However, sometimes this will mean that there may be some residual problems still existing at the end of the five sessions. Don't be concerned about that because recovering from a traumatic experience is often an ongoing process. What we are doing here is teach you the basic skills that you require to help you resolve your experience. Moreover, these skills will help you deal with any problems that might resurface in the coming months. Our main goal at this stage is to reduce the distress that you are feeling and to reduce the sorts of problems that have been getting in the way of you living the way you want to.

During treatment, I would prefer us to work as a team. I cannot "cure" you in the way that a pill might cure an illness. Rather, I would like to share with you some techniques that research has shown can overcome the sorts of problems that you have been experiencing. That's my side of the process. The other side of the process will involve you doing a range of exercises that I will ask you to practice between sessions. What that means is that doing this sort of therapy requires considerable work on your part. I will be here to help and support you with every step along the way. So after each session we will set some homework to be completed between sessions. I am feeling hopeful that if we can work together in this way, we can make some headway in dealing with these problems. It's good that we have the chance to tackle these problems so early. It often happens that if we leave these problems untreated, they can be trickier to treat in the future.

ANXIETY-MANAGEMENT SKILLS

It is useful to commence with anxiety management because it provides clients with some initial control over their distress. Be aware that most clients experience considerable distress during the initial sessions because they are confronting and expressing upsetting memories. The utility of reducing arousal in the acute posttrauma phase is also indicated by evidence that acute arousal is associated with chronic PTSD (Shalev, Sahar, et al., 1998). Giving the client some tools to assist mastery over the acute anxiety can provide both a sense of relief and a motivation to comply with more demanding therapy tasks. The general rationale for anxiety-management training is as follows:

> The first thing I will be teaching you is to learn how to reduce the arousal that your body has been experiencing. The sooner we can do this, the more you will notice that some of the problems caused by this arousal will ease. As we have discussed, it is common for the body to be very aroused after a trauma. This arousal can make your anxiety feelings worse. So by learning how to reduce your arousal, you

will have an ability to reduce some of your anxiety. This will involve you learning to do two things. First, you will practice relaxing your muscles, and then you will learn how to control your breathing. These strategies can be very useful for you in the coming weeks because they will help you cope with the distress that you will periodically experience.

Muscle-Relaxation Training

The first step in anxiety-management training is to teach muscle relaxation. This technique is based on Öst's (1987) program and aims to develop a physical response that counters the excessive arousal displayed by the acutely traumatized client. When presenting the rationale of muscle-relaxation training to clients, it is important to emphasize that muscle relaxation can (a) alleviate anxiety, (b) assist sleep, (c) reduce pain resulting from muscle tension, and (d) assist coping with later therapy tasks. It is also important to warn the client that learning to relax muscles is a gradual process that requires daily practice. Be aware that progressive muscle relaxation may not be appropriate for all clients. For example, burns patients may not be able to tense muscles because of pain associated with skin contraction. Factors contraindicating muscle relaxation should be explored before commencement of any training. The major steps in muscle relaxation training are as follows:

1. Provide a clear rationale.
2. Identify problems that the client may have with muscle relaxation.
3. Ensure that the setting is conducive to relaxation.
4. Inform the client of possible side effects.
5. Demonstrate the technique to the client.
6. Observe the client's completion of relaxation training.
7. Identify the client's difficulties with relaxation.
8. Clarify rehearsal schedule.
9. Commence homework and monitoring.

The initial step in muscle-relaxation training is to provide a rationale:

You mentioned that since the trauma, you have noticed that your body is always on edge and alert. This bodily arousal probably makes it difficult for you to sleep and concentrate and may make you more irritable. In order to reduce your arousal, I suggest that we start with muscle-relaxation training. The best way to learn this skill is for us to go through it here in the session, tape what we do, and for you to take the tape home and practice the relaxation technique. Often people think that they will derive immediate benefit from a relaxation tape.

In reality, relaxation is like any skill because it takes practice before it is mastered. Just like no one is an expert tennis player when they first start learning the game, no one is an expert at being able to relax without practice. You should remember that your body has had quite a bit of time to learn to be tense. It is not reasonable to expect your body to unlearn that tension overnight. It will take a lot of practice. As you teach your body to become more relaxed, it will gradually let go of the tension it has developed in recent times.

Relaxing your muscles requires that you can notice when you are tense. Most people get used to their tension and cannot easily identify which muscles are excessively tense. This means that we will need to do some exercises to get you more aware of the tension that exists in your muscles. The way we will do that is by tensing muscles more than you usually do and then relaxing them. This procedure will both draw your attention to the tension and also help your muscles to loosen up.

Before we start, I want you to be aware of some responses that people may have to relaxation. First, some people report feeling strange sensations. Maybe some different sensations in your stomach or chest. These may be physical signs that you were not expecting. I don't want you to worry about these because they simply reflect your increased awareness of what is happening in your body. It may also occur that you will unexpectedly have some thoughts about your trauma. This is common because you are quietly focusing on yourself and it may be at these times that you have memories of what happened. Again, I don't want you to be concerned about the fact that memories pop into your mind. You can let them come and let them go again. Don't force them out of your mind. Rather, allow yourself to come back to the job of tensing and relaxing your muscles. Finally, you may think that you are experiencing more tension as you do this exercise. This is also common but you are not actually getting tenser. Instead, you have become more aware of the tension that exists in your body, which means that you are doing your job here very well. As you continue to practice the exercise, the level of tension that you perceive will reduce.

It's important when you do relaxation exercises to make sure that you are as comfortable as possible. I suggest that you keep the following points in mind. First, always relax in a comfortable chair or lounge that supports your back and neck. This way you can experience full relaxation because you don't have to support yourself. Second, it's a good idea to loosen any clothes that are particularly tight or uncomfortable. Third, if you wear contact lenses you might like to take them out, so your eyes can fully relax. Fourth, it's a good idea to not tense muscles that are injured or prone to cramping. If there are muscles that may be a problem, you can tell me about them now and we can work with them in an appropriate way.

Okay, let's try the exercise. I would like you to sit back in the chair and wriggle around until you are really comfortable. Remember that you need not stay in a rigid position through the relaxation session.

Change positions if it makes you more comfortable. In a moment I will ask you to close your eyes and then start taking you through the relaxation procedure. That involves me asking you to concentrate on and tense up one muscle group at a time. We will start with the hands. I will ask you to tense up your left hand as hard as you can. I want you to keep it tense for about 7 seconds as you notice what the tension feels like. And then, I want you to let your hand go and loosen it so that all the tension flows out of it. As you relax the hand, say the word "relax" to yourself as you breathe out. Say it slowly and gently, as you notice the remaining tension leaving your hand. And I want you to keep noticing the tension flowing out of your hand as you continue to relax it for about 30 seconds. To give you an idea of what we will do, I want you to watch me as I do it. [Therapist demonstrates tension–relaxation cycle.] Okay, and now how about you trying it? Close your eyes, and notice how your left hand is feeling. Now make a fist with your left hand and tighten it as much as possible. That's right. Feel the tension. Continue to hold the tension. And now . . . loosen your hand, and say "r-e-l-a-x" to yourself. Slowly and comfortably. Rest your hand on the armchair, and let all the tension go out of your hand. And keep letting all the tension out of the left hand. You might notice that every time you breathe out, a bit more tension flows out of your fingertips, and your hand feels a little bit more relaxed.

Okay, now in the full exercise, we will repeat this procedure for the arms, shoulders, legs, stomach, neck, and head. That means that by the end of the exercise, we will have relaxed your whole body. [Therapist demonstrates the tension–relaxation cycle for the arms, shoulders, and so on.]

Exhibit 7.1 contains a summary of the activities that may be included in the progressive muscle-relaxation exercise. Although many clients prefer to proceed rapidly through this exercise by doing a minimal number of muscle groups, the therapist should monitor and ensure that the exercise involves most muscle groups. It is very important to clarify with clients how they should practice relaxation between sessions. Specifying the time and location in which the exercise will be conducted is important. To facilitate compliance, we typically provide clients with a tape recording of the relaxation session to take home. In preparation for its use, we give the following instructions:

This technique will only work if you can practice it every day. It will be important for you to take the tape of our session home and practice it daily. There are a couple of important things to remember when you are practicing relaxation at home. The first is that you need to find a place where no one will disturb you. For example, you need to take the phone off the hook, and tell others not to disturb you. Then you need to get yourself comfortable. Doing relaxation lying down on your bed is often not ideal because many people just fall asleep. It is better

EXHIBIT 7.1
Activities to Be Included in Progressive Muscle Relaxation

Clench fists . . . then relax fists
Bend hands inward at wrist . . . then relax hands
Tighten biceps . . . then relax biceps
Arch shoulders upward . . . then relax shoulders
Push shoulders back and tighten chest . . . then relax shoulders and chest
Tense stomach . . . then relax stomach
Tense buttocks . . . then relax buttocks
Curl up left toes . . . then relax toes
Stretch left leg and bend toes back . . . then relax leg and toes
Stretch left leg and stretch toes forward . . . then relax leg and toes
Curl up right toes . . . then relax toes
Stretch right leg and bend toes back . . . then relax leg and toes
Stretch right leg and stretch toes forward . . . then relax leg and toes
Arch back . . . then relax back
Bend head forward to chest . . . then relax head back to normal
Bend head right to shoulder . . . then relax head back to normal
Bend head left to shoulder . . . then relax head back to normal
Clench jaw . . . then relax jaw
Frown tightly . . . then relax forehead

to use a reclining chair, much like the one you are using now, to sit in. It is important that your neck and back are fully supported and your legs should not be crossed. It is usually good to not do it just before you go to bed because you may simply fall asleep. Remember, this technique is trying to teach you to be relaxed when you are awake. Also, you need to make sure that you can give yourself sufficient time to do the entire exercise. Try to allow 45 minutes, so you can complete the exercise and also enjoy some of the relaxation at the end of it. How realistic is it for you to find a quiet, comfortable place to do the exercise? [Discuss with the client the exact details about how relaxation will be conducted between sessions.]

Breathing Control

The next step in anxiety management is to teach breathing control. This should commence by the therapist modeling appropriate breathing to the client. It is important that the therapist instructs the client to not take too deep a breath initially because this may elicit an anxiety response in acutely traumatized clients. Clients with ASD can be very sensitive to physiological responses that occurred during their traumatic experience, and taking a very large breath may be overly reminiscent of their initial trauma reaction. Therapists should be careful when using breathing control techniques with clients who have been traumatized by attempted suffocation or choking or who have suffered injuries in which their breathing was impaired. We present breathing control to the patient with the following rationale:

> Breathing is a very simple, but very critical, mechanism that influences how relaxed we feel. We typically breathe very quickly when we are frightened or upset. You can probably recall times when something has scared you and you immediately responded with a gasp. These experiences can literally "take our breath away." Breathing too fast can bring on a number of physiological reactions that we associate with feeling anxious. These include breathlessness, a feeling of choking, chest pains, and light-headedness. Fast breathing is also called *hyperventilation*. This occurs when people are frightened because they feel they need to breathe more air in. In fact, at times like this, we need to actually take in less air because hyperventilation actually disrupts the balance between oxygen and carbon dioxide in our bodies. It is this imbalance that causes the symptoms like light-headedness and dizziness. Because of this, the way out of this situation is to slow down our breathing and ensure that we are taking less air into our bodies. The result of this will be a feeling of greater relaxation and control.
>
> The technique that we are going to learn, like any other skill, needs to be practiced. The more you practice it, the better you will become at using it. So don't be concerned if initially you have difficulty applying it. It does take time. It's important that you practice it twice daily, and it's best if you try to practice it at times when you are not very anxious or uptight. By doing this, you will be better prepared to use it effectively when you are feeling anxious.
>
> Now, in a moment, I am going to ask you to take a normal breath in. Not a deep breath but just a normal one and inhale through your nose. Okay, now take a normal breath in through your nose. That's good. Now, I want you to breathe out slowly and easily. And as you breathe out, I want you to say the word "relax" [or a comparable cue word that the client is comfortable with] to yourself. Okay, and again. And say "r-e-l-a-x" to yourself as you slowly breathe out. Now keep breathing in and out. To help you get the timing right, try saying to yourself, "1 ... 2 ... 3 ... in" and then as you exhale: "1 ... 2 ... 3 ... out." And say the word "relax" every time you breathe out. This procedure should produce a breathing rate of 10 breaths per minute, which is a good rate to help you remain relaxed and steady.

The client should rehearse this procedure as the therapist observes her or his progress. During this rehearsal, the therapist can count out loud as the client breathes in and out. For example, the therapist can lead the client's breathing by saying, "Now breathe in ... 1 and 2 and 3 ... and exhale, re-lax." It is useful to have the client continue this exercise for approximately 5 minutes. This period allows the therapist ample opportunity to observe the client's breathing rate.

Isometric Relaxation

We often teach ASD clients isometric relaxation because it provides them with a brief technique that can quickly interrupt an anxiety response and facilitate relaxation. Isometric relaxation involves briefly tensing and subsequently relaxing muscles that are not actually moved. This procedure can result in rapid reduction of muscle tension and has the additional advantage of allowing clients to do a muscle-relaxation exercise in public settings where they do not wish to be observed as they attempt relaxation. Exhibit 7.2 contains a summary of the steps involved in training isometric relaxation.

We provide the following rationale and instructions for clients.

Isometric relaxation is another technique I want you to learn because it is a simple strategy that can help you relax very quickly without drawing attention to yourself. *Isometric relaxation* refers to the process when you tense muscles without actually moving them and then relax them. The useful thing about this exercise is that it allows you to relax your muscles in places where it is not appropriate for you to do your full muscle-relaxation exercise. For example, imagine that you are in a doctor's waiting room and you suddenly felt very anxious. You would not be able to stretch out and do your progressive muscle-relaxation exercise because of all the people around you. Isometric relaxation allows you to briefly tense and relax your muscles in a way that nobody need see you doing it.

Let's go through the steps of isometric relaxation. First, decide on a set of muscle groups that you can tense without moving them. We can try this just now. In a moment I will ask you to clench the muscles in the top half of your leg, your quadriceps [point this area out on your own body]. So, without sticking your legs out in front of you, tighten this muscle. Can you feel it? You need to tighten them as much as you can. And this bit is important. Tighten them for about 7 seconds. If you tighten them for more than that, the muscles will tire, and it will be difficult for you to relax them. When you do relax the muscles, just say "r-e-l-a-x" to yourself, slowly, and notice the muscles loosening up. And keep letting them loosen up for about 30 seconds. Okay, let's try it. Tighten your muscles now. . . . Feel the tension. . . . 1 . . . 2 . . . 3 . . . 4 . . . 5 . . . 6. . . . And relax. Breathe out and let ALL the tension

---

EXHIBIT 7.2
Steps for Isometric Relaxation Training

1. Tense a muscle group for 7 seconds
2. Relax the muscles fully
3. Say "relax" to yourself as you exhale
4. Continue to relax for at least 30 seconds
5. Repeat the exercise if you still feel tense

TABLE 7.2
Isometric Relaxation Options

Situation	Exercise
Sitting in public	Clench your fists in your lap
Sitting in public	Lock your fingers together and tense
Standing in public	Tense your legs by straightening your knees
Standing in public	Pretend to stretch and tighten your arm muscles
Standing in public	Lock your fingers behind your neck and push forward as you force your neck back
Sitting in the car	Clench the steering wheel as tight as you can (when the car is stationary)

flow out of those muscles. That's it. Just take your time, and let the muscles loosen up and remember to say "relax" to yourself as you breathe out. . . . Good. Keep letting the muscles relax. More and more. Okay, that was good. Now often you will still feel tense after doing this. If you do, you can simply repeat the exercise several times. It is much better to do this than try to continue the tension for longer than 7 seconds. And there are many muscle groups that you can use to do this exercise. The handout lists some of the exercises you can do (see Table 7.2).

Problems

Several problems can arise when teaching anxiety management to acutely traumatized clients. First, requesting clients to close their eyes can be a threatening experience if they have concerns about losing control. It is not uncommon for ASD clients to feel an immediate sense of distress when they close their eyes in the context of therapy. It is wise to always ask clients if they feel comfortable closing their eyes and to reassure them that they can open their eyes at any time during the exercise. Second, a proportion of ASD clients may suffer hyperventilation and panic during muscle relaxation or breathing exercises. The therapist should carefully assess for the presence of panic symptoms before commencing treatment. If an ASD client reports panic, the therapist should address the panic response before proceeding to other therapy components. Specifically, the therapist should teach the client to identify catastrophic interpretations of physical sensations and ensure that panic responses are controlled before proceeding with more demanding tasks (for a detailed review of managing panic, see Craske & Barlow, 1993). Third, it is common for clients to report an increase in anxiety during the initial stages of anxiety management. These clients should be told that this is a common response and that this perceived increase in arousal simply reflects their heightened awareness of their internal states. Clients should be informed that this is an important step because perceiving their bodily tension will permit them to start reducing their tension levels. Finally, many clients will complain that they cannot reduce their anxiety levels. These concerns should be addressed by reassurance that their high levels of muscle tension will require daily practice and that only after a sustained period of rehearsal will they reap the benefits.

COGNITIVE THERAPY

We introduce the rationale and practice of cognitive therapy early in therapy to allow clients to use it during subsequent exposure programs. We have found that clients can use cognitive therapy techniques more effectively if they have previously learned this approach before focusing on distressing memories during exposure therapy. Based on the notion that emotional dysfunction results from maladaptive interpretations of events, this approach aims to correct clients' unrealistic perceptions of their trauma and their current environment (Beck, Rush, Shaw, & Emery, 1979). There are two major levels of cognitive dysfunction that are targeted by cognitive therapy. The first is *automatic maladaptive* thoughts, which are thoughts that elicit a negative emotional reaction. The second is more *pervasive* beliefs, which underlie automatic thoughts. That is, a person's belief that he or she will never be safe again may lead them to an automatic thought about the threatening intentions of a man seen in a shopping mall.

A range of studies have indexed the types of cognitive distortions that traumatized people display. Epstein (1991) pointed to four central themes that are modified by a traumatic experience: (a) The world is benign, (b) the world is meaningful, (c) the traumatized individual is worthy, and (d) other people can be trusted. Similarly, Janoff-Bulman (1992) focused on beliefs about the worth of the individual and the trustworthiness of others. McCann and Pearlman (1990) cited beliefs about safety, trust, power, esteem, and intimacy. Foa, Ehlers, et al. (1998) extended this list of beliefs to include beliefs about initial posttraumatic stress symptoms and permanent changes of one's belief about the self. Table 7.3 provides some common (but not exhaustive) problematic beliefs that acutely traumatized clients report.

Applying Cognitive Therapy With ASD Clients

Several issues need to be recognized when applying cognitive therapy to ASD populations. First, it should be acknowledged that many of the beliefs that acutely traumatized clients present with are based on recent and threatening experiences. Accordingly, their beliefs that they are not safe or that the world is inherently dangerous appear to them valid in the context of their recent trauma. Therapists need to be cautious that they

TABLE 7.3
Examples of Dysfunctional Thoughts and Beliefs

Emotion	Belief	Automatic thought
Fear	I will never be safe again.	This bus will hit me.
	Only crazy people have flashbacks.	I will be locked away.
	All men are dangerous.	He might have a knife in his coat.
Anger	I never get what I deserve.	These cops don't care.
	I didn't deserve this.	I hate this world.
	No one can be trusted.	I can't stand this.
Depression	Only sluts get raped.	My partner doesn't love me.
	I attract disaster.	I would rather be dead.
	I have no control.	Everything is hopeless.

are not perceived by their clients as invalidating their perceptions of the threat they have survived. The possible price of invalidating the acutely traumatized client's perception of her or his vulnerability is that the client may reject any form of cognitive therapy and may even become hostile to all therapeutic interventions. To avoid this situation, it is useful for the therapist to carefully explain the rationale for cognitive therapy in terms of learning how to think about one's traumatic experience in a way that does not exaggerate the event or compound the negative emotional responses. The therapist should suggest that although the client's reactions are perfectly understandable in the wake of his or her experience, the client needs to distinguish between realistic and unrealistic perceptions. Moreover, one particular focus of cognitive therapy in the acute phase is to encourage the client to recognize that the perceptions that she or he currently holds may change with time. It is sometimes unrealistic to expect someone who has recently been traumatized to modify his or her threat-related beliefs within weeks of the trauma. It can be very helpful for the client to recognize that the beliefs he or she holds in the acute phase may not be permanent and that they can change as time elapses. This recognition can pave the way for clients to explore other interpretations of their experience.

Rationale for Cognitive Therapy

We commence cognitive therapy by ensuring that the client has a clear understanding of the rationale of this technique. Below is an example of a rationale given to a client:

We all have a constant stream of thoughts running through our minds —we call this *self-talk*. These thoughts are automatic. That is, we don't try to have these particular thoughts, they just come to us, and they reflect our beliefs and attitudes about our world, other people, and ourselves. Occasionally, something happens that makes us change our way of thinking. The recent trauma you have been through may have resulted in a marked change to the way you see yourself and the world. For example, some people suddenly see the world as much more dangerous, uncontrollable, and unpredictable. As a result, they feel scared and unsafe a lot of the time. They believe that they should always be on guard to protect themselves from further trauma. This can leave a person feeling constantly on edge and at risk. Or perhaps a person might be feeling very guilty about something that happened, and they feel extremely responsible for the unpleasant things that have occurred. This can lead a person to feeling very down and bad about themselves. These sorts of thoughts can also lead a person to feeling that they may not overcome their recent trauma because they feel that the world and their future is too overwhelming.

For example, before your recent trauma, you probably felt that you could drive your car and feel pretty safe as you drove to wherever you needed to go. That is, you believed that the roads were basically a safe place if you drove sensibly. After your accident, however, you are now feeling very unsafe on the road and do not want to drive again because you feel that you might be harmed again. You now believe that every time you get behind the wheel of your car you are putting yourself at risk of being seriously hurt. Whereas you previously thought that you were safe, you now think that the world is dangerous and you are vulnerable. Of course, when you think this, you feel scared and nervous, cannot sleep properly, and want to avoid all the things that may put you in places where you are at risk. What I want you to understand is that all these reactions are occurring because of your new belief that the world is a dangerous place and that you are very vulnerable.

These new beliefs can be hard to change unless you become aware of them and recognize that this way of thinking is unhelpful and unrealistic. I want you to understand that my goal here is not to change the way you think about things. The trauma that you have been through is a very personal experience, and the things that you are thinking about since that time are entirely understandable considering what you have been through. What we need to do here is to work out which beliefs are realistic and which are not. I appreciate that what you believe at the moment is real for you, and I don't want you to think that I am doubting how strongly you feel about what you have experienced. We are just going to explore the sorts of thoughts that you have, so that any that are not helpful for you can be understood in a different light. For example, if you're believing at the moment that you can never feel safe again . . . for the rest of your life . . . , then you are most probably going to feel pretty hopeless about the future. On the other hand, if you can consider that you feel very unsafe now but that some things may happen in the future that might make things safer for you, then you may feel a bit more optimistic. Does that make sense? So what we are going to do here is learn how to interrupt the automatic thought process and become aware of your automatic thoughts. Once we've done that, we are going to learn how to challenge any unrealistic thoughts with more realistic and positive thoughts. We will do this at a comfortable pace, and it's something that we will be doing together. Probably the best way for you to think of this exercise is to imagine that we are both experimenters and that we are testing available evidence to see whether a particular theory fits or not. That is, we look at your thoughts, test them against whatever evidence we have at that time, and work out how valid these thoughts are.

It is important to demonstrate this exercise to the client because identifying negative thoughts is an unfamiliar task for most people. This demonstration should use the client's own thoughts and should encourage the client to adopt an active role in this discussion. We typically commence this process with a benign thought because it allows the client to learn the process without the distress associated with trauma-related issues. Below is an example of an interaction that attempts to identify a negative thought. Notice that wherever possible, we ask questions that allow the client to learn, for themselves, the irrational nature of the target thought and to draw his or her own conclusions on the basis of this insight.

Therapist: As we discussed before, the way you feel about anything is going to be strongly influenced by what you think. For example, imagine that you are walking down the road and you hear a sound in the bushes. You immediately think that there's a thug hiding in the bushes. What would you be feeling?

Client: Petrified.

Therapist: Sure, that's how I'd feel too. Most people would be very scared if they thought a crook was hiding in bushes as they passed by. But what if you found out that it was only a cat in the bushes? What would you be feeling then?

Client: Oh, that's no problem. I would just say to myself that it's a cat and keep on walking.

Therapist: What different reactions did you notice within your self to these different perceptions? Although it's the same noise, did you feel different depending on what you believed was making the noise?

Client: Well, yeah, when it was a thug in the bushes, I felt very scared, but there was no problem when I thought it was a cat.

Therapist: Okay, so it looks like it is what you believe about an event that matters. It is not the noise that makes you scared but rather the belief that there is a thug in the bushes. So what we need to do first is to learn to identify your thoughts, particularly the unrealistic ones. For example, a lot of people who have experienced a trauma think things like "it is only a matter of time before I have another accident," "no one can be trusted," "no place is safe," "I was probably asking for it," "I have no control over what is going to happen to me," "there is no point planning for the future anymore." I want you to think of some of the thoughts that you have had since the trauma. Can you think of any examples of negative thoughts that you have had since the trauma? [Prompt the client to discuss this issue with you.]

Okay, that's the idea. Now what I am going to ask you to do during the week is to complete a diary that records the negative thoughts that you have. This diary will ask you to write down what you were doing at the time you had the thought, what the actual thought is, and how you were feeling at the time. It's best to complete this diary each time you notice that you are feeling down or anxious. Try to write it down as soon as possible because if you leave it till later, you may forget what you are actually thinking. What you write down is important because this is the material that we will work with in our next session. I want you to bring along to our sessions examples of what you have felt and thought. Then we can work on these thoughts together and evaluate the extent to which these thoughts are realistic or not. Later, we will also work out the ways to think about these things that may be more helpful for you. If we look at the Thought Record Form (see Figure 7.1), we can see that it asks you to write down the situation in which the thought occurred to you. In the next column, you can write down what the thought actually is. I want you to also write down how strongly you believe that thought on a scale of 0 (*not at all*) to 100 (*extremely strongly*). In the next column, I want you to write what you feel and how strongly you feel that emotion on a scale of 0 (*not at all*) to 100 (*extremely intensely*). You can see that in the other columns there is room to write down how you challenge the thought, but we can leave that until later. For the moment, we are just going to work on how we identify the thought.

Challenging Negative Thoughts and Beliefs

The next step in this process is to help the client to modify negative thoughts and to compare them with available evidence. Through system-

Situation	Thought	Belief in thought (0 = not at all, 100 = extremely)	Emotion	Rating of emotion (0 = not at all, 100 = extremely intense)	Evidence for thought	Evidence against thought	Rating of emotion (0–100)
Someone knocking at the door	It's an intruder who is going to assault me	90	Terrified	95	I wasn't expecting anyone to come over	There might be an alternative explanation. Possibilities: 1. The person may be knocking at my door by mistake. 2. Maybe it is someone collecting for a charity.	50

Figure 7.1. Sample Thought Record Form.

atic questioning, the therapist can direct the client's attention to incongruities between her or his thoughts and available evidence. It is important to remember that the acutely traumatized client has only recently developed many trauma-related beliefs and that it would be detrimental to challenge beliefs in a dogmatic fashion. It is also important to tell the client that cognitive therapy is not identical to positive thinking because the goal of therapy is to lead the client to perceiving events in a realistic fashion. This is particularly true of acutely traumatized clients who are still experiencing stressful events in the acute posttraumatic phase. The therapist can begin to challenge thoughts in the following way:

> The second step involves challenging these thoughts. We find that one of the best ways to do this is to ask yourself a series of questions that draw your attention to the evidence underlying these thoughts. Remember that the point of these exercises is not to change all your thoughts. It is simply to test these thoughts against reality. These sorts of questions may help you. [It is useful to provide a handout with sample questions on it to facilitate the client's challenging.]

- What did I think about this issue before the trauma?
- Has anything in the world really changed except for my perception?
- How would someone else view this situation?
- How would I respond to someone else who had this thought?
- What is the evidence that my thought is true?
- Is there any evidence that it is not true?
- What effect is this way of thinking having on me?
- Is this thought helpful or harmful to me?
- Is my thought extreme?
- Am I focusing on only the bad things and ignoring the good?
- Am I overestimating the chances of disaster?
- Am I assuming a disaster will take place in a place that is really quite safe?
- Am I assuming responsibility for something that I had no control over?
- Would I blame someone else for the same event?

Below is an example of an interaction between therapist and client as they work on challenging an irrational thought.

Therapist: Okay, Martin, on your Thought Record Form, you mentioned that you were very frightened when someone knocked on your door the other day. According to your form, you say you thought that it was an intruder and that he was going to hurt you. Is that what you thought?

Client: Yes. I wasn't expecting anyone to come over. When there was the knock on my door, I was just overcome with fear.

Therapist: Okay. On a scale of 0 to 100, how scared were you?

Client: I was pretty terrified. I'd say about 90.

Therapist: Okay, now could you tell me what thoughts were running through your head at this time?

Client: Well, I figured it was an intruder and he was going to get me. I had no way of protecting myself.

Therapist: How strongly did you believe this?

Client: Well, I would say about 90. I felt pretty sure about it. Why else would someone be knocking on my door? I wasn't expecting anyone.

Therapist: Okay. Can you think of any other reason why someone might be knocking at your door other than being an intruder?

Client: Well, I guess they might be lost and asking for directions.

Therapist: Good. What other reasons?

Client: They might be knocking on my door by mistake. Or maybe they are collecting for a charity. . . . Or maybe they're selling something.

Therapist: Okay, so it sounds like you think there are a bunch of reasons why someone might knock on your door. They might be lost, knocking on the wrong door, collecting for charity, or selling something. When you adopt one of these alternative interpretations of the situation, how scared do you feel then?

Client: Well, not that scared. Probably only about 50.

Therapist: Okay, so what conclusion do you draw from the change in how anxious you feel? It was 90 when you thought it was an intruder and 50 when you adopted one of the alternative possibilities.

Client: Well, I guess that when I considered the less harmful possibilities, I felt less anxious.

Therapist: So it looks like simply altering the way you interpret things makes a huge difference to how you feel.

Client: Okay, but I still can't be sure that there is not an intruder out there.

Therapist: Sure, it is not possible to be 100% sure. I wonder if you could tell me more about what happened when you heard the knock on the door.

Client: I immediately went quiet so I wouldn't be heard. And then I waited.

Therapist: What happened?

Client: Well, I heard a woman's voice outside the door.

Therapist: A woman's voice?

Client: Yeah, at that point, I laughed at myself for getting my knickers in a knot unnecessarily.

Therapist: Okay, this is really interesting. . . . Are you saying that a woman wouldn't attack you?

Client: No, not likely.

Therapist: What did you do next?

Client: Well, I went to the peephole and looked outside. There was a woman standing there with a man. She looked pregnant.

Therapist: So how likely do you think it is that a couple is going to attack someone, especially when one of them is going to have a baby soon?

Client: It's not very likely.

Therapist: So what happened next?

Client: He was helping her lean against a wall. She didn't look well.

Therapist: Okay, so let's take a moment to pull it all together. You were sitting at home and heard a knock on the door. It sounds like you automatically assumed that it was an intruder who was going to harm you. But instead you found that it was a couple, one of whom was a pregnant women who was clearly not well. Have I got that right?

Client: Yes, I guess the reasonable conclusion is that they were wanting help because she wasn't feeling well.

Therapist: That sounds right to me. . . . But I can appreciate why you jumped to your conclusion because it's only a few weeks since you were badly beaten up. It's very common for people to assume that they are going to get into trouble again when something happens that even remotely resembles what you experienced when you were assaulted. What I want you to understand here is that you can slow your thoughts down and evaluate them in the light of objective evidence. As you do that now, how scared do you feel by that event?

Client: Well, it's probably dropped to about 10. I guess it shouldn't even be that high, but I still feel a bit nervous about it.

Note that in this excerpt the therapist did not engage in an argument with the client when he maintained his belief in his vulnerability. The therapist responded to this response by recognizing the client's position and then evaluating the evidence for the objections that were raised by the client. Furthermore, the therapist explicitly communicated to the client that his interpretations were understandable in the light of his recent assault. That is, the distinction was drawn between the legitimacy and the irrationality of the client's perception.

Challenging Irrational Beliefs

After the client has become familiar and rehearsed in the practice of identifying and challenging automatic thoughts, it is timely to proceed to understanding and correcting the beliefs that mediate these thoughts. Many clients find identification of these beliefs difficult because they are more abstract than automatic thoughts. Consequently, these beliefs require some degree of insight to perceive the attitudes or beliefs that are contributing to the ASD. The most common means of comprehending the underlying belief is repeated questioning about the significance of an automatic thought for the client (Burns, 1980). Asking questions that probe the client to further explore their reasoning for their automatic thought typically leads to greater awareness of the underlying belief (Clark, 1989; Foa & Rothbaum, 1997). The following are useful questions:

1. If this were true, what would it mean for me?
2. What does this say about me?
3. What would happen if this event did occur?
4. What would be so bad if this thing did happen?

The following is an example of a therapist–client interaction that attempts to identify and challenge a belief:

Therapist: Martin, the last little while we have been discussing a number of thoughts that have led you to feel scared. I would like to turn our attention to explore whether there is a common thread between these thoughts.

Client: I just feel scared. All the time.

Therapist: Okay, let's take it a bit more slowly. Let's focus on the last example we worked on. The other day, you were sitting in your office, and you felt very scared when a new client walked in. Tell me more about that.

Client: Well, I was feeling pretty okay, and then he walked in. I wasn't expecting him. He just knocked, opened my door, and gave me a terrible fright.

Therapist:	When you say he gave you a fright, what were you actually scared of?
Client:	I thought he was going to beat me. Just like the other guy. He had me cornered.
Therapist:	Okay, if he actually did that, what would it mean for you?
Client:	I'd be dead, of course. He'd hurt me . . . like the other guy did. I feel like this everywhere. I get scared at the office, at home, in the car. Even with the family.
Therapist:	So you're saying that you can't feel safe anywhere. It doesn't matter where you are or who you are with, you can't feel safe.
Client:	What's more, I know that I can't ever feel safe again. Not after what happened.
Therapist:	Okay, so what you are saying is that the main belief underlying many of these scary thoughts is that "I can't feel safe anywhere, with anyone, ever again." Is that right?
Client:	Yes. That's right. And if you had been through what I have, you'd agree with me.
Therapist:	So are you saying that there is absolutely no place that you can feel safe?
Client:	Absolutely.
Therapist:	Do you feel safe here?
Client:	Sure. But that's different. I know nothing can happen to me here.
Therapist:	Well, what about other places. You mentioned your home?
Client:	If those guys got me at home, they'd hurt me there too.
Therapist:	How often have you been assaulted in your home?
Client:	Never . . . yet.
Therapist:	How long have you lived there?
Client:	Getting onto 10 years.
Therapist:	So you've lived there for 10 years but have never been assaulted there. How often has someone tried to assault you there?
Client:	Never.
Therapist:	How often has someone you have lived with been assaulted in your home?
Client:	I guess never.

Therapist: All right, so how likely is it ... just looking at the evidence ... that you will get assaulted in your home?

Client: Based on the evidence, I guess it's not likely.

Therapist: All right, let's turn to the next part of your belief. You said that you can't feel safe with anyone. Do you really mean that?

Client: Yes. Nobody can make me safe.

Therapist: So you don't feel safe with me?

Client: No, I feel safe with you.

Therapist: What about your family?

Client: I don't necessarily feel safe with them.

Therapist: How often have you been assaulted when you've been with them? How often have they assaulted you?

Client: Never. And I know your next question.... I've known them for 30 years, and I've never been assaulted when I have been with them.

Therapist: Good, you're getting the idea of this. You need to apply some logic to the way you're thinking. You need to base these conclusions on reason and evidence. What about the third part of that belief? The one where you said that you can never feel safe again.

Client: I can't help that. It's just the way I feel.

Therapist: I understand that, but let's ask the question, how often have you been assaulted?

Client: Only once, thank God.

Therapist: How do you know then that you won't feel different in a few weeks or months? What experience are you basing that on?

Client: None.

Therapist: Have you ever felt bad in the past about something for a while but then the feeling passed or changed?

Client: No ... I mean I have felt bad about a whole bunch of things, but it always passes.

Therapist: So is it reasonable to assume that there is a chance that this feeling may pass?

Client: You're right. It probably will pass. Although it doesn't feel as though it will at the moment.

Therapist: That's understandable. But let's just sum all this up. You are saying that you can actually feel safe in certain places, feel safe when you are with numerous people, and probably feel safer some time in the future. Is that correct?

Client: Yes, guess so.

Therapist: Okay, on the basis of the evidence that you have available at this time, it sounds like you have concluded that it's not justified to feel unsafe all the time. So it looks like it's the case that if you apply this line of reasoning to this belief, you are able to change that belief. So by entertaining these other options and balancing your belief with the evidence, you are beginning to put a more realistic slant on your outlook. Let's turn to the Thought Record Form and fill out the final columns. I want you to write down the reality-based response to each of your beliefs and rate how strongly you believe that at the moment. This is what I want you to do each time you have one of these thoughts that make you feel bad. Think about the evidence, weigh it up with an open mind, and record the outcome. The more you do this, the more you will be able to have conviction in the realistic beliefs.

PROLONGED EXPOSURE

Perhaps the most critical component of therapy is PE. The major steps in PE are as follows:

1. Assess the client's suitability for PE.
2. Provide the rationale for PE.
3. Establish a contract for conducting PE.
4. Obtain a narrative in the present tense and ensure emotional engagement.
5. Continue exposure to the narrative for at least 50 minutes.
6. Obtain Subjective Units of Distress Scale (SUDS) ratings throughout PE.
7. Discuss the client's experience after PE.
8. Implement cognitive restructuring with thoughts elicited in PE.
9. Initiate PE as daily homework after habituation is observed.

The first stage in considering PE is determining the client's suitability for this procedure. We discuss the reasons for withholding PE in the next chapter. It is very important to clarify the rationale of PE with the client to engage the client in the exercise. The therapist should keep in mind that clients are being asked to confront those memories and emotions that they are trying to avoid with extreme effort. A clear understanding of the rationale for PE will assist the client in persevering with PE even when she or he is feeling distressed. A clear rationale also is important because clients need to make an informed decision about proceeding with PE. A commitment to PE is essential to reduce poor motivation. We provide the following rationale for PE:

As we discussed earlier, people who go through a trauma tend to avoid thinking about their painful experience because it eases some of the distress they feel. Although this is an understandable response, it does not usually help in dealing with the trauma because it prevents you from understanding and processing the memory. In fact, no matter how hard you try to push away thoughts about the trauma, they come back to you in distressing ways, such as nightmares or flashback memories. These symptoms are a sign that the trauma is still unfinished business. To illustrate this process, I'd like you to sit back, relax, close your eyes, and picture a big white polar bear for a moment. Tell me when you have that image clearly in your mind. . . . Okay, now I would like you to spend the next couple of minutes trying to suppress that image of the white polar bear. Don't let the thought enter your mind for a second. . . . Okay, what happened when you tried to suppress it? [The client will typically report thoughts of the bear.] Right, this is exactly what happens with your memories of the trauma. If you try and suppress the memories, they will usually pop into your mind. Instead of letting these memories pop into your head and distress you, we are going to tackle them head-on, by having you focus your attention on them. I am going to ask you to think about your memories in a way that I don't think you normally do. From the discussion we have had, I think we agree that like most people who have suffered a trauma, you typically respond to trauma memories by attempting to avoid them. That is, you think of something else, distract yourself, or do something to take your mind away from the distress. The problem with this approach is that it prevents you from ever processing and resolving these memories and feelings effectively. It takes time for the mind to get used to things. Have you ever got into a hot bath or shower? When you first get in, it feels really hot, and you feel that you can't handle it. If you stay there for a few minutes, however, your body gets used to the temperature, and it actually feels comfortable. If you got out of the bath straight away, your mind would never get the chance to get used to the heat. It's a bit like that with your memories. You are not giving your mind a chance to get used to these memories because you're avoiding them every chance you get. By focusing attention on these memories, you will actually find that they do not distress you as much as they do now. Moreover, people typically report that as they do this exercise, they get to understand the experience in a way that makes a lot more sense. To use another example, have you ever walked out of a very dark room into bright sunlight? It's virtually impossible to see anything because it all seems so bright. After a few moments, however, you are seeing normally because your eyes and brain have adapted to what's around you. It's the same with your memories. When you first think about them, they will cause great distress, but after you stay with them for a while, your mind will get used to them, and you will see them more clearly and understand them with less distress.

Obtaining a narrative from the client is very important because this represents the stimuli that is the focus of exposure. It is important to convey to the client that they are not being asked to recount what occurred. Many clients will have done this repeatedly to police, doctors, or other authorities in the wake of their traumatic experience. The therapist needs to emphasize that the client is required to relive the experience by narrating the trauma in the first person and present tense. Emphasis should be placed on engagement with the range of emotions experienced during the trauma. The client should be informed that the exposure will continue for at least 50 minutes. The therapist should explain the SUDS rating scale and tell the client that he or she will be asked to describe the level of distress regularly throughout the exposure by providing a SUDS rating. It is useful to obtain a SUDS rating every 10 minutes. Tell the client that if he or she completes the narrative in less than 50 minutes, to simply repeat the exercise until 50 minutes have expired. The narrative may be audiotaped, which permits the client to listen to it in a structured manner during homework exercises. Below is an example of instructions given to a client in the first exposure session.

> I am now going to ask you to focus on your memories for a prolonged period, about 50 minutes. This is different from thinking back to something in the past. I am going to ask you to walk me through exactly what happened by being as fully aware of your experience as you can. I want you to feel everything that you felt at the time and be aware of everything that you thought. In a sense, I want you to relive the experience because this is the most effective way for you to process the event and resolve it. We will do this over and over until you feel more comfortable and less anxious about the trauma. I realize that this sounds like a demanding task, but we are doing this because we know that this approach leads to less distress and fear. Now what questions would you like to ask before we start?
>
> Okay, let's begin. I would like you to describe your trauma to me. I don't want you to tell me about it in the past tense. Instead, I want you to tell me about it as if it were happening now. So tell me about it talking from your position. Use the words "I am" and "he is" to put us there in the here and now. And remember to focus on how you are feeling. Close your eyes if you feel comfortable. It will help you focus on what happened. And as you are telling me what's happening, try to focus on the details of the experience. Tell me about your surround-

ings, what you can see and hear, as well as what you are doing. I also want you to tell me how you are feeling emotionally, what is going through your mind, and also what your body is feeling.

As we do this, I want you to be able to tell me how distressed you feel. Let's use the SUDS scale, on which 0 means that you do not feel at all anxious and 100 means that you feel extremely anxious. So when I ask you how you are feeling, you can just tell me a number that best describes how you are feeling. Okay, you can start now.

CASE EXAMPLE

Background

Martin was the victim of an assault. He had taken a woman out for their first date, and as they left a restaurant, they were accosted and assaulted by two men. Martin was referred to us by his local doctor, whom he had consulted after the assault. When Martin initially presented 2 weeks after the assault, he displayed marked numbing and denial. He reported that he was reluctant to discuss the event but felt that he needed help because he had not slept much since the assault, had terrifying nightmares about the incident, and was frequently distressed by intrusive memories of it. He reported marked avoidance of any reminders of the night and stated that he had not spoken to anyone about the assault. It was eventually revealed that his response to the trauma was compounded by the fact that the woman that he was with that night had been sexually assaulted by one of the men. Martin admitted to pervasive avoidance behaviors since the trauma, including actively trying to suppress thoughts and conversation of them. He reported that he had not spoken to his girlfriend since that night. Martin canceled two appointments before actually attending his first appointment. On the first session, he admitted that he feared attending because he could not bear the thought of revealing the traumatic experience to anybody.

Imaginal Exposure Transcript

Therapist: Now, Martin, tell me exactly what's happening. Remember, I don't want you to describe to me what happened as if you're telling a story. I want you to relive the experience by telling me what is happening in the here and now. I want you to talk in the present tense. Use words like "is" and "am" rather than "did" or "was." And I want you to talk in the first person. That means I want you to keep using the word "I" because this will help you engage with all the feelings and concerns that you have about this event. As we discussed before, this can be distressing, but we need to tackle this problem head-on, so we can get a hold on these memories. During this exercise, I am going to ask you how you are feeling. As we agreed on earlier, I want you to tell me how distressed you feel on that scale of 0 to 100, where 0 means that you don't feel at all distressed and 100 means that you feel extremely distressed. You can tell me a number on that scale that describes how distressed you are at any particular time. Is that okay? As we discussed earlier, you might be able to connect with these things better if you close your eyes and are not distracted by things around you here. Would that be okay if you closed your eyes?

Martin: Ummm, I don't know. If you want me to.

Therapist: I think it might help.

Martin: Okay. Marge and I are leaving the shop. We've bought some take-away chicken, which we took back to the car.

Therapist: Wait a moment, Martin. Remember to talk in the present tense. Try to remember to say "we are now taking it back to the car."

Martin: Oh yeah. Okay. Sorry. . . . Well, we're walking back to the car. I am just putting the keys in the car door and I feel a terrific blow to my back. I am thrown against the car door. I can't say anything because I'm winded. When I turn around there are two guys in front of me. What are they doing? . . . They've got knives, and they're pushing me against the car. I don't know where they've come from. There was nobody here a minute ago. They're laughing . . . . They're big. . . . The knives are enormous. . . . I can't speak I am terrified. . . . I don't know what Marge is doing. All I am thinking about is these guys. This has never happened before. . . . What am I meant to do? . . . The darker one is telling me to open the door. . . . I am trying to open it. I am scared. . . . I can't get the damn keys in the lock. He is pushing me and telling me to hurry up. He's yelling at me to get it open or he'll put my head through the window. He grabs my hair, and he is shoving my face up against the door window. I can't open the door like this. . . . He shoves me to the ground and opens the door himself. My mouth is full of gravel, and I think a tooth is chipped. I can taste blood in my mouth. He is forcing me behind the wheel. . . . He's pointing the knife at the back of my neck. I am trying to get in the car as fast as possible because he's pushing the knife harder against my skin. I'm begging him to let me go. . . . I think he's going to kill me. . . . The other guy is getting in the back with Marge. They stink of beer. He sticks his face right in front of me and breathes right in my face. Why is he doing this? What does he want me to do?. . . . I am closing my eyes. I don't want to see him. . . . He laughs again and tells me to look into his eyes. I do as he says. . . . I think this is it. . . . He is looking right at me and asks me if I'm scared. . . . I nod because I can't speak. . . . He then backs away and tells me to drive. . . . He is holding the knife against my throat. It's just resting against my skin. . . . He is telling me that I better drive carefully because if I don't, his knife might slip. . . . I know that if we go over a hole or I do something dumb it'll cut my throat. . . . He is making some joke about getting blood off the car seat. I can feel the knife scraping against my skin. . . . He is telling me to drive faster, but I don't want to. I have to do what he says. I don't even know if I'm bleeding yet or not. . . . I can't go on. . . . I want to stop.

Therapist: I know it's tough, but you're doing very well. Just stay with this, Martin. This is how we are going to deal with all this. Can you tell me how you are feeling just now on that scale we mentioned?

Martin: It's about 95. It's pretty bad.

Therapist: Okay. We're just beginning here. I know it's tough, but if you can, I want you to continue telling me.

Martin: Okay. . . . I'll try. . . . This guy is just laughing. He thinks it's a real joke. He tells me to drive up to some park that's in the middle of nowhere. I haven't been there before. He tells me to stop the car. . . . Now I'm really scared. . . . I am stopping the car and just looking straight ahead. I think he's going to cut my throat. . . . He's letting the knife slide up and down my throat. . . . Why is he doing this? . . . He's making jokes about what I'd look like without a head. . . . I am crying like a baby. . . . I don't know what to do. . . . I don't know what Marge is thinking of me. A part of me tells me that I should be doing something to stop all this. . . . But I can't. I can't do anything. . . . I just want to close my eyes and not be here. Now the guy in the back seat is pulling my hair back and he is putting his knife to my throat. . . . I can hardly breathe. He is bending my neck back over the seat. Now he is leaning over the seat and talking into my ear. He's telling me he wants to get to know Marge better. . . . He is asking me all the sorts of questions about Marge's body. . . . Disgusting things. . . . I don't want to remember this. . . . I can't talk about this, no way. . . .

Therapist: That's okay, maybe move on to what happened next.

Client: Now he lets go of me. . . . Marge starts screaming. . . . He's pulling her out of the car. I don't dare turn around. She's calling out to me. . . . But there's nothing I can do. . . . I feel so guilty, I should be trying to save her. . . . I knew what was about to happen to her. . . . I just keep staring straight ahead. I close my eyes again. . . . I don't know where they are going. . . . I can't see them. . . . It's weird, but I can see all this happening. I can see him pulling her out of the car, but I am not here. I mean I am not in the car. . . . But I am. . . . But it's like I am seeing it from the other side of the park. I don't know what's happening next. It's a blur. . . . I am sitting in the car with the other guy. He keeps talking about Marge and is asking me personal things about sex. I don't remember these things. The next thing I know is that Marge is back in the car. . . . I turn around and look at her. . . . She looks terrible. Her clothes are ripped, and she is not talking. . . . I think she's bleeding. She's just staring at her lap. . . . I can't look at her. . . . There's nothing I can do to help. . . .

The guy in the front seat is now leaning over to me with his knife. He is whispering in my ear, "We've had our fun. Now what will we do?" And then he puts the knife in my mouth. . . . I stretch my mouth as wide as I can. I can feel it against my tongue as he turns it around. . . . He's pressing it right to the back of my mouth. I can't push back any more. The knife is getting further down my throat. . . . I want to scream out to him to stop but I can't move my mouth. . . . And then he just stops. He takes the knife out of my mouth. He is laughing at me. He grabs my chin and he is forcing me to look at him. Now he looks at Marge and tells her she has a "chicken shit boyfriend" because I didn't do anything to help her. . . . Then he laughs, gets out of the car, and walks off with his mate. . . . That's it. I then drive the car to the police station. I don't look at Marge. Neither of us say a word. I am in automatic pilot now. I don't feel anything. I don't think anything. That's it. There's nothing more.

Therapist: Martin, how are you feeling? Maybe rate how you are feeling now on that scale?

Martin: About 90 . . . 95. It's still bad. I thought you said I would feel better. I don't think this is going to work.

Therapist: It takes time. Most people don't find relief after doing this just once. We are going to have to do this again and again. I can't make you any promises, but I think it will get better as we do this more often. What's most important at this stage is that you felt as distressed as you did and you stayed with it. That's critical. The fact that you could do that is a great sign for how you are going to cope with this program.

Martin: I can't believe how real it was. I haven't done that before. Thought about it like that, I mean. It was all happening again. I could see his face. I can still smell the beer on his breath. Is that normal?

Therapist: Yes. It's very common for people to be very aware of all those sorts of details. And to feel the same emotions that you had at the time. Was there any point that was particularly difficult for you?

Martin: Yeah. Two things mainly. When he made me drive faster and the knife is against my throat. I really thought I was going to die then. I hate thinking about that. The other one was when they took Marge out of the car. They shouldn't have done that. It's not right. I should have done something to stop them. I will never get over that.

Therapist: Did you allow yourself to think about those things just now?

Martin: To be honest, I didn't. They're too bad. I thought about them, but I wanted to skid over them and get to other things.

Therapist: That's okay. Being able to focus on the things that you did was fine for now. We've got time to focus on those other aspects as we move on. I think you will feel more comfortable in tackling them after we've done this a bit more. How are you feeling now that it's over?

Martin: Relieved. I really didn't think that I would cope with it.

Therapist: But you did cope with it. In fact, you did very well. . . . You have been able to focus on this whole event, and you have survived it. You are now sitting here with me, in one piece, and have been able to discuss it with me. That's really important because it tells us that thinking about these memories doesn't really hurt you. You can think about them and be okay after it.

Case Example Analysis

This narrative is noteworthy because it not only illustrates the process of imaginal exposure but also highlights a number of features of the ASD client's response to the trauma. Note that Martin presented with several dissociative symptoms. His report of perceiving the assault from outside the car in which he was seated represents an example of depersonalization. He also reports dissociative amnesia of much of the time that Marge was out of the car. It is difficult to know if Martin was actually amnesic of this event or whether he intentionally did not focus attention on it during this stage of therapy. Subsequent therapy indicated that this phase of the assault was particularly threatening for Martin because he felt severe helplessness for not being able to assist Marge. He also described emotional numbing when he referred to being in "automatic pilot" and not feeling anything. This narrative also highlights the importance of encouraging the client to describe his or her feelings and thoughts during the trauma. Martin's admission that he expected himself to be able to protect Marge indicated to the therapist a potentially important area that would require attention in therapy. It is common for clients to want to withhold certain aspects of the traumatic experience because it is excessively distressing. It is worthwhile to encourage the client to continue with the narrative if it is within her or his capacity. It is important to communicate to the client that experiencing the narrative is important, although focusing on the most distressing details of the experience is not essential in the early sessions. Some clients may not disclose the most distressing features of their experience until the second or third exposure session. It is preferable for the client to be able to participate in exposure to a limited extent as opposed to being overwhelmed by the experience and subsequently avoid this exercise. It is equally important to ensure that all features of the narrative are eventually addressed within exposure.

Martin's initial exposure to the narrative took approximately 15 minutes. Accordingly, the therapist requested him to repeat the procedure for a second time. This exposure took about 20 minutes because Martin focused in more detail on some aspects and was visibly more distressed as he allowed himself to engage with the narrative. The therapist then asked Martin to repeat the procedure for a third time, which again took approximately 20 minutes. In total, the initial exposure session lasted for 55 minutes. Martin's anxiety levels did not decrease over this time. This is not uncommon in a proportion of acutely traumatized clients. In such cases, it is important to communicate to the client that his or her capacity to cope with the distress is important and that habituation will occur in future sessions. Martin was scheduled for another appointment 2 days later to permit continuation of the exposure program. When a client does not display habituation in the initial session, it is advisable to continue with the exposure in a subsequent session that occurs within several days. Clients should not be instructed to continue with exposure as homework until they have demonstrated a capacity for habituation in the presence of the therapist.

After the initial exposure session, the therapist should engage the client in a detailed and frank discussion about the exercise. The therapist should focus on any particular difficulties that the client experienced. Special attention should be directed to any features of the narrative that were avoided in some manner. Many clients will prefer to give less attention to more distressing aspects of the experience. The therapist should be sensitive to these sorts of strategies because they may develop into persistent avoidance that can undermine the effectiveness of the exposure. If the client does not report habituation during the initial exposure exercise, the therapist should reassure the client that it is common for habituation to occur only after several sessions. We suggest scheduling another exposure session within several days and repeating the exposure. Once habituation has commenced and the therapist feels confident that the client is able to conduct exposure independently, exposure should be commenced as daily homework. The client should complete a Prolonged Exposure Monitoring Form each time exposure is done (see Figure 7.2). The client records (a) starting and finishing times, (b) the scene that was the subject of exposure, (c) the SUDS rating soon after commencing exposure, (d) the SUDS rating at the completion of exposure, and (e) any salient thoughts that occurred during or after the exposure. Monitoring is important because it allows the therapist and client to note patterns of habituation, compliance, and trauma-related cognitions. The latter is important because exposure usually results in many irrational beliefs that can be usefully addressed with cognitive therapy. Accordingly, cognitive therapy needs to be integrated into sessions after each exposure session.

In Vivo Exposure

We initiate *in vivo* exposure toward the end of therapy because we believe that clients' ambivalence about participating in *in vivo* exposure is reduced after completing the other treatment components. The reluctance that many clients have in approaching feared events requires that a clear rationale be given. Although the rationale for *in vivo* exposure is the same as that for imaginal exposure, it needs to be explained to clients in the context of *in vivo* procedures. We provide the following rationale for clients:

> As we have discussed before, one outcome of your traumatic experience is that you have learned that things that remind you of your trauma make you anxious. Whereas before the assault you felt that you could go home and feel safe, since that man broke into your house you have felt that home is a dangerous place. There are now all sorts of things in your house that remind you of the experience. Things that you see every day, or noises that you hear, or smells that you notice. All these things remind you of what happened when he assaulted you. What you need to realize is that before the assault, all these things were there

Name: Anne			Date: 7/12/98		
Start time	Finish time	Describe the scene	SUDS rating on commencing exposure	SUDS rating on completion of exposure	Thoughts during exposure/General comments
10:45	11:30	The crash, seeing my husband dying, hearing my kids in the back seat of the car crying	95	65	It was pretty hard to stick with the image, it made me feel very upset initially. I kept thinking "Why me? why me?" and "Why don't they get us out quicker?"

Figure 7.2. Sample Prolonged Exposure Monitoring Form. SUDS = Subjective Units of Distress Scale.

but they did not cause you to feel anxious. What we will need to do in therapy is to teach you that these things are no longer dangerous. We can do this by gradually confronting these situations and learning that nothing bad will happen to you. Another way of thinking about this is that your body has learned to respond to many of the cues that remind you of the trauma. That is, your body becomes tense because it associates these cues with danger signals. In therapy, we must give your body and your mind the chance to learn that these things do NOT necessarily signal danger. This means exposing you to some situations that may remind you of the trauma. By remaining in these situations, you can learn that your initial anxiety will decrease, and you can develop confidence in those situations.

Let's take the example of children learning to swim. They are very fearful when they initially enter the water. When they go in the shallow end of the pool, however, they learn that the fear subsides a bit. Next time, they have slightly less fear when they enter the water. Each time they enter the water, they go a little further into deeper sections. The decrease in fear continues to occur and becomes more and more rapid as they practice. This continues until they are no longer scared. If children were removed from the water the first time they became scared, it would become even harder for them to go swimming the next time.

This is the basic principle to treat all fears. We need to face our fears and stay in the situations that we are afraid of long enough to learn that nothing bad will happen. In fact, we need to repeat this over and over until the anxiety diminishes. Avoiding the situations that we are afraid of actually strengthens our belief that they are scary because this avoidance teaches us that staying away from these things makes us feel better. In effect, avoiding the situations that scare you makes it even harder to face them the next time.

A very important part of *in vivo* exposure is to try and predict what will happen before you go in to the situation. For example, let's say a woman has had a motor vehicle accident and she has decided to go back to where the accident happened. I would ask her to make a specific prediction about what is likely to happen. She may say that she predicts that she will have another car accident. Then I would get her to rate the probability of having another accident during the exposure exercise. Let's say she said 80%. Then when she goes into the situation she can experience for herself whether the prediction she made was realized. Also, I would ask her to prepare a series of strategies to help her cope with being in this situation. For example, she may ask herself what the evidence is that she will be the victim of another accident. Finally, I would ask her to rehearse these strategies before going into that situation, so that she is very familiar with them when she actually has to use them. The most important point of this exercise is that you only leave the feared situation after you have felt relief. Remember, leaving before the anxiety subsides only reinforces the belief that it is a fearful scene.

Hierarchy Development

After explaining the rationale, the next step in *in vivo* exposure is to develop a hierarchy of feared or avoided situations. This procedure involves having the client determine a graded series of situations that elicit varying degrees of anxiety. The most effective way to create a hierarchy is to have the client evaluate avoided situations in terms of SUDS ratings. That is, the therapist asks the client to allocate a rating of 0 (*not at all distressing*) to 100 (*the most distressing I have ever felt*) to a series of events or situations. This exercise requires a joint effort by the client and therapist because most clients have some difficulty in determining gradations of anxiety-eliciting situations. This difficulty can be especially evident in the acute phase, when many clients perceive all trauma-related situations as being extremely aversive.

There are several options available to facilitate hierarchy development. The client can be given a Trauma Hierarchy Form, which requires the client to write down 10 to 15 situations which he or she avoids (see Figure 7.3). Each situation is given a SUDS rating, and this permits development of a graded hierarchy. Alternately, the client can write down each situation that is avoided on a small card. When 10 or 15 cards have been completed, the client can sort the cards in a graded fashion, and this

Trauma Hierarchy Form	Name: MARTIN	
Situation		SUDS
1.	Talking to a man I don't know on the telephone	10
2.	Talking to a woman I don't know	20
3.	Turning my back on a woman	25
4.	Driving in the day with a friend	30
5.	Talking to a man I don't know with my friend	40
6.	Talking to a man I don't know by myself	45
7.	Walking by myself in the day	50
8.	Turning my back on a man I don't know	55
9.	Driving in the day by myself	60
10.	Driving at night with a friend	75
11.	Going into a men's restroom with a friend	80
12.	Going into a men's restroom alone	85
13.	Walking with a friend at night	90
14.	Driving at night by myself	95
15.	Walking by myself at night	100

Figure 7.3. Sample Trauma Hierarchy Form. SUDS = Subjective Units of Distress Scale.

allows a hierarchy to be established and SUDS ratings to be allocated to each situation. This method has the advantage of allowing the client to repeatedly shuffle the order of situations so that it most accurately reflects the levels of anxiety that the situations elicit. Whatever method is chosen, the client should be encouraged to focus on events that are realistic and can be practically integrated into an exposure program. For example, an assault victim might nominate his or her worst fear as meeting the assailant in a dark alley again. Although this fear is genuine, it does not reflect a situation that the therapist would want the client to be able to approach. A more adaptive step that may be included in the hierarchy is walking down a safe alley alone at a time when there is minimal risk. The therapist and client need to identify situations that are avoided in a maladaptive way and that impede the client's functioning. The therapist should also be aware that the hierarchy nearly always needs to be modified once exposure has commenced because acutely traumatized clients often have difficulty accurately perceiving the level of fear that certain situations will evoke.

> Therapist: To help you gradually reduce your avoidance of these events, we need to make a list of the things that you do avoid. It's best that you approach each of these things in a gradual manner. So let's make a list of things you avoid that cause you lots of distress, moderate distress, and only a little distress. If we can describe each situation with the SUDS rating that we have used before, it will help us put each situation in a position on the hierarchy relative to other situations. Let's remember that we are going to get you to go into each of these situations, so they need to be realistic ones that you can practically do. How about we start with the hardest ones? What would be the toughest situations for you to approach?

> Client: That's hard. There are lots. I definitely will not walk by myself. There is no way I will do that. It's asking for trouble.

> Therapist: Is your fear of walking alone the same whether it's during the day or night?

> Client: Oh, it's much worse at night. That's when I was mugged. I won't walk at night.

> Therapist: Okay, how about if you are with someone or on your own?

> Client: It's worse on my own. There's some safety in numbers, you know.

> Therapist: What SUDS rating would you give a situation involving walking at night when you're by yourself?

Client: Oh, probably 100. I can't think of anything worse.

Therapist: Okay, let's write that down so we can remember it.

Client: Wait, you're not going to ask me to go walking out at night. That's dangerous.

Therapist: I agree that it's dangerous to go walking downtown at night. I certainly wouldn't want to ask you to do that. But you've told me that you won't go walking anywhere at night. Even in your own neighborhood, where you've told me that the streets are busy until 11 p.m. How about we put at the top of the hierarchy walking at night by yourself in your neighborhood at 7 p.m.?

Client: Okay, it sounds reasonable.

Therapist: What about walking with someone else at night?

Client: That would also be scary but not so bad. Maybe 95.

Therapist: Okay, how would it be driving at night?

Client: I hate that. You're not safe in your car.

Therapist: How does it compare to walking?

Client: It's a bit safer than walking. I would say about 90.

Therapist: Okay, so walking at night is a bit worse than driving at night. Is it easier driving with someone else than driving alone?

Client: You bet.

Therapist: Okay, so let's write these situations down on the cards. We've got walking alone at night, walking with a friend at night, driving alone at night, and driving with a friend at night. Can you put these in the order that you feel is most to least scary?

Client: Walking alone at night is definitely worst. That's 100 . . . without a doubt. Then it would be driving alone at night. I'd say that's 95. Then it would be walking with a friend at night . . . say 90. And then driving with a friend at night. That would be 85.

Therapist: Excellent. Now what other situations do you think we need to put on the hierarchy?

Client: Men's restrooms. I despise them. You never know what's going to happen there, and when you've got your back turned, you can't protect yourself.

Therapist: So being in a public restroom is difficult. And turning your back on people is difficult, is it?

Client:	Oh, yeah, I never turn my back on anyone. You never know who might try and get you when your back is turned.
Therapist:	Does it matter if you're in the restroom on your own or with a friend you can trust?
Client:	It's much easier with a friend.
Therapist:	Okay, and what SUDS rating would you give being in a restroom with a friend?
Client:	About 60.
Therapist:	And being there on your own?
Client:	About 75.
Therapist:	Good. Now you mentioned that it was difficult turning your back on people. Tell me more about that.
Client:	Well, I never know if someone is going to hurt me if I turn my back on them. So I never do. If I am in a room or near someone, I always watch them. I always stand next to walls so people can't get behind me.
Therapist:	Does it make any difference whether the person is male or female?
Client:	Oh, yes. I am much worse if it's a man.
Therapist:	So what would the SUDS rating be for you if you had to turn your back on a woman in a shopping mall?
Client:	Only about 25.
Therapist:	And what about turning your back on a man?
Client:	Oh, that's worse. I haven't let that happen since I was mugged. It would be about 40.
Therapist:	Okay. Would it make any difference if you were alone or with a friend?
Client:	Yes. It's a bit easier with a friend because I know that someone's there that I can trust. If I was on my own, it would be 45. But if a friend was there, it might be about 40.
Therapist:	Okay, so let's put those situations on the cards and sort them in the right order.

Implementing In Vivo Exposure

After the hierarchy is complete, the therapist should ask the client to commence with the situation that is lowest on the hierarchy. It is advisable to start with a situation that the client can cope with relatively easily because this can facilitate confidence in her or his ability and enhance compliance with more demanding items. Many in vivo exposure exercises do not work effectively because they are not structured in a regimented manner. We follow a number of guidelines to ensure that the client does achieve habituation to each step on the hierarchy. First, ensure that the client remains in the situation for at least 30 to 40 minutes, or less if the anxiety has fully subsided. Second, we operationalize habituation by requiring that the SUDS rating decrease by 50% before leaving the situation. To recognize reduction in anxiety, it is important that the client uses the *In Vivo* Exposure Form (see Figure 7.4) to monitor progress by describing (a) the situation, (b) the time spent in the situation, (c) SUDS

Name: _____ Date: _____

Situation: _____

_____

_____

_____ Expected SUDS:_____ /100

BEFORE

Time Commenced: _____ Initial SUDS: _____ /100

What do you predict will happen in the situation?

_____

_____

AFTER

Time Finished: _____ Final SUDS:_____ /100

Did your predictions come true?

_____

_____

Additional Problems/Comments:

_____

_____

OBSERVER'S RATING (please tick **one** of the choices below)

☐ Task fully completed   ☐ Task partially completed   ☐ Task not completed

☐ Observer not present

Figure 7.4. In Vivo Exposure Form.

ratings at the beginning and end of the exercise, and (d) his or her thoughts during the exercise. Third, it is extremely useful to have someone accompany the client during exposure, especially in the early stages. This can assist the client because (a) many situations on a hierarchy initially involve the presence of a supportive person, (b) the person can encourage the client to remain in the situation, and (c) the person can remind the client to engage in adaptive strategies to assist coping with the situation. The person assisting the client may be the therapist, a therapist aide, or a friend or partner of the client. It is always important that the additional person participating in the exposure is fully aware of the rationale and techniques of exposure. Fourth, we encourage the client to contact us by telephone if a situation is avoided because the anxiety is excessively distressing. In these cases, we suggest modifications of the hierarchy that serve to build in intermediate steps. Fifth, it is important to expose the client to all situations that elicit anxiety and contribute to avoidance behavior. This requires the therapist to be sensitive to covert means of avoidance during exposure. For example, an assault victim may agree to remain in a shopping mall but will carry a knife in his pocket as a means of protection. Such safety behaviors serve to minimize full exposure to the situation and should be removed from the exposure exercise. Below is an example of reviewing the previous week's exposure homework and making plans for the next step:

Therapist: Looking at your record form, it seems that you had problems in going into a public restroom. What happened?

Client: I just panicked. A few days before I had gone in with a friend and I coped okay. I mean it was pretty distressing, but I was able to hang in there. But yesterday, I tried it on my own, and I just lost it. I walked in and felt that I was going to handle it. But then it all went haywire. I started to panic, my heart went wild. . . . I thought my chest was going to explode. I just felt that something bad would happen in there.

Therapist: What did you do?

Client: I ran out. I know I wasn't meant to but I had to get out. To be honest, I really didn't think it would be as bad as that.

Therapist: Okay, how about we build in a few more steps so you can handle this. As we have discussed before, the most important thing here is that you can stay in these situations that cause you distress. Leaving them will only reinforce the belief that they are scary and you can feel better if you leave them. Tell me more about what scared you when you went in to the restroom.

Client: Well, it was dark, and I didn't know who was around.

Therapist: So you went at night?

Client: Yes.

Therapist: Do you think it would have been easier if you went during the day?

Client: Probably. Now you mention it, I was worried about the dark because that's when those guys got me.

Therapist: Okay. How about going into the restroom in the middle of the day? Would that make it easier?

Client: Yes, that'd be better. But I have to tell you, I am not looking forward to this.

Therapist: Well, you say that you coped last week with it when you went in with your friend. How about we try it initially with your friend waiting outside the restroom for you?

Client: That would be much better.

Therapist: What do you predict will happen when you go to the restroom during the day with your friend?

Client: I reckon there is a good chance we will be attacked.

Therapist: How much of a chance?

Client: Well . . . I would say 50%.

Therapist: Okay, how does that sound for a plan? The next step is for you to go into the restroom during the day and with your friend waiting outside. After you've managed that, you can try going into the restroom by yourself during the day without your friend being there. After you've managed that, you can then try going in there later in the day. You're predicting that you will be attacked—so by going there, you will get to check that out. How does that sound?

Client: Much better.

Relapse Prevention

The final component of treatment is relapse prevention (for a review, see P. H. Wilson, 1992). This is a critical component because it is very common for acutely traumatized clients to experience numerous setbacks in the months following a trauma. Identifying likely problems and rehearsing means to overcome them can assist the client's longer term adaptation to the trauma. This component is particularly important because many ASD clients have ongoing stressors, including legal proceedings, ongoing medical complaints, and social difficulties that can directly compound their posttraumatic stress.

The steps for relapse prevention are as follows:

1. Identify areas of poor therapeutic gain.
2. Initiate remedial steps to enhance therapy gains.
3. Predict possible situations when relapse may occur.
4. Develop strategies to deal with expected difficulties.
5. Rehearse strategies to increase familiarity with problem solving.
6. Initiate relapse prevention steps (a) before expected difficult situations and (b) when symptoms increase.

First, the therapist should begin relapse prevention by asking the client to identify the aspects of therapy he or she have found most beneficial. This allows the therapist to determine (a) areas that may not have been given enough attention during therapy and (b) areas that match with the client's coping abilities. The therapist and client can use this information to decide whether further sessions are required to enhance the client's skills. Second, the therapist assists the client to identify foreseeable situations that may exacerbate his or her condition. For example, anniversaries of the trauma, appearing in court, or surgical procedures may be nominated as possible situations in which the client may experience a resurgence of symptoms. Third, the therapist should identify those particular therapeutic skills that will assist the client to manage these expected difficulties. Inherent in this work is the assumption that the client will not need therapeutic support each time she or he experiences problems. Instead, it is important to convey to clients that they have learned important skills that they will be able to use at problematic times to master symptoms that may arise. Fourth, the therapist should encourage clients to rehearse the particular skills necessary to cope with foreseeable problems. This stage of therapy may involve role-playing with the client the expected difficult situations and assisting the client to refine his or her coping strategies. Finally, it is useful to routinely plan for two or three monthly booster sessions after therapy. These sessions permit useful monitoring of the client's longer term adaptation as well as provision of any assistance to facilitate coping. We explain relapse prevention in the following way:

Therapist: Well, we are coming toward the end of therapy, and so it is probably a good time to look back to the progress you have made and look forward to the next few weeks and months. As I am sure you are aware, the end of therapy is not the end of the process of dealing with your trauma. There will inevitably be ups and downs. Sometimes the memories of the trauma will bother you, and sometimes they won't. During therapy, you have developed a collection of coping strategies and ideas for managing the trauma. Each of the strategies is fairly new, so it will be important to keep practicing them. Then, if ever you do come across a period when the memories of your trauma are bothering you, you will able to go back to these strategies and continue your own therapy. In your sessions, we have learned a number of strategies to deal with your trauma. Which ones do you find most useful?

Client: I think I probably benefited most from the relaxation and the imaginal exposure.

Therapist: What were your thoughts about the cognitive therapy?

Client: Well, I guess it was an eye-opener. I feel like I am doing that pretty automatically now in all situations.

Therapist: What part of therapy do you think is still a bit difficult?

Client: Well, I guess the real-life exposure is tough. I know I've managed the early steps, but some of these later ones are not easy.

Therapist: So perhaps our immediate plan should focus on real-life exposure. What areas still cause you some distress?

Client: Well, none really cause me a huge amount of distress. But there are still one or two that cause me a little bit of discomfort. Like on my way to work I can take one of two routes. One goes past where I had the accident. This is the most direct route. But I still take another way that doesn't go past the accident site, even though it's 20 minutes longer.

Therapist: Well, I am pleased that you are aware when you are avoiding. This ability will serve you well. As soon as you detect avoidance, you will be able to work out what you are fearful of in the situation and then go into the situation to test out if your feared outcome occurs. So what do you think you should do about your driving to work?

Client: I guess make a plan to drive there every day. But I know what you'll say next. You think I should stay there for half an hour until I am not edgy about it anymore. Am I right?

Therapist: Absolutely. We are starting to think alike. I know it won't be pleasant but by staying there for prolonged periods, I think you'll be surprised how quickly this anxiety will subside. If there are any things that still cause you distress and you are doing things to avoid them, now is the time to tackle them. If you deal with them in the near future, it is less likely that they will be problems later.

Client: Do you think I will have more problems?

Therapist: I don't know. Most people have some hiccups at some time or another. That doesn't mean they go back to where they started. It just means that you need to apply the skills that you have learned here to master the situation. What helps is if you can plan for those occasions in advance. Can you think of any situations in the coming months that will be stressful for you?

Client: Definitely. In a couple of months I have to go to court and give evidence against the men who ran me over. The cops have told me that I can do it so I won't be recognized. But I am terrified. I know it's going to bring it all back.

Therapist: Well, Ed, I think you're right. It will be a tough time, but you have the advantage of planning for it now. What sorts of things are you worrying about? How do you think they will affect you?

Client: It's hard to know at this stage. To be honest with you, I have been considering leaving town so the cops can't find me. I think if I can just get away from that whole scene, I will feel better. Since I have been thinking about it over the last week, I've stopped reading papers and watching the news so I don't get confronted by it all.

Therapist: What I hear you saying, Ed, is that you want to avoid the reminders of the experience. I would agree with you if I thought that you were in any danger. But it seems to me that you are trying to avoid things because they are stirring up memories of what happened in the past. Now we have spoken often about how important it is for you to not allow avoidance to develop. I suggest that you use the opportunity of this court episode to deal with your avoidance more effectively. I suggest that you make a plan to intentionally watch the news and read the papers until you notice that your anxiety has subsided. I think you should also return to your imaginal exposure in the period before going to court because this will help to reassure you that you don't need to be afraid of these memories. There are also a range of practical strategies you can use to help you cope with your stress. Your relaxation techniques will be very helpful at that stage. In fact, I suggest that we actually make a detailed plan about the strategies you will use to deal with this period. Then we can rehearse them here, so you can feel confident in using them when the time arrives.

8

TREATMENT OBSTACLES

The treatment of acutely traumatized individuals often can be difficult. The particular symptoms of ASD, the social upheaval associated with the recent trauma, and the presence of ongoing stressors all can contribute to problems in the therapy process. Although the treatment protocol we described in chapter 7 outlines treatment strategies that have been proven to be successful, it is unusual for any treatment of ASD to proceed as neatly as a treatment manual would suggest. Accordingly, in this chapter, we describe the difficulties that can arise in treating ASD and discuss a range of options for overcoming these obstacles.

EXCESSIVE AVOIDANCE

A common obstacle to treating ASD is the extent to which the person actively avoids confronting his or her traumatic memories or feared situations. Although strong avoidance tendencies will be present in nearly all clients with ASD, in a proportion of individuals, avoidance impedes any form of exposure-based therapy. Avoidance is frequent during therapy for a number of reasons. First, in the acute trauma phase, many people feel they have lost control over their responses to events, and they attempt to regain some control by avoiding those things that will threaten that control. Second, avoidant styles are common in individuals with ASD and may even be a predisposing factor to the development of ASD (Guthrie & Bryant, in press). Third, the distress elicited by exposure often evokes further avoidance in clients because they feel they cannot cope with the resulting anxiety. Fourth, disclosing details about one's traumatic experience to a therapist often can be difficult because of fears about how the information will be used or how the therapist will react. Many acutely traumatized people have already been forced to disclose details about the trauma to police, organizational authorities, or legal counsel before seeing a therapist. These earlier experiences can result in avoidance of disclosing personal experiences when working with a therapist.

When confronted with extreme avoidance of traumatic memories, the therapist should first consider the utility of this avoidance. A client's extreme avoidance is sometimes an important warning sign to the therapist that the client needs support and containment rather than exposure-based intervention that may further compound his or her elevated anxiety. Pushing an acutely traumatized client to surrender her or his avoidance in the acute phase may precipitate further crises. In such cases, more active therapeutic intervention may be more appropriate several months later. It is important for therapists to remember that treatment need not always be offered in the acute phase and that taking a supportive approach until they are more able to use therapy effectively can often lead to better outcomes.

If the therapist determines that the client can cope with exposure, several strategies can be implemented to minimize the avoidance. First, the therapist can repeat the rationale for exposure in a way that clarifies the need for habituation of anxiety. Second, one can use motivational techniques that compare the benefits and disadvantages of proceeding with therapy. Third, more attention to cognitive therapy can assist the client in perceiving his or her response to exposure more realistically. Fourth, it is often useful to implement a graded exposure regime that commences with less distressing aspects of the traumatic experience. For example, although one client we worked with could focus attention on two men beating him around the head during an assault, he was resistant to thinking about the assailants stabbing his younger brother. After contracting with him that his brother's assault would not be the focus of exposure, he was compliant to completing exposure to his own assault. After initial habituation of his anxiety about his own assault, he suggested that we proceed with exposure to the features of the assault that involved his brother's experience. When therapists initiate graded exposure because of a client's stated reluctance to confront critical aspects of the trauma, it is imperative that all features of the narrative are eventually integrated into the exposure.

DISSOCIATION

The emotional detachment associated with dissociative responses can impede engagement with traumatic memories (Foa & Hearst-Ikeda, 1996). A person may be able to relate the events that happened to him or her but will not feel the distress associated with the experience. This problem can occur commonly in ASD because of the prevalence of dissociation in this condition. Therapists should be sensitive to the presentation of marked dissociation because it may indicate a defense against overwhelming distress that the person may not be able to manage in the acute phase.

Acute dissociation is more evident in very severe or prolonged traumas (Zatzick et al., 1994). This pattern suggests that dissociative responses may reflect reactions to particularly disturbing experiences. Breaching dissociative responses in the acute phase may often be unwarranted because it may reduce the individual's control in this period. Therapists should be sensitive to the defensive and potentially protective role that dissociative responses can play in the acute phase. Respecting this function of dissociation, therapists should consider clients' psychological resources and their capacity to tolerate the distress from which they are distancing themselves. Those individuals who display signs of not being psychologically robust may fare better with supportive therapy that allows them to stabilize their acute reaction before more direct therapeutic intervention. Those dissociative individuals who are considered capable of managing their distress may require modified exposure techniques. For example, clients who do not feel anxiety when recalling their traumatic experience may be able to experience distress when imagining a loved one suffering the same traumatic event. Alternately, directing clients to imagine a scene that they can feel emotional about and then switching to the traumatic memory can facilitate emotional engagement. It has been suggested that hypnosis can facilitate breaching acute dissociative reactions because it allegedly involves dissociative techniques (Spiegel, 1996). It should be recognized, however, that there are no outcome studies concerning the use of hypnosis with ASD.

ANGER

Anger is a very common response after a traumatic experience (Hyer et al., 1986; Yassen & Glass, 1984). Anger responses are particularly prevalent in victims of violent crime (Riggs, Dancu, Gershuny, Greenberg, & Foa, 1992). There is convergent evidence that anger responses to a trauma do not respond effectively to exposure treatments. Factor analyses of PTSD indicate that anger responses are more associated with numbing than anxiety (Foa, Riggs, & Gershung, 1995). It has been suggested that anger may serve to inhibit anxiety after a trauma, especially when effortful avoidance is unsuccessful (Riggs, Hearst-Ikedo, & Perry, 1995). Furthermore, both self-reported anger before treatment and facial expressions of anger during the initial exposure session are associated with poor therapeutic gain (Foa, Riggs, & Gershung, 1995; Jaycox, Perry, Freshman, Stafford, & Foa, 1995). These findings suggest that exposure may not be the optimal treatment for those acutely traumatized individuals whose primary presentation is anger. Recent CBT programs that have specifically addressed posttraumatic anger have demonstrated that integrating anxiety management and cognitive therapy into treatment can be effective (Chemtob, Novaco, Hamada, & Gross, 1997).

GRIEF

Grief is a very common condition after a traumatic experience (Raphael & Martinek, 1997). Moreover, posttraumatic stress and grief interact to compound the clinical presentation (Goenjian et al., 1995; Horowitz, Weiss, & Marmor, 1987). The use of exposure in the acute trauma phase should be exercised cautiously with people who present with grief issues. Acute grief reactions are often characterized by intrusive symptoms, numbing, and a degree of avoidance. The bereavement process requires time, however, and it may not be appropriate to provide the acutely grieving client with exposure when she or he is coming to terms with her or his loss. For example, a woman was referred to us after a motor vehicle accident in which her 2-year-old child died. She was trapped in the car for several hours with her dead child lying on her lap. This scene represented the primary content of her intrusive memories. The referral expressly asked us to use an exposure-based approach to help this client manage her distressing images of this scene. We decided that requesting this woman to complete exposure to this image several weeks after the loss would have placed excessive strains on her at a time when she was only just managing to grieve for her lost child. Therapists need to be aware that whereas ASD can be considered a psychopathological condition because it leads to ongoing disorder, acute grief reactions are normal and not necessarily indicative of later psychopathology. Recognizing the need for people to proceed through the grieving process often involves not overburdening clients with exposure in the acute phase.

EXTREME ANXIETY

Recent commentaries have noted that exposure can be impeded by a participant's excessive anxiety because the experience can be perceived as overwhelming (Jaycox & Foa, 1996). Activating traumatic memories can result in an anxiety state that will not be managed by the individual if he or she lacks the necessary resources to cope with the distress. Any individual who suffers panic attacks in the acute phase should be monitored carefully because exposure can elicit a panic that can be perceived as further traumatization. Such a response often results in poor compliance with subsequent therapeutic attempts.

Individuals who display extreme anxiety require instruction in anxiety management before any exposure therapy. Following Meichenbaum's (1974) SIT program, we teach the client relaxation, breathing control, self-talk, and, if required, panic control. Only when the anxiety is manageable should exposure be considered. It is not uncommon for exposure to result in extreme anxiety and requests by the client to cease exposure. In such a situation, the therapist has two options. One is to give more attention to cognitive therapy to assist the client to appraise the exposure in a more adaptive way. The alternative is to cease exposure. The latter option is problematic because it can reinforce to the client that avoidance of the memories is associated with fear reduction. If the client cannot tolerate the anxiety, however, it is wiser to temporarily suspend exposure and return to it at a later time when the distress of the acute phase has stabilized. We emphasize that the decision to suspend exposure should be based on the client's inability to tolerate anxiety rather than the therapist's own discomfort with administering exposure. Many therapists avoid exposure because they are reluctant to elicit strong anxiety reactions in traumatized clients. Although this tactic may be more comfortable for the clinician, it may be depriving the client of a therapeutic intervention with proven efficacy.

CATASTROPHIC BELIEFS

Clients who complete exposure but continue to ruminate on catastrophic thoughts about their experience often do not benefit from exposure. A recent study found that exposure was not successful if the person's narrative of the trauma was characterized by mental defeat or lack of mastery over the situation (Ehlers, Clark, et al., 1998). This situation highlights the need for exposure to be accompanied by cognitive restructuring. Clients who manifest entrenched beliefs arising from their experience should receive substantive cognitive therapy. Proceeding with exposure without addressing their interpretations of the recalled memories may simply reinforce their maladaptive beliefs.

PRIOR TRAUMA

We noted in chapter 3 the likelihood that many people who develop ASD have a history of previous traumas. It is common for people who have suffered unresolved traumatic experiences before the recent trauma to be confronted with both the recent stressor and a resurgence of the earlier memories. For example, a woman who survived a recent motor vehicle accident had seen her mother commit suicide 20 years earlier. Soon after the motor vehicle accident, she began experiencing severe posttraumatic stress symptoms relating both to the motor vehicle accident and to her mother's death. In terms of network theory, the two sets of memories are stored within associated networks that promote merging of the multiple traumas. This scenario is especially common in populations that are frequently exposed to traumatic events, such as police, ambulance workers, and military personnel. Therapists need to decide whether the longer term traumatic experience will disturb the acutely traumatized individual to an extent that is beyond her or his tolerance. We have decided to not treat a proportion of ASD individuals in the acute phase because the distress associated with memories of longer term traumas was excessively upsetting in the context of the recent trauma. Allowing the posttraumatic upheaval to settle before addressing the traumatic memories can lead to a better outcome. If the therapist decides that a client who presents with symptoms relating to multiple traumas is able to manage therapy, it is useful to prioritize the memories that will be addressed. The therapist and client can mutually agree on compartmentalizing the intrusive memories into an order that the client feels comfortable addressing. In most cases, we would address memories of the recent trauma first because they tend to be more accessible and were the reason for the presentation.

COMORBIDITY

We noted in chapter 3 that depression, substance abuse, anxiety disorders, and other Axis I and Axis II disorders are common comorbid diagnoses in posttraumatic stress populations (Barton et al., 1996; Davidson & Fairbank, 1993; Davidson, Hughes, & Blazer, 1991; Keane & Wolfe, 1990; Southwick, Yehuda, & Giller, 1993). Individuals who suffer a psychiatric disorder at the time of being exposed to a traumatic event are likely to respond in a more complicated manner than those who had no prior disorder. Therapists need to be particularly aware of disorders that may be exacerbated by the distress elicited by exposure. Some of the more problematic preexisting disorders include borderline personality disorder and psychosis. People with these backgrounds can experience marked deterioration, including psychotic episodes, severe dissociative states, and self-destructive tendencies when confronted with exposure to traumatic memories in the acute phase. Caution is required with these vulnerable people, and it is probably wiser to offer support to contain their preexisting disorder than to resolve their traumatic experience in the acute phase.

SUBSTANCE ABUSE

Substance abuse is also a common posttraumatic response (Keane & Wolfe, 1990; Kulka et al., 1990) that is conceptualized as a form of avoidance behavior that assists distraction from distressing intrusive symptoms (Keane, Gerardi, Lyons, & Wolfe, 1988). There are several reasons to index the level of substance abuse in any acutely traumatized client before treatment. First, marked substance abuse can result in poor ability to engage with anxiety during exposure. Second, people who have a tendency toward substance abuse may increase their reliance on the substance as a means of coping with the distress associated with exposure. Third, reliance on substances in the acute phase is often a sign of one's inability to cope with the posttraumatic stress and a tendency to use avoidant coping mechanisms. These are poor prognostic signs for exposure. It is common in exposure programs to require sobriety of several months before commencing exposure (Foa & Rothbaum, 1997). Accordingly, we typically do not provide exposure therapy to someone in the acute phase who presents with substance abuse because we need evidence of prolonged sobriety. This typically results in treatment being offered several months after the trauma.

DEPRESSION AND SUICIDE RISK

Depression and suicidal ideation are prevalent risks after a trauma. Studies of rape victims have indicated that over 40% of victims have contemplated suicide and at least 17% have actually attempted suicide since the rape (Kilpatrick et al., 1985; Resick, 1988). It is for this reason that the level of depression needs to be assessed carefully both before treatment and throughout the therapy process. Although there is some evidence that posttraumatic depression can be reduced through treatment of the primary posttraumatic stress symptoms (Bryant, Harvey, Dang, Sackville, & Basten, 1998; Nishith, Hearst, Mueser, & Foa, 1995), there is also evidence that depression can coexist independently of posttraumatic stress (Shalev, Freedman, et al., 1998). Individuals who are considered a suicide risk in the acute phase require support, containment, and possibly antidepressant medication or hospitalization. The risk of providing suicidal clients with exposure is that it may enhance their attention toward the negative aspects of their experience. There is considerable evidence that depressed people have poor retrieval of specific positive memories (Williams, 1996), and so they may have difficulty reinterpreting their traumatic memories after exposure. Our practice is to ensure that acutely traumatized clients who are also severely depressed are provided with the appropriate assistance to stabilize their depression before exposure therapy.

POOR MOTIVATION

Poor motivation to engage in treatment is often a feature of individuals who are traumatized. This is particularly prevalent in the acute phase because many individuals are referred for therapy by other people. This practice can place considerable strain on therapy because often the client is not adequately motivated to participate in therapy. Therapists should always try to ascertain the level of motivation that a client has for therapy, and when there is clear ambivalence, there should be attempts to educate the client about the advantages of proceeding with therapy. Proceeding with therapy when the client is not motivated can be counterproductive because unsuccessful attempts at therapy can sabotage the possibility of subsequent effective therapy. It may be better to not proceed with therapy in the acute phase if the client is not willing. In postponing therapy, however, the therapist should attempt to have the client own responsibility for the decision to not proceed with therapy and to realize the merits of considering therapy when she or he is more motivated. It is common in the acute phase for other events to distract the client from giving therapy priority, and in such cases, the chances of therapeutic success may be better after the disruptions of the acute phase settle.

ONGOING STRESSORS

The presence of ongoing stressors in the acute phase also can represent an obstacle for effective therapy. Severe pain or other medical problems, financial losses, criminal investigations, property loss, and media attention are some of the stresses that are demanding on the acutely traumatized individuals. Accordingly, therapists need to evaluate the client's available resources that can be allocated to therapy, especially in the acute phase. Asking a client to complete exposure exercises when he or she is attempting to manage many other demands can result in insufficient attention being given to therapy or unnecessarily high levels of distress. Furthermore, the demands of therapy can result in the person experiencing further distress that impedes her or his capacity to deal with the ongoing stressors. For example, a burn patient who is attempting to cope with the severe pain of daily debridements and physiotherapy may require psychological support to assist her or him through these procedures. Attempting exposure may create additional distress at a time when the individual requires all available energy for managing his or her medical condition.

It is also common for acutely traumatized clients to perceive that there are still threats to their safety. For example, it is not uncommon for assailants to inform victims of home invasions, assaults, and domestic violence that they will be harmed again. The therapist needs to decide whether the actual risk to the client is likely to impede that client bene-fiting from therapy. For example, one of our clients who was stuck with a hypodermic filled with possibly contaminated blood during an assault was preoccupied with the possibility that he would contract AIDS. Because final pathology evidence indicating his health status would be available after a short delay, it was decided to delay active treatment untill he was aware of his condition. In another case, however, a client was terrified that an assailant would be released on bail and kill him before he could testify against him. Considering that the issue of bail was not going to be finally determined for a long time, we decided that therapy needed to proceed immediately with a strong focus on his appraisals of future harm.

CULTURAL ISSUES

Therapists need to be aware that a traumatic experience can differ-entially affect people from different cultural backgrounds (Manson, 1997). Moreover, one's cultural perspective can influence response to therapeutic interventions (Lee & Lu, 1989). Exposure can be interpreted differentially by people from different cultures. For example, one Buddhist client com-plained that she did not want to participate in exposure because she be-lieved that focusing on a negative memory would be detrimental to her future prosperity. Similarly, a Taoist client reported that he believed that the assault that he suffered was a result of fate and it was not appropriate through exposure to challenge or modify the events that had happened to him. In such cases, the rationale for exposure needs to be integrated into the client's value system in a way that is congruent with his or her view of recovery. Cognitive restructuring that attempts to reconcile therapy techniques with the client's epistemology can be useful. If there is a per-sistent discrepancy, however, the therapist needs to recognize that a client's culturally driven outlook must be recognized and validated.

APPROPRIATE VERSUS INAPPROPRIATE AVOIDANCE

One of the difficulties in working with acutely traumatized clients is deciding when avoidance behavior is maladaptive. In cases of longer term trauma, the identification of avoidance behaviors that need to be targeted in treatment is more straightforward. There are many instances in the in-itial period after a trauma when avoidance behavior may be regarded as reasonable because of the recency of the trauma. For example, one client we treated came to us after a home invasion. The invader had viciously attacked our client for several hours, leaving him with multiple knife wounds and burns. As the invader left, he told our client that he would return one day and "finish the job." Our client was reluctant to return to his house because he feared future attacks, every room in the house was bloodstained, and the assailant had not been apprehended. We considered that to urge the client to return to the house through a graded *in vivo* regime in the initial weeks after such an ordeal was not constructive. In a case such as this, there are realistic concerns and understandable reasons to avoid very salient reminders of the trauma. This client was willing to participate in a range of other *in vivo* exercises that actively encouraged him to confront certain other situations. Alternately, another client who was also the victim of a home invasion was adamant in therapy that she wanted to sell her house, leave the city, and impulsively engage in a wide range of avoidance behaviors. In this case, we encouraged the client to commence *in vivo* exercises on a selected number of situations and persuaded her to restrict her avoidance to a temporary change of residence until her acute stress symptoms stabilized. Therapists should recognize the functional, and sometimes safety-enhancing, roles of some avoidance behaviors in the acute phase. Avoidance behaviors that need to be targeted are those that clearly contribute to ongoing anxiety and a longer term pattern of phobic avoidance.

MULTIPLE TRAUMA SURVIVORS

It is common for a client's adjustment to be directly influenced by the responses of others who were also involved in the traumatic event. The individual's perceptions of the event, appraisals of future harm, and compliance with therapeutic aims can often depend on how other trauma survivors are coping with their own experiences. One of our clients, who had been assaulted with her husband, had significant difficulties in responding to treatment because her husband repeatedly expressed his catastrophic concerns about their vulnerability and the need for pervasive avoidance strategies. Other clients have displayed considerable difficulty in allocating sufficient attention to therapy for themselves because they are preoccupied by caring for their loved ones who have also suffered the experience. We have seen many parents who are reluctant to participate in exposure because they believe they must contain their emotional responses to the trauma so they do not communicate fear to their children. Therapists need to index the impact of others' traumatic responses on the client and to integrate this factor into the treatment plan. In some cases, it is appropriate to involve others in therapy. In other cases, it may be more appropriate to directly work with the client on strategies for managing the impact of others' reactions. In rare cases, we have suggested that clients remove themselves from their environments because they are contributing to their posttraumatic stress. One client, who was a member of a street gang, was very disturbed in the weeks after a very violent assault because the gang insisted that our client rehearse a planned revenge attack. Although leaving the gang involved its own risks, our client agreed that he could not resolve the recent assault as long as he remained in this environment.

Therapists should also be careful when treating more than one person who has survived the same traumatic event. It is often difficult for the therapist to keep the multiple clients' narratives and interpretations of the trauma separate. Whenever possible, we allocate clients from the same traumatic event to different therapists. If this is not possible, the therapist needs to be aware of the ease with which details and attributions reported by different clients can be confused. In these situations, the therapist needs to keep detailed notes concerning each client's idiosyncratic response to the traumatic experience.

WHEN EXPOSURE SHOULD NOT BE USED

Although exposure can be a powerful therapeutic tool, it is clear that this intervention can cause a number of problems in trauma survivors. Kilpatrick and others have criticized exposure for rape victims because (a) in aiming to reduce anxiety it may focus on symptom change rather than modifying irrational thoughts, (b) it may contribute to excessive noncompliance with therapy because of its distressing nature, (c) it may inappropriately reduce anxiety to nonconsensual sex, and (d) it does not directly teach coping strategies (Kilpatrick et al., 1985; Kilpatrick, Veronen, & Resick, 1982). Although others have countered these criticisms (see Foa & Meadows, 1997; Rychtarik, Silverman, Van Landingham, & Prue, 1984), therapists do need to be aware that exposure can exacerbate a number of problems. Note that Pitman et al. (1991) have reported that they terminated a study that used imaginal exposure because of the significant adverse effects it had on their participants. Similarly, Vaughan and Tarrier (1992) have reported that one of their sample of 7 participants suffered a marked deterioration after exposure. We suggest that caution be exercised and the use of exposure be seriously questioned when the acutely traumatized client presents with one of the following problems:

- Extreme anxiety
- Panic attacks
- Marked dissociation
- Borderline personality disorder
- Psychotic illness
- Anger as primary trauma response
- Unresolved prior traumas
- Severe depression or suicide risk

- Complex comorbidity
- Substance abuse
- Marked ongoing stressors

Although these types of presentations are seen in relatively few acutely traumatized clients, clinicians should be sensitive to their presence prior to commencing any therapy. In cases where exposure is contraindicated, other techniques, including anxiety management, cognitive therapy, or pharmacological intervention, may be effective.

IV

SPECIAL CONSIDERATIONS

9

SPECIAL POPULATIONS

Although the same ASD criteria apply to all trauma survivors, there can be important differences between various trauma populations. In recent years, there has been increasing awareness that PTSD needs to be studied in specific trauma populations. For example, prospective studies of PTSD after sexual and nonsexual assault (Riggs et al., 1995; Rothbaum et al., 1992) indicate that the recovery process is not identical after these related, but distinct, types of trauma. Furthermore, Riggs et al. (1995) have found different recovery rates for females and males after nonsexual assault. Whereas 70% of females and 50% of males satisfied PTSD criteria (excluding the duration criterion) an average of 19 days posttrauma, this rate decreased to 21% for females and 0% for males 4 months posttrauma. Accordingly, our understanding of acute trauma response and the ways we manage it should take into account the specific clinical needs that are associated with different trauma populations. We recognize that because the study of ASD is in its infancy, we know relatively little about how different trauma populations react in the acute trauma phase. This limitation notwithstanding, clinicians need to be aware that there are distinct issues associated with a number of trauma populations that require particular attention.

TRAUMATIC BRAIN INJURY

A significant proportion of traumatized individuals sustain brain injuries in the course of their trauma. Motor vehicle accidents, industrial accidents, and assaults frequently involve injuries to the head, which may result in loss of consciousness and some form of brain injury. For many years, it was commonly believed that individuals who sustain a brain injury in the course of their traumatic experience do not develop PTSD (Mayor, Bryant, & Duthie, 1993; Sbordone & Liter, 1995). This argument is based on the premise that because traumatic brain injury involves some period of loss of consciousness at the time of the trauma, the impaired encoding of traumatic events precludes reexperiencing symptoms. That is, it is held that because events were not stored in memory at the time of the trauma, there are no memories to distress the person.

In contrast to the view that PTSD does not occur in traumatic brain injury patients, recent studies indicate that both ASD and PTSD occur frequently after mild traumatic brain injury. Brain injuries that result in posttraumatic amnesia of less than 24 hours are considered mild traumatic brain injuries (American Congress of Rehabilitation Medicine, 1993). Although these patients have impaired consciousness for a period at the time of their trauma, they typically report memory for events that occurred after consciousness has resumed. Consequently, they can frequently recall distressing aspects of their experiences. For example, the motor vehicle accident survivor who temporarily loses consciousness when his car collides with a tree may have total recall of lying in the car and waiting for the ambulance to arrive. Studies of PTSD after mild traumatic brain injury indicate that the frequency of PTSD is between 17% and 33% (Bryant & Harvey, 1998b; Middelboe, Anderson, Birket-Smith, & Friis, 1992; Ohry, Solomon, & Rattock, 1996). In a comparison of PTSD rates in patients who either had no head injury, suffered whiplash, suffered an injury to the head, or suffered loss of consciousness, Hickling, Gillen, Blanchard, Buckley, and Taylor (1998) found no differences in PTSD prevalence rates. Few studies have investigated ASD after mild traumatic brain injury. In an earlier study that predated the diagnosis of ASD, Bryant and Harvey (1995a) administered the IES and the PTSD-I (Watson et al., 1991) to motor vehicle accident survivors who either sustained a mild traumatic brain injury or no traumatic brain injury. This study reported that although having sustained a mild traumatic brain injury was associated with less acute posttraumatic stress and fewer intrusive symptoms, a proportion of the mild traumatic brain injury sample reported high levels of intrusions and avoidance. Furthermore, according to the PTSD-I, 27% of the mild traumatic brain injury sample and 42% of the no-traumatic-brain-injury sample met criteria for PTSD (excluding the duration criterion).

Diagnosing ASD after mild traumatic brain injury is potentially problematic because of the overlap of ASD symptoms and postconcussive symptomatology. The dissociative symptoms of reduced awareness, depersonalization, derealization, and amnesia are commonly reported during posttraumatic amnesia in individuals with a mild traumatic brain injury

(Grigsby, 1986; Grigsby & Kaye, 1993; Gronwall & Wrightson, 1980). In addition, irritability and concentration deficits are components of the criteria for ASD and also are common after mild traumatic brain injury (Bohnen & Jolles, 1992). Although there are some suggestions concerning differential diagnosis of dissociative and organic amnesia (Sivec & Lynn, 1995), there are currently no reliable means to differentiate between the overlapping ASD and postconcussive symptoms. The differential diagnosis is particularly difficult when there are no external indications of brain injury (e.g., lacerations or bruising) after acceleration–deceleration injuries (e.g., motor vehicle accidents). These diagnostic problems indicate that clinicians should approach the task of diagnosing ASD in brain-injured individuals with caution.

In the only study to date that has diagnosed ASD after mild traumatic brain injury, Harvey and Bryant (1998a) found that 14% of their sample of motor vehicle accident survivors met criteria for ASD. When these patients were assessed 6 months later, 24% met criteria for PTSD (Bryant & Harvey, 1998b). In terms of those diagnosed with ASD, 82% met criteria for PTSD 6 months posttrauma. In terms of those not diagnosed with ASD, 11% subsequently met criteria for PTSD. In a 2-year follow-up of the initial sample, Harvey and Bryant (in press-f) found that 80% of those who initially satisfied ASD criteria still suffered PTSD. The utility of the ASD criteria in identifying mild traumatically brain-injured individuals who develop chronic PTSD is particularly impressive considering the overlapping symptoms between ASD and postconcussive symptoms. Interestingly, whereas Bryant and Harvey (1999a) found that people with no traumatic brain injury reported more fear and more intrusive memories in the acute posttrauma phase than those with mild traumatic brain injury, this difference was not apparent 6 months later. Specifically, whereas the rate of intrusions decreased over time in the no-traumatic-brain-injury group, they increased in those who suffered a mild traumatic brain injury. These patterns point to the differential course of posttraumatic adjustment in people with and without brain injury.

To date, there are no studies of ASD in severe traumatically brain injured populations. Severe traumatic brain injury includes posttraumatic amnesia of more than 24 hours, which prevents a person from recalling significant components of the trauma (American Congress of Rehabilitation Medicine, 1993). Several case reports describe patients who satisfy PTSD criteria after severe traumatic brain injury (Bryant, 1996b; McMillan, 1991). A recent study of a cohort of severe traumatic brain injury patients in a brain-injury rehabilitation service indicated that 27% of this sample satisfied criteria for PTSD 6 months after their hospital discharge (Bryant, Marosszeky, Crooks, & Gurka, in press). This rate probably overestimates the incidence of PTSD in this population because the sample was partially self-selective. Nonetheless, it points to the possibility of PTSD after severe traumatic brain injury. It is likely that research of acute stress reactions in this population will be very difficult to conduct because of the significant problems associated with assessing psychological response to trauma during prolonged posttraumatic amnesia. Moreover, the patient who is still in posttraumatic amnesia several weeks after the trauma could not be diagnosed with the dissociative symptoms described in the ASD criteria. This scenario indicates that the ASD diagnosis may have limited application for some trauma populations.

The traumatic brain injury population represents a theoretically interesting sample because their impaired consciousness informs us about the role of memory in trauma response. That is, people who develop ASD or PTSD after brain injury suffer reexperiencing symptoms despite limited awareness of their trauma. Recent conceptualizations of trauma response have recognized that reexperiencing symptoms can be mediated by verbal (i.e., consciously recalled) or nonverbal symptoms that result in a sense of reliving feelings or sensations of the trauma (Brewin et al., 1996). This proposition is consistent with recent findings that reexperienced symptoms after severe traumatic brain injury are more likely to be experienced as psychological distress or physiological reactivity than as discursive memories of the trauma (Bryant, Marosszeky, et al., in press). This observation is also consistent with biological theories that propose that PTSD is mediated by fear conditioning in limbic structures that may be independent of higher cortical processes (van der Kolk, 1996b). These proposals suggest that ASD and PTSD after traumatic brain injury may be characterized by distinct memory processes. Interestingly, many traumatic brain injury patients report traumatic memories (or more accurately, pseudomemories) that are reconstructions of events that they cannot accurately remember. For example, Bryant (1996b) reported a case of a traumatic brain injury patient in which the intrusive memories of his motor vehicle accident were based on a newspaper photograph of his wrecked car. Although his memories were inconsistent with police reports of what occurred in the accident, the patient reported strong belief in the reality of this intrusive imagery. This pattern has been reported in larger samples of both mild brain injury (Bryant & Harvey, 1998b) and severe brain injury (Bryant, Marosszeky, et al., in press). These findings support recent commentaries that caution against interpreting intrusive thoughts or images as veridical accounts of historical events (Frankel, 1994). It is more appropriate to regard intrusive phenomena as narratives of the person's psychological state.

The distinctive pattern of ASD symptoms in the brain-injured population suggests that they may have specific treatment needs. The finding that brain-injured individuals report fewer intrusive thoughts and images (Bryant & Harvey, 1995a) than non-brain-injured individuals suggests that exposure-based treatments may need to be modified. That is, it may be difficult to treat a brain-injured trauma survivor who is amnesic of the trauma and reports no verbally accessible memories of the experience. As noted above, such individuals may meet criteria for ASD by virtue of suffering psychological or physiological distress when exposed to reminders of the trauma. The anxiety experienced by these individuals suggests that exposure-based therapy that will facilitate habituation should be beneficial. In practice, however, this form of exposure cannot rely on mental images. We have found that in most cases, these individuals can readily elicit anxiety by focusing on salient triggers of their reexperiencing symptoms. For example, one man who had no memory of his trauma experienced marked anxiety and a sense of a collision when he witnessed cars driving in traffic. His anxiety was successfully reduced by requiring him to repeatedly watch a 50-minute videotape of cars in traffic. After daily practice of this activity for 1 week, he was able to sit by a busy intersection and watch the traffic for 90 minutes. He reported marked habituation during this time, and after 1 week of this exercise, he reported diminished reexperiencing symptoms. Although we conceptualize his reexperiencing symptoms within a similar information-processing framework as non-brain-injured trauma survivors, we recognize that the limited access to mental images of the trauma requires more concrete means to activate the fear network.

The acute effects of brain injury typically involve postconcussive symptoms, which can include headaches, dizziness, sensitivity to light or sound, and fatigue (Bohnen & Jolles, 1992). These symptoms can be very distressing for patients in the acute trauma phase and can contribute to their posttraumatic impairment. There has been debate over the extent to which postconcussive symptoms are the product of psychological distress (Lishman, 1988), neurological damage (Levin et al., 1987), or a combination of both (Rutherford, 1989). Bryant and Harvey (1999b) have reported that postconcussive symptoms are more frequently reported by mild traumatic brain injury patients who have PTSD than those who do not have PTSD and also those PTSD patients with no traumatic brain injury. Moreover, postconcussive symptoms are associated with the severity of intrusive, avoidance, and arousal symptoms. This pattern accords with Rutherford's (1989) view that postconcussive symptoms are mediated by an interaction of psychological and neurological factors. These findings suggest that treating ASD after brain injury may reduce postconcussive symptoms. To test this proposal, Bryant, Guthrie, and Moulds (1999) provided ASD clients who had suffered a mild traumatic brain injury with either supportive counseling or CBT. In keeping with previously reported treatment studies, those clients who received CBT reported greater improvement than those who received counseling. Interestingly, the reduction in ASD symptoms was associated with reduced postconcussive symptoms at 6-month follow-up. This study demonstrates that an additional benefit of treating ASD in people who have sustained a mild traumatic brain injury is that troublesome postconcussive symptoms can also be alleviated. The actual process that mediates this improvement may involve (a) reduced arousal, (b) less attention to negative symptoms, (c) reduced cognitive load on available resources, or (d) more adaptive evaluations of the postconcussive symptoms.

Therapists need to be aware of a range of comorbid problems that can exist in traumatically brain-injured populations. This group often experiences other psychiatric conditions, including depression, substance abuse, and impulse-control disorders (Middelboe et al., 1992). They are also prone to develop a range of physical complaints, including chronic pain (Lahz & Bryant, 1996). The comorbid difficulties associated with traumatic brain injury can contribute to poor posttraumatic adjustment and higher prevalence of ASD. Furthermore, the cognitive deficits that are often evident after mild traumatic brain injury (Jennett & Teasdale, 1981) may be compounded by the attention and memory deficits commonly associated with PTSD (Bremner et al., 1993; Dalton, Pederson, & Ryan, 1989). The cognitive deficits that result from the combined effects of traumatic brain injury and posttraumatic anxiety can impede effective treatment. Therapists often need to structure treatment carefully by providing clients with detailed homework exercises, assisting attentional focus on exposure exercises, simplifying cognitive therapy techniques, and ensuring that all therapy tasks are written in a format that can prompt client adherence to treatment tasks between sessions.

EMERGENCY WORKERS

Previous writers have commented on the specific acute responses of emergency workers, including police, firefighting, paramedic, and military personnel (Hartsough & Myers, 1985; Mitchell & Dyregrov, 1993; Raphael, 1986; Wilson, 1989). These populations can often be distinguished from primary victims of traumas because of (a) the environmental demands placed on them, (b) their tendency to identify with victims, (c) the organizational structure that the emergency worker operates within, (d) the tendency for these individuals to experience multiple traumas, and (e) the common expectation for these individuals to be resilient in the face of trauma. Each of these individual and organizational factors has significant implications for managing ASD in these populations.

Environmental Demands

A salient point for mental health practitioners to note is that emergency workers often have to work under extremely demanding pressures. These demands may include time pressures, physical exertion, environmental and climatic extremes, and community expectations. These conditions typically result in stress reactions in most people. Indeed, it is probably adaptive that people do display stress reactions to survive and manage the situation. Practitioners need to be aware that stress reactions are not necessarily psychopathological or even maladaptive. Accordingly, one should consider the emergency worker's reaction in terms of the proximity to these stressors. Although one could make a diagnosis of ASD after 2 days, it may be premature to do so when emergency personnel have only just removed themselves from a traumatic situation. Intervention is contraindicated at this stage because (a) emergency workers need to allocate their resources to immediate duties, (b) their capacity to attend to therapeutic factors is reduced by operational demands, (c) therapeutic intervention may temporarily heighten distress that could impede functioning, (d) ongoing duties may result in continued activation of trauma-related cognitive schema in a way that does not allow habituation, (e) material that may need attention in therapy may not be finalized because of the ongoing involvement in the trauma, and (f) unsuccessful and premature intervention may result in the emergency worker feeling discouraged about future therapy. After evaluating the needs of the emergency worker in the immediate postdisaster phase, the therapist may decide that he or she does not have a role to play until the pressing demands of the disaster situation have abated.

Identification

Emergency personnel are at risk of identifying with the people they are trying to help. J. P. Wilson (1989) has noted that emergency personnel often display strong countertransference responses to trauma victims (see also Berah, Jones, & Valent, 1984; Raphael, 1986). These individuals often display a strong sense of commitment to those whom they are helping. The therapist needs to be aware of the personal attributions that emergency workers make about their perceived accomplishments and perceived failures. Many emergency workers have high expectations about their performances, and it is common for them to feel failure and self-blame when rescue operations have not been successful. The therapist can address these reactions by identifying emergency workers' preexisting beliefs about their professional identities and highlighting the reasons for the dissonance between their expectations and the actual outcomes of the traumatic situation. Effective cognitive therapy commences with frank discussion of these issues in a way that recognizes the emergency worker's perspective of the trauma. Modification of beliefs about the trauma can then be attempted by testing the individual's perceptions against available information. In most cases, the therapist's goal will be to modify the emergency worker's self-image to permit more realistic expectations concerning his or her performance and reactions.

Organizational Structures

The organizational structure that the emergency worker operates within can play a crucial role in posttraumatic adjustment. Different emergency organizations have distinct attitudes to stress reactions, and these can heavily influence how emergency personnel respond to traumatic experiences. Organizations that actively educate their personnel about stress reactions, encourage discussion of traumatic experiences, and promote help seeking are more likely to foster an environment in which personnel will participate in therapy. Therapists need to be aware of the organizational structure and ethos because these issues can be critical in therapeutic discussions. For example, a firefighter who works in a unit that equates expressions of distress with professional weakness may be reluctant to honestly communicate his reactions to a therapist. Developing rapport with emergency personnel often can depend on the therapist demonstrating either knowledge of the organization's operations or a desire to learn about them. For example, it is unrealistic for a therapist to expect a police officer, whose work involves undercover activities, to modify his cognitive schema so that he can trust people with whom he works. Such ignorance of the context in which the client is operating is likely to result in diminished rapport and reduced respect for the therapeutic process. Although therapists cannot be knowledgeable about all organizations, they should make a concerted effort to learn from the client how his or her organization operates and how this influences his or her trauma response.

Previous Trauma

Therapists need to be sensitive to the emergency worker's previous traumatic experiences. There is strong documentation that emergency workers are repeatedly exposed to traumatic events, and this repeated exposure places them at greater risk of developing psychological problems (Bryant & Harvey, 1995c, 1996b). We have seen many emergency personnel who have presented after a recent trauma and who during therapy have reported distress associated with previous traumas. It is critical during assessment of emergency workers to identify their responses to past traumas because their capacity to manage those traumas may influence treatment choice. For instance, in an assessment of one police officer, it became apparent that he had long-standing concerns over being molested when he was a child. It was decided that proceeding with exposure-based therapy of his recent trauma might be detrimental to the management of this pre-existing issue. We focused on anxiety management and cognitive therapy in the acute phase, and after several months, this client commenced an exposure-based therapy program. In another case, we treated a firefighter for ASD after a narrow escape from a bushfire, and after several sessions of exposure he revealed that he was ridden with guilt because he blamed himself for not saving two people who burned in their house in a fire several years earlier. If this firefighter had not been provided with considerable cognitive therapy to adequately resolve this guilt, it is likely that his treatment response would have been less than satisfactory.

Resilience

One of the difficulties often faced by emergency workers is the perception that they should be resilient to the effects of stress (O'Brien & Hughes, 1991). Clinicians need to be aware that emergency workers' professional identities often rely on this self-image of strength and resilience (Solomon, 1989). Accordingly, therapists should be careful to recognize the strengths of the emergency worker and to explicitly state at the outset of assessment that symptoms of extreme stress do not reflect weakness or incompetence. As therapy proceeds, there is typically a need to allocate considerable cognitive therapy to issues of poor self-esteem, failure, and the equation of professional capability with resistance to the effects of stress. In cases where the emergency worker decides to leave the profession because of the effects of stress, special attention should be given to reducing attributions of guilt and failure.

CHILDREN

There is currently little empirical investigation to guide our understanding of acute trauma responses in children. Although there is an increasing number of commentaries on childhood ASD (DeBellis, 1997; Milgram, 1998), there is virtually no published research on this disorder with children. Accordingly, many common beliefs about acute trauma responses of children may not be well founded. In discussing childhood trauma reactions, DeBellis (1997) has suggested that "the assessment and treatment of ASD is similar [to PTSD] except for the duration of symptoms" (p. 459). Such claims appear to be made without firm evidence and highlight the importance of disentangling myths and facts in acute stress responses in children (see also Garmezy, 1986; Yule, 1992).

The relative lack of investigation of childhood acute stress reactions is unfortunate when one considers the prevalence of exposure to stressors in childhood. For example, in the United States, it is estimated that each year there are approximately 100,000 children kidnapped (Lewis, 1978), 33,000 children hospitalized after burns (Garmezy & Rutter, 1985), and up to 200,000 new instances of child sexual abuse (Finkelhor & Hotaling, 1984). Moreover, there is increasing evidence that children can develop rates of PTSD that are at least comparable to adults. For example, Kinzie,

Sack, Angell, Manson, and Rath (1986) reported that 50% of Cambodian adolescents met criteria for PTSD 4 years after emigrating. Terr (1983) reported that all children who were kidnapped in a school bus exhibited symptoms 4 years later. Yule (1992) reported that a year after the sinking of the ship *Jupiter*, nearly half the surviving children on board met criteria for PTSD. Yule reported that these children displayed comparable levels of intrusive and avoidance symptoms as adults who survive similar disasters. The comparability of adult and childhood PTSD has been reported in numerous studies (Eth & Pynoos, 1985; Goodwin, 1988; Pynoos et al., 1987; Schwarz & Kowalski, 1991a, 1991b; Wolfe, Gentile, & Wolfe, 1989). Furthermore, in a meta-analysis that was based on 2,697 traumatized children and 3,495 traumatized adults, Fletcher (1996) reported that an average of 36% of children were diagnosed with PTSD compared with 24% of adults.

Note that *DSM–IV* stipulates that PTSD may manifest itself differently in children and adults. For example, a child's fearful response may be observed through "disorganized or agitated behavior" (American Psychiatric Association, 1994, p. 428). Reexperiencing symptoms may be observed in young children through playing out aspects of the trauma. Dreams may also involve generally distressing themes that may not contain recognizable content. Fletcher (1996) has presented data from his meta-analysis that indicate that children and adults report generally similar rates of each of the *DSM–IV* symptoms of PTSD. In addition, children reportedly suffer other symptoms that are not described in the *DSM–IV*. For example, Fletcher has found that children often report dissociative reactions, guilt, generalized anxiety, low self-esteem, depression, and separation anxiety after traumas. The incidence of specific symptoms appears to be related to the type of stressor suffered. Children who suffer a chronic and abusive trauma more often display more avoidance, distress on reminders of the trauma, heightened startle responses, and irritability than those who suffer acute traumas. Child victims of acute and nonabusive traumas, on the other hand, more frequently report intrusive thoughts, hypervigilance, generalized anxiety, concentration deficits, separation anxiety, somatic complaints, and social withdrawal.

Few studies have investigated acute reactions in children. One study indexed PTSD reactions in 492 Israeli children who wore gas masks and survived the bombings of the Gulf War (Weisenberg, Schwarzwald, Waysman, Solomon, & Klingman, 1993). Three weeks after the war, 26% met criteria for PTSD (minus the duration criterion). Yule and Udwin (1991) reported that their screening battery of the IES, Fear Survey Schedule, and Birleson Depression Inventory administered 10 days posttrauma predicted psychopathology at 5 months posttrauma. Whereas there is some evidence that PTSD is reasonably stable in children across the 1st year posttrauma (Nader, Pynoos, Fairbanks, & Frederick, 1990), there also are indications that prevalence of the disorder decreases over time (Kinzie et al., 1986; Milgram, Toubania, Klingman, Raviv, & Goldstein, 1988; Sack et al., 1993; Saigh, 1989).

Although there are an increasing number of measures of childhood posttraumatic stress (see Nader, 1997), there are no measures of acute stress response that allow for the assessment of ASD in children. In this context, it should be noted that the *DSM–IV* criteria may not be ideal for assessing PTSD in children. It has been argued that the avoidance criteria may be overly restrictive in children because symptoms of denial and numbing may be difficult to assess (Schwarz & Kowalski, 1991b). Furthermore, it has been proposed that the *DSM–IV* criteria may not adequately encompass those symptoms that are more sensitive to children's reactions to trauma (Armsworth & Holaday, 1993). It is probable that these criticisms are equally applicable to the ASD criteria. Most important, at this time, the utility of the ASD diagnosis to children is untested because there are no prospective studies of ASD and PTSD in children.

There are several specific issues that need to be considered when assessing children in the acute trauma phase. First, there is convergent opinion that parents and teachers often underestimate the severity of children's responses to a trauma (Earls, Smith, Reich, & Jung, 1988; Gordon & Wraith, 1993; Kinzie et al., 1986). Accordingly, clinicians need to listen carefully to the child's own responses. Second, there is evidence that children who do not display disturbance immediately after the trauma can develop subsequent problems (McFarlane, 1987; Terr, 1979). Third, the reliance in the ASD criteria on dissociative symptoms being predictive of subsequent pathology may not be as applicable to children. Younger children have stronger skills in fantasy and dissociation (Spiegel & Spiegel, 1987), and their use of such cognitive strategies to manage stress may not be identical to that seen in adults. Fourth, there is considerable evidence that childhood responses to trauma are influenced, to varying degrees, by familial and parental factors (Nash et al., 1993).

Intervention strategies for children depend largely on their developmental stage. In terms of acute intervention, Pynoos and Nader (1993) have suggested three categories of intervention that address the needs of (a) preschoolers through children in Grade 2, (b) children in Grades 3 to 5, and (c) children in Grades 6 and older. Whereas the younger children receive more help in terms of support and protection, labeling emotions, and education, older children or adolescents receive more adult-oriented therapy that includes discussion of trauma responses and understanding one's interpretations (DeBellis, 1997). One popular method follows the interview developed by Pynoos and Eth (1986) for assessing children who have been recently traumatized. This procedure comprises three steps. The interview commences with establishing rapport and focusing the child on the purpose of the interview. The second stage requires the child to draw his or her experiences or reactions to the traumatic experience, and this material becomes the focus of discussions that attempt to concretize the child's reactions. The final step attempts to integrate this material and facilitate realistic perceptions of the experience and the child's future coping abilities. Pynoos and Nader have pointed out that such exercises may not be helpful and may even be detrimental if they are not based on theoretical frameworks of trauma response. They have reported that the common practice of asking schoolchildren affected by the 1989 earthquake in Northern California to draw the impact of the quake may have aggravated children's anxiety. In contrast, Galente and Foa (1986) have reported that after an Italian earthquake, children's fears diminished after they engaged in play of the destructive aspects of the quake and subsequently reenacted the reconstructive process of building safe houses. These discrepant reports highlight the need for controlled outcome studies to evaluate early-intervention strategies with children.

In terms of evaluation of early intervention, as mentioned earlier, Yule (1992) administered a modified form of the Fear Survey Schedule for Children (Ollendick, Yule, & Ollier, 1991), the Birleson Depression Inventory (Birleson, 1981), and the IES to child survivors of the *Jupiter* ship disaster 5 to 9 months posttrauma. They compared the responses of 24 children from one school who received a single debriefing 10 days after the trauma and 15 children from another school who did not receive debriefing. Those who received intervention reported lower IES and Fear Survey Schedule scores than those who did not. Yule proposed that these results offer evidence for the potential benefits of early intervention in children. Note, however, that this study's conclusions were limited by the lack of random allocation to groups, inadequate controls over the exact interventions provided, and uncertainty concerning preintervention severity levels.

We suggest that significant caution is required in extrapolating assumptions about acute interventions for adults and directly applying them to children. For example, it is commonly argued that the optimal time for intervention is in the acute phase because reexperiencing symptoms are still salient and the associated affect is readily accessible (Pynoos & Nader, 1993). There is currently no evidence, however, to support this claim. Furthermore, although flooding techniques have been successfully reported in child trauma survivors (Saigh, 1986), there is no evidence that prolonged exposure is helpful in reducing acute stress symptoms in children. There is a possibility that children may (a) have difficulty in understanding the rationale of exposure, (b) be further traumatized by focusing on traumatic images for prolonged periods, especially if their personal coping resources or developmental stage renders them unable to manage the associated anxiety, or (c) be incapable of using cognitive strategies to modify beliefs about the images. Further study is required that evaluates the utility of early provision of exposure and cognitive therapy with children at different developmental stages after a variety of traumas.

There is increasing evidence that childhood responses to trauma can be significantly influenced by family environment. For example, there is evidence that the effects of childhood abuse can be strongly influenced by the family environment in which it occurred (Nash et al., 1993). Furthermore, family cohesion (Conte & Schuerman, 1987), maternal distress (Deblinger, McLeer, & Henry, 1990), and family help-seeking behavior (Waterman, 1993) are strong predictors of recovery after abuse. Moreover, initial evidence indicates that treatments that include parental involvement may result in different therapy outcomes than those that only treat the abused child (Deblinger, 1994). Treatment of ASD in traumatized children also may need to take into account the long-term effects of the trauma that may be observed only at subsequent developmental stages (Briere, 1992). This possibility points to the need for long-term follow-up of treated children. One study has reported that deterioration after abuse is most likely in children with fewer initial symptoms (Gomes-Schwartz, Horowitz, Cardarelli, & Sauzier, 1990). Accordingly, treatment studies need to identify the optimal timing of intervention because onset of symptoms may occur either in the acute stage or at later stages. The utility of CBT has not been adequately tested in childhood ASD or PTSD. Future research needs to systematically evaluate CBT in children after acute and longer term traumas and apply strict experimental rigor to permit firm inferences about the components of CBT that may be effective, the suitability of CBT at different developmental states, and the long-term outcomes of CBT.

We stress that one should maintain the distinction between single traumas in childhood and prolonged or intrafamilial trauma, such as childhood abuse. There are relatively few controlled treatment studies of psychological disturbance arising from childhood abuse (see Finkelhor & Berliner, 1995). A major reason for the scarcity is difficulty in identifying target symptoms that are to be treated. Recent work indicates that childhood abuse does not lead to a definitive constellation of symptoms but can result in a wide range of disorders (Kendall-Tackett et al., 1993). Accordingly, this population represents a very heterogeneous group. Moreover, it is unclear how relevant the diagnosis of ASD is to children who may have suffered ongoing abuse over an extended period of time. That is, the result of ongoing abuse may be a long-standing disorder that precludes the notion of an acute stress reaction. In terms of current knowledge, it is premature to apply the treatment modalities currently in use for adult ASD to children who have recently suffered a trauma that is one component of ongoing abuse.

10

THE ROLE OF DEBRIEFING

One of the most prolific developments in recent years in the field of trauma management has been the acceptance of posttraumatic debriefing (Raphael, 1986). This practice was initially introduced as an attempt to ameliorate the longer term effects of posttraumatic stress. The notion that frontline intervention can facilitate recovery was based on early reports that managing immediate effects of stress in combat troops would facilitate return to duties (Bloch, 1969; Jones & Johnson, 1975; Solomon & Benbenishty, 1986). Although this practice was subsequently criticized in terms of its ethical standards and dubious benefits (Camp, 1993; Kulka et al., 1990), it has been extended to civilian contexts. The momentum for debriefing has exploded in recent years for a number of reasons. First, it is attractive to people who subscribe to crisis-intervention policies. Second, it is a simple procedure that can be provided inexpensively and by personnel with minimal training. Third, it permits an informal intervention that does not require individual commitment by participants. Fourth, many government and private agencies have adopted debriefing because of fear that if such protocols are not activated after potentially traumatic events, the organization may be liable for managing the clinical and financial consequences of chronic psychiatric conditions. The explosion of debriefing practices has been premature, however, in that there is currently little structured empirical support for debriefing. In this chapter we discuss debriefing in the context of ASD, review the evidence for debriefing,

163

and highlight the critical differences between critical incident stress (CIS) and ASD.

CRITICAL INCIDENT STRESS

There is no doubt that individuals who participate in traumatic events can experience elevated levels of stress. Numerous studies indicate the frequency of stress symptoms in emergency workers, military personnel, and disaster survivors (see Mitchell & Dyregrov, 1993). CIS is a generic phrase that refers to a very broad range of responses that occur after a stressful experience. An underlying assumption of CIS is that the stress response is a normative reaction to a difficult situation. Whereas it is common and probably adaptive in many cases for people in critical incidents to experience heightened levels of stress, this response should not be considered a disorder. This proposition highlights the distinction between CIS and ASD. CIS is conceptualized as comprising four major types of symptoms (Mitchell & Dyregrov, 1993). The *cognitive* problems associated with CIS include confusion, poor concentration, memory lapses, and diminished attentional focus (Sedgwick, 1975; Wilkinson & Vera, 1985). These problems are commonly associated with elevated arousal (Eysenck, 1989; Pallak, Pittman, Heller, & Munson, 1975). The *physical* effects include fatigue, insomnia, gastrointestinal problems, muscle tension, and heightened autonomic activity (Byl & Sykes, 1978; Illinitch & Titus, 1977; Mitchell, 1982). These symptoms can be understood as somatic effects of sustained arousal. The *emotional* effects of CIS may include anxiety, depression, guilt, anger, and denial (Cohen & Ahearn, 1980; Mitchell, 1982). Finally, the *behavioral* symptoms of CIS can include social withdrawal, listlessness, substance abuse, and aggressive behaviors (Blackmore, 1978; Glass, 1959). It is important to note the conceptual and definitional differences between CIS and ASD. First, whereas ASD has been explicitly defined in *DSM–IV*, CIS lacks any standardized definition. Individuals experiencing CIS vary both in the number and severity of stress symptoms. This ambiguity about its parameters renders CIS somewhat resistant to structured study of purported CIS responses. Second, the lack of a demonstrated relationship between CIS and longer term adaptation raises questions about the role of interventions that attempt to reduce CIS. Third, the aim of any intervention of CIS should not be regarded as treatment of a disorder. As Raphael, Wilson, Meldrum, and McFarlane (1996) have noted, there is marked confusion concerning the extent to which managing CIS is a preventative step to reduce subsequent disturbance or a treatment of the initial signs of a disorder. This issue raises the question concerning the distinction between debriefing CIS and treating ASD.

DEBRIEFING VERSUS TREATMENT

One of the most popular models of debriefing is Mitchell's (1983) critical incident stress debriefing (CISD). The stated goal of this procedure is to assist people who have experienced a stressful event to progress to a healthy adjustment. Whereas this process was initially conceptualized as a structured group format that was conducted within 24 and 72 hours post-trauma, these parameters have been modified to permit more flexible interventions. Mitchell (1983) has proposed that debriefing comprises seven phases: (a) an introductory phase, which outlines the purpose and benefits of debriefing; (b) a fact phase, in which participants relate what happened to them; (c) a thought phase, in which participants relate their initial thoughts about the critical incident; (d) a feeling phase, which requires participants to focus on the worst aspects of the incident and engage their emotional reactions to the incident; (e) an assessment phase, in which participants are asked to note their physical, cognitive, emotional, and behavioral symptoms; (f) an education phase, which provides information about the stress responses and means to manage them; and (g) the reentry phase, which summarizes information and offers possible referral information. These phases may take 1 to 5 hours and are usually coordinated by a trained mental health professional. There have been several other models of debriefing outlined since Mitchell's (1983) initial proposal (see Raphael et al., 1996).

Although Mitchell (1983) has stated that debriefing is not intended to be a substitute for therapy, there is confusion over the exact goal of debriefing. Implicit in many commentaries on debriefing is the expectation that it will result in diminished posttraumatic psychopathology (Dyregrov, 1989; Mitchell, 1983). This tendency is reflected in the pattern of studies that have attempted to index the efficacy of debriefing by using measures of posttraumatic stress symptomatology at follow-up (Griffiths & Watts, 1992; Hytten & Hasle, 1989). Others have argued that the mechanism by which debriefing may prevent posttraumatic psychopathology is that it facilitates help seeking in those who require more intensive intervention (Mitchell & Dyregrov, 1993).

Table 10.1 contains a summary of the major differences between CISD and treatment of ASD. On the basis of notions of crisis intervention, CISD tries to prevent subsequent psychopathology in all trauma survivors. In contrast, treating ASD assumes the existence of a psychopathological state. Inherent in the construct of ASD is the notion that most people will recover from their trauma without formal intervention and that treatment is only indicated for the small proportion of people who are at risk of long-term PTSD. CISD holds that encouraging ventilation and providing education can facilitate recovery. This emphasis on ventilation traces its roots back to earlier notions of acute grief, which placed considerable

TABLE 10.1
Differences Between Debriefing and Therapeutic Interventions

Variable	Debriefing	Therapy
Underlying theory	CISD model	Information processing–biological theories
Core dysfunction	Confusion, unexpressed affect	Arousal–anxiety, maladaptive beliefs, avoidance behavior
Goal	Prevent a disorder	Treat a disorder
Process	Education–ventilation	Exposure, cognitive therapy, anxiety management
Duration	1 session	Multiple sessions
Participants	All trauma survivors	Participants with ASD diagnosis
Format	Group–individual	Individual
Timing of intervention	Within 72 hours of the trauma	After 2 weeks posttrauma
Evidence	No supporting evidence	Initial supportive evidence

Note. CISD = critical incident stress debriefing. ASD = acute stress disorder.

importance on working through the loss of the loved one. ASD, on the other hand, is based on the premise that the individual is suffering from an anxiety disorder that is characterized by heightened arousal, erroneous beliefs about vulnerability, and avoidance of feared stimuli. Accordingly, treatment attempts to habituate individuals to their feared memories, desensitize them to feared events, teach anxiety-management skills, and modify cognitive distortions. These different conceptualizations of intervention result in CISD being completed in one or two sessions, often in group formats, and within 72 hours of the trauma. In contrast, treating ASD requires multiple sessions combined with intensive homework, is always done on an individual basis, and typically commences after the immediate aftermath of the trauma has settled. That is, CISD and treatment of ASD involve different goals, theoretical premises, populations, and strategies.

EVIDENCE FOR PRETRAUMA TRAINING

A common belief is that one's capacity to effectively manage a critical incident can be enhanced by education and preparation for this event. There is indirect evidence to support the notion that pretraining for a stressful experience may enhance coping. Severity of PTSD is associated with uncontrollability and unpredictability (Foa & Rothbaum, 1989). Within the stress management literature, there is considerable attention given to stress inoculation as a means of providing the individual with necessary skills and opportunity to rehearse them before the actual stressful event (Meichenbaum, 1974). Mitchell and Dyregrov (1993) have proposed six steps that may be beneficial in preparing one to cope with a traumatic incident. First, they give emergency workers education about general stress responses and their causes. Second, they provide information about CIS. Third, they explain the differences between everyday hassles and the acute stress of an emergency situation. Fourth, they teach individuals to identify the specific behavioral, emotional, physical, and cognitive symptoms that may appear in the acute phase. Fifth, they provide simple strategies to manage the stress symptoms. These may include taking breaks, limiting exposure to particularly distressing events, and talking to colleagues. Sixth, they provide stress-mitigation strategies to the spouses and others who will be interacting with the affected personnel in the acute phase. Numerous similar pretraining programs also have been proposed (e.g., Howarth & Dussuyer, 1988; Myers, 1989).

There is tentative evidence for some benefits of pretraining individuals who may experience a traumatic event. In a study of 123 survivors of an industrial fire, Weisaeth (1989a, 1989b, 1995) found that adaptive response to the disaster was positively correlated with levels of prior training and experience. Interestingly, even though the pretraining in this situation was received within the context of military and maritime service, it appears to have enhanced coping responses. Hytten's (1989) survey of helicopter crash survivors indicated that the aspect of training that was perceived as most beneficial was to remain calm and evaluate their situation objectively. On the basis of findings from their study of firefighters, Fullerton, Mc-Carroll, Ursano, and Wright (1992) proposed that training emergency workers to not identify with victims, to utilize social supports, and to express emotional reactions may be beneficial. Finally, in a comparison of torture survivors who were and were not political activists, the nonactivists showed higher levels of subsequent torture-related psychopathology and general distress (Basoglu et al., 1997). This report assumes that political activists would have had more psychological preparedness than the nonactivists. In contrast, Sarason, Johnson, Berberich, and Siegel (1979) reported that whereas police who were provided with 12 hours of stress management (including relaxation and cognitive techniques) were rated as "significantly superior" to untrained colleagues, there was not evidence of long-term benefits. Similarly, a range of studies have found that pretraining has not been effective in reducing subsequent stress responses (Janis, 1971; Zuckerman & Spielberger, 1976). This failure may be related to the difficulty in preparing individuals for the severity of actual traumas. Ersland, Weisaeth, and Sund (1989) found that although rescue personnel who attended an oil rig disaster were trained for disaster responses, they perceived that this event was beyond the scope of their training.

The possible utility of pretraining is supported by findings that prior experience of traumatic events may enhance response to subsequent traumas. In a study of those who participated in body handling during Operation Desert Storm, those who had no previous experience in body han-dling had greater intrusion and avoidance symptoms than those who did have experience (McCarroll, Ursano, Fullerton, & Lundy, 1995; McCarroll et al., 1993). Similarly, Solomon, Mikulincer, and Jakob (1987) found that soldiers with no prior combat experience were more likely to experience combat stress reactions than those who had experience. This pattern has been interpreted as evidence of the inoculating effect of previous traumatic experiences (Ursano, Grieger, & McCarroll, 1996). It is possible that one develops a sense of self-mastery and a framework in which one can un-derstand and respond to traumatic events if one has the advantage of hav-ing rehearsed these procedures (Quarantelli, 1985). This conclusion needs to be qualified, however, by findings that the inoculating effect of previous traumas may occur only when the previous experience is similar to the current trauma (Norris & Murrell, 1988). Furthermore, there is evidence that severity of PTSD may be mediated by the accumulated stress that develops after multiple traumas (Bryant & Harvey, 1996b). Although there is some evidence that pretraining may play a role in enhancing posttrauma coping mechanisms, there is currently no firm evidence that pretraining does mitigate the effects of significant trauma. The potential benefits of pretraining indicate that there is a need for controlled outcome studies to determine the extent to which pretraining can reduce posttraumatic stress reactions. This research needs to consider the parameters of pretraining, the interplay between pretraining and trauma factors, and the capacity of participants to use pretraining during a traumatic experience.

EVIDENCE FOR DEBRIEFING

Proponents of debriefing claim that there is convergent evidence that supports the efficacy of this practice. For example, Mitchell and Bray (1990) have cited estimates, based on anecdotal reports, that CISD results in diminished mental health problems. Similarly, Robinson and Mitchell (1993) have reported on a survey of 172 emergency service, welfare, and hospital personnel who participated in 31 separate debriefings. An evalu-ation questionnaire was completed 2 weeks after the debriefings, and it was reported that 60% of participants reported stress reduction after debriefing and attributed this improvement to the debriefing. Note, however, that these reports do not represent controlled studies.

A number of studies suggest some benefits of debriefing. For example, an analysis was conducted of survivors of a major fire that occurred during rush hour in London's King's Cross Station, in which 31 people died and hundreds were affected. This study found that people who discussed their reactions with others seem to have fared better than those who did not (Turner, Thompson, & Rosser, 1993). A study of a North Sea oil rig disaster demonstrated that there was no long-term disturbance in one group of workers who were provided with the opportunity to discuss their experiences; in contrast, there were significant problems in another group that was not given this opportunity (Ersland et al., 1989). These groups were not randomly designated, however, and there are numerous factors that could account for these differences in long-term adjustment. In a recent study, Chemtob, Thomas, Law, and Cremniter (1997) reported that a debriefing provided to survivors of a natural disaster 6 months posttrauma was effective in reducing scores on the IES. However, given that the debriefing was conducted 6 months posttrauma, this study does not represent a test of the effectiveness of acute phase debriefing.

Numerous studies indicate that debriefing activities do not prevent serious long-term psychological disturbance. Although Weisaeth (1989a) intensively interviewed survivors of an industrial accident, there were still marked levels of PTSD at follow-up. Similarly, Tyrer (1989) found that a significant proportion of a sample displayed psychiatric morbidity after supportive interventions. Creamer, Burgess, Buckingham, and Pattison (1993) found that following comprehensive support and debriefing to survivors of a multiple shooting, 33% were symptomatic. McFarlane (1988a) found that debriefing was not predictive of diminished longer term posttraumatic stress among 315 firefighters. These findings are consistent with the finding of Bryant, Harvey, Dang, Sackville, and Basten (1998) that 67% of individuals who met criteria for ASD and who were provided with supportive counseling for five sessions still met criteria for PTSD 6 months posttrauma. The failure of debriefing to reduce posttraumatic stress is further indicated by a number of studies that used the IES to index the outcome of debriefing. Hytten and Hasle (1989) found no differences in IES scores between firefighters who received formal debriefing and those who had casual conversations about their experiences with colleagues. Griffiths and Watts (1992) administered the IES to emergency personnel who attended bus crashes and who either received formal debriefing or who did not. They found that those who attended debriefing had higher intrusion and avoidance scores than those who did not. This difference may be attributed, however, to the possibility that the more distressed personnel attended debriefing. A better controlled study was conducted after a major earthquake in a large industrial city in Australia; in 1989, the quake, which measured 5.6 on the Richter scale, caused 13 deaths and resulted in $660 million damage. Emergency personnel who were involved in the earthquake were divided into two groups: those who received debriefing (n = 56) and those who did not (n = 117; Kenardy et al., 1996). These two groups generally did not differ on demographic factors or disaster variables. At follow-up, there were no differences in IES scores between groups. Interestingly, the debriefed group did report higher General Health Questionnaire (Goldberg & Hillier, 1979) scores. A similar result was reported by Bisson, Jenkins, Alexander, and Bannister (1997), who randomly allocated burn survivors to debriefing or to a control condition. At a 13-month follow-up by an independent assessor, 26% of the group that received debriefing met criteria for PTSD compared with 9% of controls. The significance of this finding is dubious, however, because the debriefing group was more distressed before the debriefing. A study of Gulf War soldiers involved in body handling reported that those who received debriefing and those who received no debriefing showed equivalent levels of posttraumatic stress nine months posttrauma (Deahl, Gilham, Thomas, Searle, & Srinivasan, 1994). Another study that compared women who had suffered a miscarriage indicated no differences in IES scores 4 months posttrauma between those who were provided with debriefing and those who were not (Lee, Slade, & Lygo, 1996). In summarizing their conclusions of a review of six available controlled studies of debriefing, Wessely, Rose, and Bisson (1997) concluded that "there is no current evidence that psychological debriefing is a useful treatment for the prevention of post traumatic stress disorder after traumatic incidents" (p. 1).

We recognize that adequately testing the efficacy of debriefing is very difficult in the context of disasters. The possibilities of random allocation to debriefing, equating preintervention severity and motivation levels, assessing expectancy of intervention, and ensuring intervention adherence by debriefers can be difficult within the acute posttrauma phase. Nonetheless, the efficacy of debriefing cannot be accepted until adequately controlled studies indicate that debriefing is useful (Raphael, Meldrum, & McFarlane, 1995). There are reasons to suggest that future studies of debriefing will only replicate the previously documented finding that CISD does not prevent PTSD. Shalev (in press) has cogently argued that PTSD results from a combination of factors, including vulnerability and personality features that have existed for many years prior to the trauma. Considering this complex etiology of PTSD, it is unrealistic to expect a brief interaction, like CISD, to have a significant impact on posttraumatic adjustment.

PROBLEMS WITH DEBRIEFING

There is increasing concern that debriefing may actually be detrimental to some trauma survivors (Lieberman, 1982). This pattern is tentatively suggested by some of the findings that those who receive debriefing display more subsequent disturbance than those who cope without debriefing (Bisson et al., 1997; Kenardy et al., 1996). Moreover, there are conceptual reasons for suspecting that debriefing may have toxic effects. Shalev (in press) has interpreted evidence of an association between heightened arousal in the acute phase and long-term psychopathology as grounds for focusing on arousal reduction immediately after a trauma. He has proposed that verbalization and elaboration of a traumatic experience may exacerbate distress. Moreover, he has suggested that information provided during the acute phase may result in consolidation of long-term memories that may have long-term adverse effects. The likelihood of debriefing contributing to poor adjustment also is indicated by the manner in which exposure to traumatic memories is conducted. PE involves structured exposure to the memories until habituation occurs. In contrast, the practice of discussing one's experiences within a debriefing context may result in an individual exposing herself or himself to traumatic memories in a way that elicits strong anxiety but does not permit habituation of the anxiety. This practice may enhance, rather than reduce, acute stress reactions. Finally, we have noted earlier that many acutely traumatized people display dissociative and other avoidance patterns as means of coping with their distress. It is possible that these strategies serve an important protective function in the immediate posttrauma phase and that dismantling them through debriefing practices may be detrimental. In this context, it is useful to remember that Bryant, Sackville, Dang, et al. (in press) found that the more severely distressed ASD clients did not manage therapy and tended to drop out of treatment. All of these reasons are possible explanations for reported findings of detrimental effects of debriefing. In any case, they serve as a warning to practitioners that encouraging all trauma survivors to disclose and ventilate their reactions immediately after a traumatic event may cause numerous problems that are difficult to detect in a group setting.

In recent times, there has been an unfortunate tendency for the boundary between debriefing and therapy to be blurred. Techniques that have been developed for individuals with acute anxiety disorders have been applied within debriefing contexts. This development can be attributed to a number of factors. There is a common perception that one should assist all trauma survivors to resolve their traumatic experience as soon as possible and that procedures such as PE can facilitate this process. This desire is occasionally motivated by financial reasons, especially when organizations perceive that a brief and early intervention may enable traumatized personnel to resume normal duties. The introduction of therapy techniques into debriefing contexts also seems to have occurred as a result of mental health professionals, who often work within therapeutic settings, being introduced into acute trauma care.

The use of therapeutic techniques in acute disaster settings is potentially damaging. In a large-scale Australian bushfire in 1994, Richard A. Bryant was invited to observe debriefing procedures during the disaster. There were many instances of well-meaning therapists attempting to provide care to traumatized firefighters with inappropriate means (Bryant, 1994). These interventions included requesting firefighters to challenge their thoughts about their responses within hours of fighting the fires, initiating PE before the firefighters had even rested after their duties, and providing feedback about officer's coping abilities in the presence of subordinates. Each of these instances resulted in hostile responses from the firefighters and placed additional stress on individuals who were attempting to deal with the acute stages of an intense trauma. These instances highlight the problems associated with involvement of personnel who are inappropriately prepared to deal with acute trauma care. On the one hand, there were problems of poorly qualified people attempting to provide interventions for which they were not adequately trained. This deficiency resulted in signs of significant pathology not being detected. On the other hand, there were cases of clinically qualified practitioners attempting to provide therapy in contexts that were not suited to this intervention. These situations highlighted the important distinction between attempts to debrief people immediately after a trauma and treatment interventions that require a different setting, time frame, and goal. Blurring this distinction can have detrimental effects for trauma survivors and those who are attempting to assist them.

It is probable that debriefing practices will come up under more scrutiny in the future for forensic and investigative reasons. There is increasing concern that the practice of group debriefings immediately after critical incidents can result in memory contamination of participants. That is, acutely traumatized individuals sharing their recollections of events in the hours or days after a traumatic event may obstruct the ability of organizations to obtain uncontaminated reports from participants about the event. For example, after a recent naval accident in Australia in which several personnel were killed on board, debriefings occurred on the same day of the accident and before the ship arrived back at port (Commonwealth of Australia, 1998). During the inquiry of this event, there were concerns from naval authorities that formal statements were obtained only after those personnel who were involved had participated in group debriefings. It is likely that the issue of memory contamination during group debriefings will lead to more cautious use of debriefings in situations that require accurate and untainted recollections of the event.

The assumption that debriefing can reduce subsequent psychopathology can also lead to inadequate assessment of traumatized individuals. It has already been noted that posttraumatic stress reactions may not necessarily be evident immediately after a trauma in some individuals who subsequently develop disturbances. A danger in believing in the efficacy of debriefing is that proper assessments are not conducted on people who have been initially debriefed. It is interesting to note that studies of survivors who received debriefing have indicated that a significant proportion still suffer marked posttraumatic stress at follow-up (Deahl et al., 1994; Kenardy et al., 1996; Lee et al., 1996). The ineffectiveness of debriefing to prevent

PTSD indicates that decisions to assess trauma survivors should not be influenced by whether debriefing was provided.

Although there is no strong evidence for the efficacy of debriefing, we do not suggest that there is no value in this practice. It is possible that the educational components, the legitimizing of symptoms, and the distribution of referral information may facilitate help seeking in those who may otherwise avoid professional assistance. Furthermore, debriefing may have benefits for organizational structure and morale among groups involved in disasters. In this context, there is evidence that reviewing a traumatic event can enhance group cohesion of those involved (Shalev, in press). We emphasize, however, that these benefits are distinct from prevention of PTSD, which lies in the domain of empirically based treatment.

11

LEGAL ISSUES

In recent years, lawyers have developed an interest in PTSD that is not paralleled by any other psychiatric disorder (Stone, 1993). The inherent link between the symptoms of ASD and PTSD and a precipitating event has made both disorders highly amenable to compensation claims (Bryant, 1996a). Although not as popular as compensation issues, the use of PTSD in criminal cases also is becoming increasingly popular (Pitman, Sparr, Saunders, & McFarlane, 1996). As the legal world continues to focus attention on trauma reactions, the role of ASD is becoming increasingly prominent. In compensation cases, there are issues of immediate duty of care, the relative contributions of debriefing and therapy to manage trauma response, the responsibility of organizations to assess and treat ASD, and the possible relationship between ASD and longer term PTSD. In criminal matters, there are issues of diminished responsibility during dissociative episodes, impaired memory for events, and aggression associated with acute arousal. The law is currently trying to come to terms with these issues at a time when the empirical knowledge base of ASD is in its infancy. In this chapter we review the major legal issues in ASD and provide guidelines concerning assessment and treatment that clinicians should consider when managing acutely traumatized individuals.

ASD AND COMPENSATION

Compensation and trauma response have long been associated. During much of this century, the genuineness of posttraumatic psychopathology has been questioned because of the suspicion that reports of trauma-induced distress are motivated by desire for compensation. Following World War I, authorities perceived that compensation for shell shock contributed to the persistence of symptoms after the war. This perception led the German psychiatrist Bonhoeffer (1926, p. 180) to propose that "the law is the cause of traumatic neuroses." This resulted in the National Health Insurance Act in 1926 precluding traumatic neurosis as a compensable disorder in Germany (van der Kolk, Weisaeth, & van der Hart, 1996).

Despite increasing evidence that PTSD symptoms persist after compensation has been settled (Brooks & McKinlay, 1992; Mayor et al., 1993; McFarlane, in press; Resnick, 1994), there is still strong suspicion that the desire for compensation contributes to the reporting and maintaining of posttraumatic symptoms. To support this claim, there is evidence that symptom exaggeration is more prevalent in compensation-seeking veterans than those not seeking compensation (Frueh, Smith, & Barker, in press) and that compensation status does partially predict PTSD severity after motor vehicle accidents (Bryant & Harvey, 1995b). Although sufficient evidence indicates that many posttraumatic stress responses cannot be attributed to litigation factors, the likelihood of compensation influencing a plaintiff's actual or reported symptoms has resulted in psychiatrists and clinical psychologists needing to play a cautious role in managing posttraumatic cases in which litigation is a possibility.

The introduction of ASD has a number of important legal implications. First, whereas before 1994, acute trauma responses were not recognized as a psychiatric disorder, *DSM–IV*'s recognition of ASD now permits acute stress reactions to be regarded as compensable disorders. Second, because ASD links its symptoms to a precipitating event, ASD represents an attractive diagnosis to litigators. Third, the demonstrated relationship between ASD and chronic PTSD (Bryant & Harvey, 1998b; Harvey & Bryant, 1998d) provides a strong legal claim for early assessment of trauma reaction. A plaintiff's counsel can cogently argue that adequate assessment was not conducted if ASD was not monitored during the acute trauma phase and chronic PTSD subsequently developed. Fourth, evidence that early treatment of ASD has the potential to prevent development of PTSD (Bryant, Harvey, Dang, Sackville, & Basten, 1998) raises important issues concerning duty of care. That is, counsel can argue that if an individual suffering ASD was not provided appropriate therapy in the initial month posttrauma and develops chronic PTSD, duty of care was violated. Considering the prevalence of ASD following common events, such as motor vehicle accidents, industrial accidents, and assaults (Harvey & Bryant,

1999c), it is likely that in the coming years, compensation courts will be faced with increasing numbers of plaintiffs claiming ASD.

CRIMINAL LAW

The diagnosis of ASD also has potential implications for criminal law matters. In the past, PTSD has primarily been used by defense counsel to justify the actions of a defendant. In one review, the use of PTSD as a defense strategy has risen steadily since its introduction in 1980 (Speir, 1989). Although PTSD is rarely used as an insanity defense (Applebaum et al., 1993), it is more commonly used to argue for diminished capacity. Pitman, Sparr, et al. (1996; see also Grant & Coons, 1983; Sparr, Reaves, & Atkinson, 1987) have summarized the major aspects of PTSD that can reduce one's capacity in a criminal act. These can include (a) sensation seeking because of the need to revisit the trauma, (b) need for punishment to appease guilt arising from the traumatic experience, (c) substance abuse arising from the need to self-medicate, and (d) the lack of consciousness associated with dissociated states. The latter is particularly applicable to ASD, which by its definition is characterized by dissociation in a way that is less evident in PTSD. A defendant who is charged with murder could argue that the degree to which her or his actions were volitional was diminished by reduced awareness of the surroundings, depersonalization, derealization, or dissociative amnesia. This defendant could argue that he or she was not criminally responsible for the assault because his or her mental state at the time impaired awareness of actions and their consequences. For example, one man who attended our clinic had violently assaulted an intruder who had broken into his home and held him at knifepoint. It was alleged that after being threatened for a prolonged period and eventually knifed, this client struck the intruder with a metal pipe and seriously injured him. This client, who satisfied ASD criteria, reported being unaware of much of this ordeal, including striking the intruder. He displayed marked depersonalization, reduced awareness of his surrounds, and amnesia. Although he was not charged with criminal assault because he was acting in self-defense, this example illustrates how dissociated states that occur in ASD may contribute to defense pleas. It is possible that in criminal contexts, in which individuals may engage in criminal acts during an acute trauma response, defense arguments may rely on ASD as a strategic means to reduce the responsibility attributed to the defendant.

MEMORY CONTAMINATION

One of the cornerstones of most legal testimony is the witness's capacity to accurately recall and report events that are relevant to the matter at hand. This is typically an issue in compensation matters, in which trauma victims are required to recall the events surrounding their injury. It is often on the basis of these reports that conclusions concerning causality and consequences are made. This emphasis on the trauma victim's recollection of events is potentially problematic in ASD because memory reports are often not stable, they can be influenced by therapy, and they can be impaired because of the dissociative responses associated with ASD.

There is considerable debate concerning the veridicality of trauma memories (Lynn & McConkey, 1997). Whereas one school of thought proposes that trauma memories tend to be stored in pristine form and can be recalled vividly and accurately (van der Kolk & van der Hart, 1991), another perspective suggests that trauma memories are susceptible to distortion (Kihlstrom, 1997). As we noted in chapter 4, there is strong evidence that under highly arousing conditions, encoding can be specific and selective (Kramer et al., 1990; Maas & Kohnken, 1989). Accordingly, it appears that many trauma victims may have difficulty recalling aspects of the trauma because they were not fully encoded. Indeed, the constructs of reduced awareness, derealization, and depersonalization suggest that the acutely traumatized individual may have limited encoding of both her or his surrounds and internal reactions. This caution is supported by findings that trauma memories often change over time (Wagenaar & Groeneweg, 1990) and that one's current mood influences the recall of memories for the trauma (Southwick et al., 1997) and for acute traumatic symptoms (Harvey & Bryant, 1999a).

Clinicians need to have a firm understanding of the implications of reduced encoding. If information is not encoded, it cannot be accurately recalled. Therapists who approach assessment or therapy with the assumption that a client has temporarily dissociated awareness of experiences that were initially encoded may be tempted to encourage the client to reconstruct what did occur. This practice is fraught with legal problems because the reconstruction of events may reflect therapeutic influences rather than historical truth. This process has been heatedly debated in recent years in the context of repressed memories of childhood trauma (see Conway, 1997; Lynn & McConkey, 1997; Pope, Oliva, & Hudson, in press). The major lesson we can learn from that debate is that clinicians have a responsibility to their clients to ensure that they do not wittingly or unwittingly influence their reconstruction of events.

There are several mechanisms that can mediate the influence of therapy on memory. There is evidence that exposure therapy modifies one's memory for trauma. Foa, Molner, and Cashman (1995) obtained narratives of rape victims before and after exposure. They found that after exposure, memories were more organized, less fragmented, and more elaborated. That is, the process of repeatedly focusing attention on one's memory for trauma increases recall. This hypermnesia effect is a commonly observed phenomenon in a range of settings in which individuals repeatedly attempt to recall information (Erdelyi, 1994). Performing this exercise in therapy allows possible hypermnesia to be influenced by therapist factors. Therapists should be particularly cautious when using hypnosis or hypnosis-like strategies to assist acutely traumatized individuals. Using hypnosis in cases where there may be subsequent reliance on the individual's memory can be problematic, however, because hypnosis can increase the reporting of both accurate and inaccurate memories (Lynn, Lock, Myers, & Payne, 1997). Moreover, individuals report enhanced confidence in hypnotically assisted memories. These findings represent a significant problem within legal settings because investigators may elicit testimonies that are based on narratives that were reconstructed during hypnosis rather than the individual's uncontaminated memory of the target events. It is for this reason that many judiciaries consider testimonies that are provided after hypnotic intervention to be inadmissible as evidence. This position has been taken because cross-examination of an individual who has reconstructed memories during hypnosis is impeded by the confident belief in the hypnotically assisted memories (McConkey & Sheehan, 1995).

In the context of ASD, one should be particularly careful because the dissociative processes that have limited the trauma victim's awareness of what has transpired may be particularly susceptible to therapeutic influences. That is, the need to understand the trauma and to fill in any missing gaps of knowledge may motivate the client to respond to cues from the therapist concerning the reconstructed memory. This is particularly problematic because there is considerable evidence that individuals who are more dissociative are more suggestible to memory distortion (Lynn et al., 1997). Accordingly, ASD individuals may be more prone to memory distortion because of their higher hypnotizability levels (Bryant et al., 1999a), and this vulnerability may be compounded by their need in the acute trauma phase to reconstruct events. This situation places considerable responsibility on therapists to ensure that they avoid using techniques that are known to increase the likelihood of memory distortion.

The potential problems associated with using fantasy-based strategies with ASD clients were saliently highlighted in a case that we reviewed for a medicolegal purpose. Maggie was a young bank teller who had been assaulted during a bank robbery. Observer reports indicated that the bank robber jumped behind the counter, pulled his hood off, and then brandished a shotgun into Maggie's face as he walked past her to reach some money. Maggie apparently developed ASD after this experience and reportedly displayed marked dissociative responses. These included dissociative amnesia for the episode when the robber pulled off his mask and walked past Maggie. The police investigating this crime wanted Maggie's assistance in identifying the robber because although several bank customers witnessed the robber retrieve the money, Maggie was the only person in the bank who apparently saw his face. It transpired that independent to the police investigation, Maggie was referred to a psychologist for assistance with her psychological reaction to the trauma. This psychologist, who was a hypnotherapist, used hypnosis to assist Maggie's recall of the episode. This psychologist provided Maggie with a standard hypnotic induction and suggestions that she could "wind the videotape back and see his face as clearly as if she was watching television." Maggie reported to us that this technique did not initially elicit any improved recall. She reported that after repeated hypnotic sessions that attempted to increase recall, she began to develop an image of the robber's face. She also reported that the more the hypnotherapist encouraged her to use her imagination to reconstruct the memory, the easier she would be able to remember. She stated to us that she received much reinforcement from the hypnotherapist each time she provided some more detail about the events that she previously could not recall. Maggie reported that on her fifth session of hypnotherapy she suddenly had a clear image of the robber's face and of what he did as he walked past her to retrieve the money. Interestingly, Maggie's account did not accord with multiple observers' reports of what the robber did when he passed by her. This case underscores the major problems associated with using hypnosis to facilitate recall in ASD clients. First, Maggie's testimony was no longer admissible in court because of the probable contamination of memory. Second, she perceived that she was under some degree of pressure to provide a memory, and the repeated attempts to reconstruct her memory apparently motivated her to report some images that met the demands of the hypnotist. It is probable that the motivation to recall the robber's appearance was heightened by expectations from the police that she remember that critical episode. Third, it was after direct communications from the hypnotist to suspend reality monitoring and allow imagination to dominate that Maggie developed a vivid image of the robber. This case points to the dangers of using hypnosis to enhance recall in distressed people who have strong personal needs to reconstruct events that are not accessible to awareness. This matter also highlights the pressure that both trauma survivor and clinician can experience to recall events that may be desired by investigating agencies.

In response to the controversy surrounding repressed memories, numerous professional bodies have proposed guidelines that preclude certain practices that may encourage and contribute to false traumatic memories. For example, the American Psychiatric Association (1993), the American Psychological Association (1994), the British Psychological Society (1995), and the Australian Psychological Society (1995) all have outlined the problems associated with encouraging reconstruction of childhood traumas. These guidelines converge on precluding the use of imaginative techniques that create a forum in which reality monitoring is suspended while an individual is encouraged to reconstruct memories of suspected events. Similar caution is needed in cases of ASD, in which the dissociative response can result in some forgetting of traumatic events. The combination of diminished recall of recent events because of dissociative responses, heightened suggestibility, the need to make attributions about their current functioning, and the possible contaminating influences of information learned since the trauma creates a situation in which the individual may develop a belief in memories of a trauma that are not accurate.

Many clinicians argue that these concerns are only relevant in the courtroom and that therapy that is focused on symptom reduction need not concern itself with such issues. Recent surveys have indicated that as many as 71% of professionals report using "memory recovery" techniques to facilitate recall of "dissociated memories" (Poole, Lindsay, Memon, & Bull, 1995). Although claiming disinterest in historical truth can be a comfortable position for therapists, there are dangers in adopting this belief for both therapist and client. It is common after assaults, accidents, and injuries that compensation matters or criminal charges arise and one's memory for the trauma becomes critical. If a therapist has provided a treatment that has wittingly or unwittingly contaminated the memory of the trauma, the trauma victim may be disadvantaged because his or her testimony may be considered invalid. That is, opposing counsel can readily provide evidence that casts doubt on the accuracy of the individual's testimony because the individual has been exposed to leading influences during therapy. The therapist's professional reputation can also be jeopardized both in the courtroom and within the therapist's professional body if she or he is guilty of behaving in a way that influenced a client to believe in a traumatic memory that was not accurate.

GENUINE VERSUS FEIGNED ASD

The forensic benefits of claiming ASD can result in the clinician being faced with decisions concerning the genuineness of the client's reported ASD symptoms. Although considerable energies have been directed toward this issue in the context of PTSD over recent years, there are still many limitations to our understanding of how to detect genuine from malingered traumatic stress.

Biological Indicators

Several researchers have proposed that the best objective measures of traumatic stress are those that involve biological markers (Friedman, 1991; Pitman & Orr, 1993). It has been proposed that autonomic reactivity to trauma cues represents the most promising objective measure of ASD or PTSD because these indexes are not as susceptible to feigning as self-reports. In support of this proposal is considerable evidence that people with PTSD can be distinguished from those without PTSD on autonomic responses to cues that are specific to their trauma (see Orr & Kaloupek, 1997). There are limitations to the use of psychophysiological measures, however. To date, there are few studies that have investigated the capacity for psychophysiological measures to be sensitive to malingering. In one study, veterans without PTSD were able to increase their reactivity to a level that was comparable to veterans with PTSD (Gerardi, Blanchard, & Kolb, 1989). Orr and Pitman (1993) found that whereas veterans instructed to respond as if they had PTSD were able to mimic the heart rate responses of PTSD veterans, skin conductance and electromyogram were able to distinguish these groups. On the basis of current data, it seems that psychophysiological measures cannot be regarded as reliable indicators of genuine ASD or PTSD.

Psychometric Measures

The assessment of the veridicality of a client's presentation can be facilitated by a number of psychometric measures. Probably the most studied measure to index genuineness of clinical presentation is the Minnesota Multiphasic Personality Inventory (MMPI/MMPI–2; Hathoway & McKinley, 1991). The MMPI–2 has an array of validity scales designed to index motivation underlying responses to items about psychopathology (Greene, 1991). Whereas some studies have indicated the utility of the MMPI–2 to distinguish genuine from malingered PTSD (Fairbank, McCaffrey, & Keane, 1985), others have pointed to limitations of this procedure to identify malingerers (Perconte & Goreczeny, 1990). Overall, the MMPI–2 remains the best validated index of feigned PTSD. Although the utility of the MMPI–2 Validity Scales to detect malingered ASD has yet to be established, it seems reasonable to expect that the MMPI–2 will perform comparably for people with PTSD and ASD.

Clinical Interviews

Although many experienced clinicians believe they can distinguish genuine from feigned traumatic stress, there is increasing evidence that indicates that it is very difficult to accurately detect malingering on the basis of clinical presentation. We recently tried to distinguish between the reports of intrusive symptoms of a group of motor vehicle accident survivors with PTSD and a group of controls who were instructed to simulate PTSD on the basis of their knowledge of this condition (Bryant & Harvey, 1998a). To elicit intrusive images or thoughts, we required participants to listen to a sound effect of a crashing car and then report their cognitive experiences. Their responses were audiotaped and subsequently rated on a range of domains by independent clinicians. We found that simulators and actual PTSD participants could not be distinguished in terms of their levels of imagery, involuntariness, belief in the reality of the memory, affect, or movement of imagery. Simulators only differed from PTSD participants in that the latter reported trying to distract themselves from their memories to a greater extent than simulators. This study highlights that it is difficult to identify malingerers on the basis of their reported reexperiencing symptoms.

Guidelines for Detecting Malingering

There have been numerous guidelines offered to detect possible malingering. For example, Rogers (1997) has suggested that clinicians can be sensitive to the following factors when determining a client's genuineness:

1. *Exaggerated clinical presentation.* This can include emphasizing the severity of symptoms, global endorsement of symptoms, and overestimation of impairment. For example, a client may claim to be suffering from all the ASD symptoms in a manner that obviously impresses on the examiner that the client is debilitated. In contrast, an acutely traumatized client who is experiencing numbing symptoms often does not express overt distress in describing her or his reactions.
2. *Deliberateness.* This includes careful consideration of all answers, extensive use of qualifiers, and excessive caution in committing to definitive responses. A client may ask for clarification about the meanings of questions, especially in response to queries about lesser known symptoms such as numbing, depersonalization, or derealization.
3. *Inconsistency of diagnostic presentation.* In terms of ASD, inconsistency may include reports of rapidly oscillating symptoms, amnesia of the entire traumatic event, avoidance of benign stimuli and lack of avoidance of overtly traumatic cues, and intrusive thoughts of positive experiences. One form of inconsistent presentation is reporting dissociative amnesia but later reporting aspects of the event when the examiner subsequently probes for details when apparently asking about reactions independent of amnesia.
4. *Inconsistency of self-report.* These self-reports may be characterized by divergent reports at different assessments, varying content that depends on the demand characteristics communicated by the examiner, and discrepancies between reported and observed symptoms. For example, a client may

report an exaggerated startle response but display no reactivity to a loud and unexpected noise initiated by the examiner.

5. *Endorsement of obvious symptoms.* Clients may report suffering more obvious or positive symptoms and give less attention to subtle or negative symptoms. A similar pattern is often seen when clients describe symptoms that are characterized by their content rather than their process. For example, a client may report the better known symptoms, such as flashbacks and nightmares, but not describe more subtle processes, such as emotional numbing.

GUIDELINES FOR ASSESSING ASD IN LEGAL CONTEXTS

Convergent opinion suggests that the most comprehensive manner to assess for malingered ASD or PTSD is to use multiple measures of psychopathology. These can include psychometric measures, psychophysiological indexes, behavioral observations, and clinical interviews (Pitman, Sparr, et al., 1996). In assessing for ASD within a forensic context, we suggest that the following guidelines be considered:

1. Commence the assessment with prolonged open-ended questioning that permits the client to provide uncued descriptions of his or her reported problems. If a client does not spontaneously provide appropriate descriptions of ASD symptoms, then malingering should be considered.

2. The interview can then proceed to more directive questioning about ASD symptoms. If the client describes ASD symptoms after directive questions but did not during her or his spontaneous narration, concerns about malingering would be strengthened.

3. The examiner can then provide the client with questions that intentionally cue the respondent to provide responses that are not consistent with ASD. For example, a client can be told that it is common for acutely traumatized people to suffer intrusive memories of very happy experiences as well as traumatic experiences.

4. The interviewer should require the client to provide a subjective description of each symptom rather than a dichotomous response that describes the presence or absence of specific symptoms. For example, the client should be asked to describe in detail the content of any intrusive memories, the manner in which they occur, the associated emotions, and his or her responses to them. The interviewer should be alert

to descriptions that depict popular impressions of trauma responses. For example, a malingering client may provide a "Hollywood" description of a flashback that involves a 20-minute trance in which the entire trauma is reenacted in a way that involves sustained dissociation from the person's surrounds. Although this form of intrusion is common in cinema depictions of traumatic stress, it is atypical and should be considered cautiously. The interviewer should always remember that the decision concerning the presence of a symptom relies on the interviewer's clinical evaluation of the client's reports. That is, a clinician may decide that a symptom is not present even though the client has reported it is present.

5. The interviewer should consider the objective history of the client when proceeding with the interview. In all forensic cases, objective evidence from medical reports, police statements, and other reliable sources should be given primary importance. Objective sources should be monitored carefully in decisions about the severity and nature of the traumatic event, functional impairment after the trauma, and conclusions concerning avoidance and help-seeking behaviors. Objective indicators are especially important in assisting the clinician to decide between a transient stress response and pathological functioning.

6. The interviewer needs to take a careful history of previous psychopathology, family history of psychiatric disorders, previous traumas, and prior PTSD. These factors are crucial in the forensic assessment of ASD because they aid the examiner in drawing conclusions about the relative causative roles of vulnerability factors and the traumatic event itself.

7. Psychometric measures should be applied to index the motivation of the respondent. Initial use of inventories of psychopathology that directly communicate to the client the symptoms of ASD should be avoided. Using measures that contain validity indexes (e.g., MMPI–2) that may assist interpretation about malingering or exaggeration will strengthen the clinician's decision making.

8. Psychophysiological assessment may also be used as part of the assessment. We recognize that most clinicians will not have the facilities or the expertise to use sophisticated psychophysiological measurement. Nonetheless, assessing heart rate, skin conductance, and electromyogram in response to trauma cues can assist the clinician's conclusions concerning the consistency of the client's responses with documented literature.

9. Finally, in conducting the forensic assessment, interviewers should always remember that they most probably will be required to defend their diagnostic decisions in court. This prospect is daunting for most clinicians because their assessment practices and conclusions are subjected to rigorous scrutiny under cross-examination. The clinician's position is most robustly defended in this situation by contemplating the aforementioned guidelines when preparing his or her assessment and considering diagnostic decisions in the context of current scientific literature on ASD and PTSD.

IMPACT OF LEGAL PROCEDURES

It is also important for clinicians to be aware of the effects of legal proceedings on acutely traumatized individuals. Many individuals report that an important feature of their trauma was their involvement in legal activities after the initial trauma. For example, the rape victim who has had to manage the turmoil of a life-threatening attack may be subsequently confronted with a lengthy investigative process that she feels violates her privacy and reinforces her sense of vulnerability. Similarly, the accident victim may be subjected to repeated interviews by counsel concerning the causes and effects of the accident. These events are commonplace in the acute trauma phase and can cause a number of problems for the individual. First, legal and investigative procedures are often stressful and intrusive and can serve to further increase the trauma victim's perceived loss of control in the acute phase. Second, because repeated interviewing in legal settings is not conducted therapeutically, these activities can serve to elicit reexperiencing symptoms in a way that does not allow habituation. Third, because of the temporal proximity between the trauma and the legal procedures, the legal proceedings can become associated with the trauma. In cognitive terminology, the legal proceedings can become integrated into the fear network and can compound the trauma response.

The therapist should be alert to the potentially adverse consequences of legal proceedings in the acute posttrauma phase. When managing a client who is exposed to stressful legal processes, the clinician should take the following steps:

1. Assess the client's resilience to manage the legal stresses. In cases where the client appears significantly suicidal or at risk of marked deterioration, the client should consult with the agencies involved in the legal activities. Clinicians can request that consideration be given to the client's mental state.

Several of our acutely traumatized clients attempted suicide during the course of legal investigations.

2. The clinician can adapt the therapeutic intervention to assist the client through the legal process. This may involve various strategies. We have postponed exposure-based therapies with numerous clients because we decided that the demands of therapy would place excessive strain on clients who reported extreme distress during legal investigations. In some cases we have focused on anxiety management to enhance the client's coping skills to manage with the legal proceedings. This can often involve SIT in which we role-play feared scenarios and the client's adaptive response. It can also be useful to schedule therapy appointments at times when the client is likely to be most distressed by legal events. For example, we have often seen clients immediately after identifying the body of a deceased loved one or identifying a suspect at a police lineup.

3. The client's subsequent response to the trauma can be modified by focusing on cognitive therapy during any legal proceedings. We have found that many clients have subsequently developed maladaptive beliefs that were strongly influenced by their involvement in legal proceedings. For example, numerous rape victims have reported that they developed beliefs about self-blame after police interrogations. Assisting the client to interpret events that occur within the legal system in a realistic manner can facilitate subsequent adjustment to those events.

4. The clinician needs to clarify her or his role in the management of the acutely traumatized client who is in the process of legal action. It is not uncommon for a clinician to be faced with a conflict of interests because investigative authorities are making requests from a clinician that may not be in the client's best interest. We were managing one client who had witnessed a murder and was reluctant to cooperate with authorities because the murderer had threatened her with death if she spoke to authorities. The police placed strong pressure on us to urge the client to reveal the assailant's identity, even though this would have aggravated her condition. This situation raised questions concerning the role that clinicians should play when requested to act in ways that are not motivated by their allegiance to the client. Although these situations can be very difficult for clinicians, we have always adopted the position that the therapist's allegiance is always to the client. In the previous example, we openly discussed

with the client the advantages and disadvantages of cooperating with the police and engaged in cognitive restructuring
of certain beliefs that were not realistic. In all this discussion,
however, we refrained from offering any direct advice and
informed her that we would accept whatever decision she
made about cooperating with the police.

5. Clinicians should always be aware that legal issues are outside
their domain of expertise, and they should never offer advice
about legal matters. Moreover, clinicians should be cautious
in any interactions with legal agencies because their comments may be used in legal contexts in ways that were not
envisaged.

CONCLUSION

As the ASD diagnosis becomes more widely known among legal personnel, it is likely that it will be increasingly invoked in both civil and
criminal matters. It is naive for clinicians to believe that such developments do not affect their practice. Whether one wishes to participate in
legal matters or not, clinicians who deal with acutely traumatized clients
need to be fully aware that they are most likely to be drawn into forensic
issues at some stage. Being adequately prepared by remaining cognizant of
recent developments in ASD and ensuring that one conducts clinical practice in a professional manner will assist therapists to deal with the particular demands of legal proceedings. By conducting clinical practice in a way
that recognizes the possibility of subsequent legal developments, clinicians
can more effectively protect the welfare of both their clients and themselves.

APPENDIX A

ACUTE STRESS DISORDER INTERVIEW

Name: _____ DOB _____ Sex: M F

Interviewer: _____ Referral Source: _____

Date of trauma: _____ Date of Assessment _____

Description of trauma:

_____

_____

_____

_____

Comments about client presentation:

_____

_____

_____

_____

CRITERION A	**NO**	**YES**
1) When ⟨Trauma⟩ happened did you think that you or someone else was going to be seriously injured or die?	0	1
2a) When ⟨Trauma⟩ happened, did you feel very frightened?	0	1
2b) When ⟨Trauma⟩ happened, did you feel that there was nothing you could do about it?	0	1

If Item (1) is coded 1 AND Item (2a) and/or Item (2b) are coded 1, Criterion A is met.

Criterion A met: Yes _____ No _____

CRITERION B

	NO	YES
1) During or since the ⟨Trauma⟩, have you felt numb or distant from your own emotions?	0	1
2) During or since the ⟨Trauma⟩, have you felt less aware of your surroundings?	0	1
3) During or since the ⟨Trauma⟩, have things around you seemed unreal?	0	1
4) During or since the ⟨Trauma⟩, have you felt distant from your normal self or have you felt as though you were looking at yourself from the outside?	0	1
5) Have you been unable to recall some important aspect of the ⟨Trauma⟩?	0	1

For those items coded 1, ask:
How soon after the ⟨Trauma⟩ did you first start
having these problems?   _____   _____
When was the last time you had any of these
problems?   _____   _____

If 3 or more of Criterion B items are coded 1, Criterion B is met.

Criterion B met: Yes _____   No _____

CRITERION C

	NO	YES
1) Have you kept remembering the ⟨Trauma⟩ even when you have not wanted to?	0	1
2) Have you kept having bad dreams or nightmares about the ⟨Trauma⟩?	0	1
3) Have you suddenly acted or felt as though the ⟨Trauma⟩ were about to happen again, even though it wasn't?	0	1
4) Do you feel very upset when you are reminded of the ⟨Trauma⟩?	0	1

For those items coded 1, ask:
How soon after the ⟨Trauma⟩ did you first start
having these problems?   _____   _____
When was the last time you had any of these
problems?   _____   _____

If any of Criterion C items are coded 1, Criterion C is met.
Criterion C met: Yes _____   No _____

CRITERION D

	NO	YES
1) Have you deliberately tried not to think about the ⟨Trauma⟩?	0	1
2) Have you deliberately tried not to talk about the ⟨Trauma⟩?	0	1
3) Have you avoided places or people or activities that may remind you of the ⟨Trauma⟩?	0	1

4) Have you tried not to feel upset or distressed about the ⟨Trauma⟩?

	0	1

For those items coded 1, ask:
How soon after the ⟨Trauma⟩ did you first start having these problems? _____ _____
When was the last time you had any of these problems? _____ _____
If any of Criterion D items are coded 1, Criterion D is met.
Criterion D met: Yes _____ No _____

CRITERION E	**NO**	**YES**
1) Since the ⟨Trauma⟩, have you had trouble sleeping?	0	1
2) Since the ⟨Trauma⟩, have you felt unusually irritable or have you lost your temper a lot more than usual?	0	1
3) Since the ⟨Trauma⟩, have you had difficulty concentrating?	0	1
4) Since the ⟨Trauma⟩, have you become much more concerned about danger or very much more careful?	0	1
5) Since the ⟨Trauma⟩, have you become jumpy or do you get easily startled by ordinary noises or movements?	0	1
6) When you are reminded of the ⟨Trauma⟩, do you sweat or tremble or does your heart beat fast?	0	1

For those items coded 1, ask:
How soon after the ⟨Trauma⟩ did you first start having these problems? _____ _____
When was the last time you had any of these problems? _____ _____

If any of Criterion E items are coded 1, Criterion E is met.

Criterion E met: Yes _____ No _____

CRITERION F	**NO**	**YES**
1) Have you felt very upset by the symptoms you have experienced since the ⟨Trauma⟩?	0	1
2) Have the problems which occurred as a result of the ⟨Trauma⟩ kept you from normal socializing or talking with people?	0	1
3) Have the problems which occurred as a result of the ⟨Trauma⟩ kept you from completing your normal work?	0	1
4) Have the problems which occurred as a result of the ⟨Trauma⟩ kept you from doing other things you need to do?	0	1

For those items coded 1, ask:
How soon after the ⟨Trauma⟩ did you first start
having these problems?   _____   _____
When was the last time you had any of these
problems?   _____   _____
If any of Criterion F items are coded 1, Criterion F is met.

Criterion F met: Yes _____   No _____

CRITERION G

  1) Have you taken medication or used drugs or alcohol at the time or since
       the ⟨Trauma⟩?   Yes _____   No _____

If yes, specify which _____

_____

If yes, specify when was the last time _____

_____

  2) Have you suffered any medical conditions, including head injuries or
       losing consciousness, at the time or since the ⟨Trauma⟩?
       Yes _____   No _____

If yes, specify which _____

_____

If yes, specify when was the last time _____

_____

If any Criterion G items are coded 1, consider if the substance use or medical
condition may account for the previously described symptoms. If there is no
evidence of substance use or medical condition accounting for the previously
described symptoms, Criterion G is met.

Criterion G met: .   Yes _____   No _____

CRITERION H

Have the symptoms reported in the following criteria lasted longer than 2 days
and less than 4 weeks after the trauma? This information is based on
responses obtained in the relevant sections of the interview. [Note. Criterion B
can occur during or following the trauma.]

Criterion C: Yes _____   No _____

Criterion D: Yes _____   No _____

Criterion E: Yes _____   No _____

If all Criterion H items are coded 1, Criterion H is met.

Criterion H met: Yes _____ No _____

SUMMARY SCORES

CRITERION	MET	TOTAL SCORE (Sum of items coded 1)
Criterion A	Yes _____ No _____	NA
Criterion B	Yes _____ No _____	_____
Criterion C	Yes _____ No _____	_____
Criterion D	Yes _____ No _____	_____
Criterion E	Yes _____ No _____	_____
Criterion F	Yes _____ No _____	
Criterion G	Yes _____ No _____	
Criterion H	Yes _____ No _____	

ASD Criteria met: Yes _____ No _____   TOTAL: _____

Note. © 1999 by Richard A. Bryant.

APPENDIX B

ACUTE STRESS DISORDER SCALE

Name: _____ Date: _____

Briefly describe your recent traumatic experience: _____
_____
_____

Did the experience frighten you?   Yes   No

Please answer each of these questions about how you have felt since the event.
Circle one number next to each question to indicate how you have felt.

	Not at all	Mildly	Medium	Quite a bit	Very much
1. During or after the trauma, did you ever feel numb or distant from your emotions?	1	2	3	4	5
2. During or after the trauma, did you ever feel in a daze?	1	2	3	4	5
3. During or after the trauma, did things around you ever feel unreal or dreamlike?	1	2	3	4	5
4. During or after the trauma, did you ever feel distant from your normal self or like you were watching it happen from outside?	1	2	3	4	5
5. Have you been unable to recall important aspects of the trauma?	1	2	3	4	5

	Not at all	Mildly	Medium	Quite a bit	Very much
6. Have memories of the trauma kept entering your mind?	1	2	3	4	5
7. Have you had bad dreams or nightmares about the trauma?	1	2	3	4	5
8. Have you felt as if the trauma was about to happen again?	1	2	3	4	5
9. Do you feel very upset when you are reminded of the trauma?	1	2	3	4	5
10. Have you tried not to think about the trauma?	1	2	3	4	5
11. Have you tried not to talk about the trauma?	1	2	3	4	5
12. Have you tried to avoid situations or people that remind you of the trauma?	1	2	3	4	5
13. Have you tried not to feel upset or distressed about the trauma?	1	2	3	4	5
14. Have you had trouble sleeping since the trauma?	1	2	3	4	5
15. Have you felt more irritable since the trauma?	1	2	3	4	5
16. Have you had difficulty concentrating since the trauma?	1	2	3	4	5
17. Have you become more alert to danger since the trauma?	1	2	3	4	5
18. Have you become jumpy since the trauma?	1	2	3	4	5
19. When you are reminded of the trauma, do you sweat or tremble or does your heart beat fast?	1	2	3	4	5

Note. © 1999 by Richard A. Bryant.

REFERENCES

Akil, H., Watson, S. J., & Young, E. (1983). Endogenous opioids: Biology and function. *Annual Review of Neuroscience, 7*, 223–255.

Alford, C. F. (1992). *The psychoanalytic theory of Greek tragedy*. New Haven, CT: Yale University Press.

American Congress of Rehabilitation Medicine. (1993). Definition of mild traumatic brain injury. *Journal of Head Trauma Rehabilitation, 8*, 86–87.

American Psychiatric Association. (1952). *Diagnostic and statistical manual of mental disorders*. Washington, DC: Author.

American Psychiatric Association. (1968). *Diagnostic and statistical manual of mental disorders* (2nd ed.). Washington, DC: Author.

American Psychiatric Association. (1980). *Diagnostic and statistical manual of mental disorders* (3rd ed.). Washington, DC: Author.

American Psychiatric Association. (1987). *Diagnostic and statistical manual of mental disorders* (3rd ed., rev.). Washington, DC: Author.

American Psychiatric Association. (1994). *Diagnostic and statistical manual of mental disorders* (4th ed.). Washington, DC: Author.

American Psychiatric Association, Board of Trustees. (1993). *Statement on memories of sexual abuse*. Washington, DC: Author.

American Psychological Association, Public Affairs Office. (1994). *Interim report of the APA Working Group on Investigation of Memory of Childhood Abuse*. Washington, DC: Author.

Amir, N., Kaplan, Z., Efroni, R., Levine, Y., Benjamin, J., & Kotler, M. (1997). Coping styles in post-traumatic stress disorder. *Personality and Individual Differences, 23*, 399–405.

Amir, N., Cashman, L., & Foa, E. B. (1997). Strategies of thought control in obsessive compulsive disorder. *Behaviour Research and Therapy, 35*, 775–777.

Anastasi, A. (1988). *Psychological testing* (6th ed.). New York: Macmillan.

Andrews, B., Brewin, C. R., Rose, S., & Kirk, M. (1998). *Predicting PTSD in victims of violent crime: The role of shame, anger and blame*. Manuscript submitted for publication.

Anthony, J. C., Folstein, M., Romanoski, A. J., Van Korff, M. R., Nestadt, G. R., Chalal, R., Merchant, A., Brown, C. H., Shapiro, S., Kramer, M., & Gruenberg, E. M. (1985). Comparison of the lay Diagnostic Interview Schedule and a standardized psychiatric diagnosis. *Archives of General Psychiatry, 42*, 667–676.

Applebaum, P. S., Jick, R. Z., Grisso, T., Givelber, D., Silver, E., & Steadman, H. J. (1993). Use of posttraumatic stress disorder to support an insanity defense. *American Journal of Psychiatry, 150*, 229–234.

Armsworth, M. W., & Holaday, M. (1993). The effects of psychological trauma on children and adolescents. *Journal of Counseling and Development, 72,* 49–50.

Atchison, M., & McFarlane, A. C. (1994). A review of dissociation and dissociative disorders. *Australian and New Zealand Journal of Psychiatry, 28,* 591–599.

Australian Psychological Society. (1995). Guidelines relating to the reporting of recovered memories. *Bulletin of the Australian Psychological Society, 17,* 20–21.

Bar-On, R., Solomon, Z., Noy, S., & Nardi, C. (1986). The clinical picture of combat stress reactions in the 1982 war in Lebanon: Cross-war comparisons. In N. A. Milgram (Ed.), *Stress and coping in time of war: Generalizations from the Israeli experience* (pp. 103–109). New York: Brunner/Mazel.

Bartemeier, L. H. (1946). Combat exhaustion. *Journal of Nervous and Mental Disease, 104,* 359–425.

Barton, K. A., Blanchard, E. B., & Hickling, E. J. (1996). Antecedents and consequences of acute stress disorder among motor vehicle accident victims. *Behaviour Research and Therapy, 34,* 805–813.

Basoglu, M., Mineka, S., Paker, M., Aker, T., Livanou, M., & Goek, S. (1997). Psychological preparedness for trauma as a protective factor in survivors of torture. *Psychological Medicine, 27,* 1421–1433.

Bauman, W., & Melnyk, W. T. (1994). A controlled comparison of eye movements and finger tapping in the treatment of test anxiety. *Journal of Behavior Therapy and Experimental Psychiatry, 25,* 29–33.

Beck, A. T. (1972). *Depression: Causes and treatment.* Philadelphia: University of Philadelphia Press.

Beck, A. T., Rush, A. J., Shaw, B. F., & Emery, G. (1979). *Cognitive therapy of depression.* New York: Guilford Press.

Beck, A. T., & Steer, R. A. (1990). *Beck Anxiety Inventory—Manual.* San Antonio, TX: Psychological Corporation.

Beck, A. T., Steer, R. A., & Brown, G. K. (1996). *Beck Depression Inventory—Second edition manual.* San Antonio, TX: Psychological Corporation.

Beck, A. T., Ward, C. H., Mendelson, M., Mock, J. E., & Erbaugh, J. K. (1961). An inventory for measuring depression. *Archives of General Psychiatry, 4,* 561–571.

Beecher, H. K. (1946). Pain in men wounded in battle. *Annals of Surgery, 123,* 96–105.

Berah, E. F., Jones, H. J., & Valent, P. (1984). The experience of a mental health team involved in the early phase of a disaster. *Australian and New Zealand Journal of Psychiatry, 18,* 354–358.

Bernstein, E. M., & Putnam, F. W. (1986). Development, reliability, and validity of a dissociation scale. *Journal of Nervous and Mental Disease, 174,* 727–735.

Billings, A. G., & Moos, R. H. (1981). The role of coping responses and social resources in attenuating the stress of life events. *Journal of Behavioural Medicine, 4,* 139–157.

Birleson, P. (1981). The validity of depressive disorder in childhood and the development of a self-rating scale. *Journal of Child Psychology and Psychiatry, 22*, 73–88.

Bisson, J. I., Jenkins, P. L., Alexander, J., & Bannister, C. (1997). Randomised controlled trial of psychological debriefing for victims of acute burn trauma. *British Journal of Psychiatry, 171*, 78–81.

Blackmore, J. (1978). Are police allowed to have problems of their own? *Police Magazine, 1*, 47–55.

Blake, D., Weathers, E., Nagy, L., Kaloupek, D., Klauminzer, G., Charney, D., & Keane, T. (1990). *Clinician Administered PTSD Scale (CAPS)*. Boston: National Center for Post-Traumatic Stress Disorder, Behavioral Science Division.

Blanchard, E. B., & Hickling, E. J. (1997). *After the crash: Assessment and treatment of motor vehicle accident survivors*. Washington, DC: American Psychological Association.

Blanchard, E. B., Hickling, E. J., Barton, K. A., Taylor, A. E., Loos, W. R., & Jones-Alexander, J. (1996). One-year prospective follow-up of motor vehicle accident victims. *Behaviour Research and Therapy, 34*, 775–786.

Blanchard, E. B., Hickling, E. J., Buckley, T. C., Taylor, A. E., Vollmer, A., & Loos, W. R. (1996). Psychophysiology of posttraumatic stress disorder related to motor vehicle accidents: Replication and extension. *Journal of Consulting and Clinical Psychology, 64*, 742–751.

Blanchard, E. B., Hickling, E. J., Taylor, A. E., Loos, W. R., Forneris, C. A., & Jaccard, J. (1996). Who develops PTSD from motor vehicle accidents? *Behaviour Research and Therapy, 34*, 1–10.

Blanchard, E. B., Hickling, E. J., Taylor, A. E., Loos, W. R., & Gerardi, R. J. (1994). Psychological morbidity associated with motor vehicle accidents. *Behaviour Research and Therapy, 32*, 283–290.

Blanchard, E. B., Kolb, L. C., & Gerardi, R. J. (1986). Cardiac response to relevant stimuli as an adjunctive tool for diagnosing post traumatic stress disorder in Vietnam veterans. *Behavior Therapy, 17*, 592–606.

Bloch, H. S. (1969). Army clinical psychiatry in the combat zone: 1967–1968. *American Journal of Psychiatry, 126*, 289–298.

Bohnen, N., & Jolles, J. (1992). Neurobehavioral aspects of postconcussive symptoms after mild head injury. *Journal of Nervous and Mental Disease, 180*, 183–192.

Bonhoeffer, M. (1926). Beurteilung, Begutachtung und Rechtsprechung bei den sogenannten Unfallsneurosen [Evaluation, review, and jurisdiction for the so-called accident neuroses]. *Deutsche Medizinische Wochenschrift, 52*, 179–182.

Bordow, S., & Porrit, D. (1979). An experimental evaluation of crisis intervention. *Social Science and Medicine, 132*, 251–256.

Boudewyns, P. A., & Hyer, L. (1990). Physiological response to combat memories and preliminary treatment outcome in Vietnam veterans: PTSD clients treated with direct therapeutic exposure. *Behavior Therapy, 21*, 63–87.

Boudewyns, P. A., & Hyer, L. A. (1996). Eye movement desensitization and reprocessing (EMDR) as treatment of post-traumatic stress disorder (PTSD). *Clinical Psychology and Psychotherapy, 3,* 185–195.

Boudewyns, P. A., Hyer, L., Woods, H. G., Harrison, W. R., & McCrame, E. (1990). PTSD among Vietnam veterans: An early look at treatment outcome using direct therapeutic exposure. *Journal of Traumatic Stress, 3,* 359–368.

Bowen, G. R., & Lambert, J. A. (1986). Systematic desensitization therapy with post-traumatic stress disorder cases. In C. R. Figley (Ed.), *Trauma and its wake* (Vol. 2, pp. 280–291). New York: Brunner/Mazel.

Branscomb, L. (1991). Dissociation in combat-related post-traumatic stress disorder. *Dissociation, 4,* 13–30.

Bremner, J. D., & Brett, E. (1997). Trauma-related dissociative states and long-term psychopathology in posttraumatic stress disorder. *Journal of Traumatic Stress, 10,* 37–49.

Bremner, J. D., Krystal, J. H., Putnam, F. W., Southwick, S. M., Marmar, C., Charney, D. S., & Mazure, C. M. (1997). *Measurement of dissociative states with the Clinician-Administered Dissociative States Scale (CADSS).* Manuscript submitted for publication.

Bremner, J. D., Scott, T. M., Delaney, R. C., Southwick, S. M., Mason, J. W., Johnson, D. R., Innis, R. B., McCarthy, G., & Charney, D. S. (1993). Deficits in short-term memory in posttraumatic stress disorder. *American Journal of Psychiatry, 150,* 1015–1019.

Bremner, J. D., Southwick, S., Brett, E., Fontana, A., Rosenheck, R., & Charney, D. S. (1992). Dissociation and posttraumatic stress disorder in Vietnam combat veterans. *American Journal of Psychiatry, 149,* 328–332.

Breslau, N., Davis, G. C., Andreski, P., & Peterson, E. (1991). Traumatic events and post-traumatic stress disorder in an urban population of young adults. *Archives of General Psychiatry, 48,* 216–222.

Brett, E. A. (1996). The classification of posttraumatic stress disorder. In B. A. van der Kolk, A. C. McFarlane, & L. Weisaeth (Eds.), *Traumatic stress: The effects of overwhelming experience on mind, body, and society* (pp. 117–128). New York: Guilford Press.

Breuer, J., & Freud, S. (1986). *Studies on hysteria.* New York: Basic Books. (Original work published 1895)

Brewin, C. R., Andrews, B., Rose, S., & Kirk, M. (1999). Acute stress disorder and posttraumatic stress disorder in victims of violent crime. *American Journal of Psychiatry, 156,* 360–366.

Brewin, C. R., Dalgleish, T., & Joseph, S. (1996). A dual representation theory of posttraumatic stress disorder. *Psychological Review, 103,* 670–686.

Briere, J. (1992). *Child abuse trauma: Theory and treatment of the lasting effects.* Newbury Park, CA: Sage.

Briere, J. (1997). Psychological assessment of child abuse effects in adults. In J. P. Wilson & T. M. Keane (Eds.), *Assessing psychological trauma and PTSD* (pp. 43–68). New York: Guilford Press.

Briere, J., & Zardi, L.Y. (1989). Sexual abuse histories and sequelae in female psychiatric emergency room patients. *American Journal of Psychiatry, 144,* 1602–1606.

British Psychological Society. (1995). *Recovered memories.* Leicester, England: British Psychological Society.

Brom, D., Kleber, R. J., & Defares, P. B. (1989). Brief psychotherapy for posttraumatic stress disorders. *Journal of Consulting and Clinical Psychology, 57,* 607–612.

Brom, D., Kleber, R. J., & Hofman, M. (1993). Victims of traffic accidents: Incidence and prevention of post-traumatic stress disorder. *Journal of Clinical Psychology, 49,* 131–140.

Brooks, N., & McKinlay, W. (1992). Mental health consequences of the Lockerbie disaster. *Journal of Traumatic Stress, 5,* 527–543.

Bryant, R. A. (1994). Ethical considerations in managing posttraumatic stress. *Bulletin of the Australian Psychological Society, 16,* 3–5.

Bryant, R. A. (1996a). Atomic testing and posttraumatic stress disorder: Legally defining a stressor. *Australian Psychologist, 31,* 34–37.

Bryant, R. A. (1996b). Posttraumatic stress disorder, flashbacks, and pseudomemories in closed head injury. *Journal of Traumatic Stress, 9,* 621–629.

Bryant, R. A. (1999). Cognitive behavior therapy of violence-related posttraumatic stress disorder. *Aggression and Violent Behavior: A Review Journal, 5,* 79–97.

Bryant, R. A., Guthrie, R. M., & Moulds, M. L. (1999). *Treating acute stress disorder following mild traumatic brain injury: A comparison between cognitive behavior therapy and supportive counseling.* Manuscript submitted for publication.

Bryant, R. A., & Harvey, A. G. (1995a). Acute stress response: A comparison of head injured and non-head injured patients. *Psychological Medicine, 25,* 869–874.

Bryant, R. A., & Harvey, A. G. (1995b). Avoidant coping style and post-traumatic stress following motor vehicle accidents. *Behaviour Research and Therapy, 33,* 631–635.

Bryant, R. A., & Harvey, A. G. (1995c). Post-traumatic stress in volunteer firefighters: Predictors of distress. *Journal of Nervous and Mental Disease, 183,* 267–271.

Bryant, R. A., & Harvey, A. G. (1995d). Processing threatening information in posttraumatic stress disorder. *Journal of Abnormal Psychology, 104,* 537–541.

Bryant, R. A., & Harvey, A. G. (1995e). Psychological impairment following motor vehicle accidents. *Australian Journal of Public Health, 19,* 185–188.

Bryant, R. A., & Harvey, A. G. (1996a). Initial post-traumatic stress responses following motor vehicle accidents. *Journal of Traumatic Stress, 9,* 223–234.

Bryant, R. A., & Harvey, A. G. (1996b). Post-traumatic stress reactions in volunteer firefighters. *Journal of Traumatic Stress, 9,* 51–62.

Bryant, R. A., & Harvey, A. G. (1997a). Acute stress disorder: A critical review of diagnostic and theoretical issues. *Clinical Psychology Review, 17,* 757–773.

Bryant, R. A., & Harvey, A. G. (1997b). Attentional bias in post-traumatic stress disorder. *Journal of Traumatic Stress, 10,* 635–644.

Bryant, R. A., & Harvey, A. G. (1998a). A comparison of traumatic memories and pseudomemories in posttraumatic stress disorder. *Applied Cognitive Psychology, 12,* 81–88.

Bryant, R. A., & Harvey, A. G. (1998b). The relationship between acute stress disorder and posttraumatic stress disorder following mild traumatic brain injury. *American Journal of Psychiatry, 155,* 625–629.

Bryant, R. A., & Harvey, A. G. (1999a). The influence of traumatic brain injury on acute stress disorder and posttraumatic stress disorder following motor vehicle accidents. *Brain Injury, 13,* 15–22.

Bryant, R. A., & Harvey, A. G. (1999b). Postconcussive symptoms and posttraumatic stress disorder following mild traumatic brain injury. *Journal of Nervous and Mental Disease, 187,* 302–305.

Bryant, R. A., Harvey, A. G., Dang, S., & Sackville, T. (1998). Assessing acute stress disorder: Psychometric properties of a structured clinical interview. *Psychological Assessment, 10,* 215–220.

Bryant, R. A., Harvey, A. G., Dang, S. T., Sackville, T., & Basten, C. (1998). Treatment of acute stress disorder: A comparison of cognitive behavior therapy and supportive counseling. *Journal of Consulting and Clinical Psychology, 66,* 862–866.

Bryant, R. A., Harvey, A. G., Gordon, E., & Barry, R. (1995). Eye-movement and electrodermal responses to threat stimuli in post-traumatic stress disorder. *International Journal of Psychophysiology, 20,* 209–213.

Bryant, R. A., Harvey, A. G., Guthrie, R. M., & Moulds, M. L. (in press). A prospective study of psychophysiological arousal, acute stress disorder and posttraumatic stress disorder. *Journal of Abnormal Psychology.*

Bryant, R. A., Marosszeky, J. E., Crooks, J., & Gurka, J. A. (in press). Posttraumatic stress disorder following severe traumatic brain injury. *American Journal of Psychiatry.*

Bryant, R. A., Moulds, M. L., & Guthrie, R. M. (1999a). *Hypnotizability in acute stress disorder.* Manuscript submitted for publication.

Bryant, R. A., Moulds, M. L., & Guthrie, R. M. (1999b). *Thought control strategies and the resolution of acute stress disorder.* Manuscript submitted for publication.

Bryant, R. A., Moulds, M. L., & Guthrie, R. M. (in press). Acute stress disorder scale: A self-report measure of acute stress disorder. *Psychological Assessment.*

Bryant, R. A., Sackville, T., Dang, S. T., Moulds, M. L., & Guthrie, R. M. (in press). Treating acute stress disorder: An evaluation of cognitive behavior therapy and supportive counseling techniques. *American Journal of Psychiatry.*

Buckley, P., Conte, H. R., Plutchik, R., Wild, K. V., & Karasu, T. B. (1984). Psychodynamic variables as predictors of psychotherapy outcome. *American Journal of Psychiatry, 141,* 742–748.

Burns, D. D. (1980). *Feeling good: The new mood therapy.* New York: Morrow.

Burstein, A. (1985). Post-traumatic stress disorder. *Journal of Clinical Psychiatry,* 46, 554–556.

Butler, G., & Mathews, A. (1983). Cognitive processes in anxiety. *Advances in Behaviour Research and Therapy,* 5, 51–62.

Byl, N., & Sykes, B. (1978). Work and health problems: An approach to management for the professional and the community. *Community Health,* 9, 149–158.

Calhoun, K. S., & Resick, P. A. (1993). Post-traumatic stress disorder. In D. H. Barlow (Ed.), *Clinical handbook of psychological disorders: A step-by-step treatment manual* (pp. 48–98). New York: Guilford Press.

Camp, N. M. (1993). The Vietnam War and the ethics of combat psychiatry. *American Journal of Psychiatry,* 150, 1000–1010.

Cardeña, E., Classen, C., & Spiegel, D. (1991). *Stanford Acute Stress Reaction Questionnaire.* Stanford, CA: Stanford University Medical School.

Cardeña, E., & Spiegel, D. (1993). Dissociative reactions to the San Francisco Bay Area earthquake of 1989. *American Journal of Psychiatry,* 150, 474–478.

Carlson, E. B., & Putnam, F. W. (1993). An update on the Dissociative Experiences Scale. *Dissociation,* 6, 16–27.

Carlson, E. B., & Rosser-Hogan, R. (1991). Trauma experiences, posttraumatic stress, dissociation, and depression in Cambodian refugees. *American Journal of Psychiatry,* 148, 1548–1551.

Carlson, J. G., Chemtob, C. M., Rusnak, K., Hedlund, N. L., & Muraoka, M. Y. (1998). Eye movement desensitization and reprocessing (EMDR) treatment for combat-related posttraumatic stress disorder. *Journal of Traumatic Stress,* 11, 3–24.

Cassiday, K. L., McNally, R. J., & Zeitlin, S. B. (1992). Cognitive processing of trauma cues in rape victims with post-traumatic stress disorder. *Cognitive Therapy and Research,* 16, 283–295.

Charcot, J. M. (1887). *Lessons on the illness of the nervous system held at the Salpêtrière* (Vol. 3). Paris: Progrès Médical en A. Delahaye & E. Lecrosnie.

Chemtob, C. M., Novaco, R. W., Hamada, R. S., & Gross, D. M. (1997). Anger regulation deficits in combat-related posttraumatic stress disorder. *Journal of Traumatic Stress,* 10, 17–36.

Chemtob, C., Roitblat, H. L., Hamada, R. S., Carlson, J. G., & Twentyman, C. T. (1988). A cognitive action theory of post-traumatic stress disorder. *Journal of Anxiety Disorders,* 2, 253–275.

Chemtob, C. M., Tomas, S., Law, W., & Cremniter, D. (1997). Postdisaster psychosocial intervention: A field study of the impact of debriefing on psychological distress. *American Journal of Psychiatry,* 154, 415–417.

Clark, D. M. (1989). Anxiety states: Panic and generalized anxiety. In K. Hawton, P. Salkovskis, J. Kirk, & D. M. Clark (Eds.), *Cognitive behaviour therapy for psychiatric problems: A practical guide.* Oxford, England: Oxford University Press.

Classen, C., Koopman, C., Hales, R., & Spiegel, D. (1998). Acute stress disorder as a predictor of posttraumatic stress symptoms. *American Journal of Psychiatry*, *155*, 620–624.

Classen, C., Koopman, C., & Spiegel, D. (1993). Trauma and dissociation. *Bulletin of the Menninger Clinic, 57*, 178–194.

Clohessy, S., & Ehlers, A. (1997). *PTSD symptoms and coping in ambulance service workers*. Manuscript submitted for publication.

Cohen, R. E., & Ahearn, F. L. (1980). *Handbook for mental health care of disaster victims*. Baltimore: Johns Hopkins University Press.

Commonwealth of Australia. (1998). *Report of the Board of Inquiry into the fire in HMAS Westralia on 5 May 1998*. Canberra, Australia: Defence Publishing Services.

Conte, J., & Schuerman, J. (1987). Factors associated with an increased impact of child sexual abuse. *Child Abuse and Neglect, 11*, 201–211.

Conway, M. (1997). *Recovered memories and false memories*. Oxford, England: Oxford University Press.

Coons, P. M., Bowman, E. S., Pellow, T. A., & Schneider, P. (1989). Post-traumatic aspects of the treatment of victims of sexual abuse and incest. *Psychiatric Clinics of North America, 12*, 325–335.

Coons, P. M., & Milstein, V. (1986). Psychosexual disturbances in multiple personality: Characteristics, etiology, and treatment. *Journal of Clinical Psychiatry, 47*, 106–110.

Cooper, N. A., & Clum, G. A. (1989). Imaginal flooding as a supplementary treatment for PTSD in combat veterans: A controlled study. *Behavior Therapy, 3*, 381–391.

Craske, M. G., & Barlow, D. H. (1993). Panic disorder and agoraphobia. In D. H. Barlow (Ed.), *Clinical handbook of psychological disorders* (pp. 1–47). New York: Guilford Press.

Creamer, M., Burgess, P., Buckingham, W. J., & Pattison, P. (1993). Post-trauma reactions following a multiple shooting: A retrospective study and methodological inquiry. In J. P. Wilson & B. Raphael (Eds.), *The international handbook of traumatic stress syndromes* (pp. 201–212). New York: Plenum.

Creamer, M., Burgess, P., & Pattison, P. (1992). Reaction to trauma: A cognitive processing model. *Journal of Abnormal Psychology, 101*, 452–459.

Creamer, M., & Manning, C. (1998). Acute stress disorder following an industrial accident. *Australian Psychologist, 33*, 125–129.

Dalton, J. E., Pederson, S. L., & Ryan, J. J. (1989). Effects of post-traumatic stress disorder on neuropsychological test performance. *International Journal of Clinical Neuropsychology, 11*, 121–124.

Dancu, C. V., Riggs, D. S., Hearst-Ikeda, D., Shoyer, B. G., & Foa, E. B. (1996). Dissociative experiences and posttraumatic stress disorder among female victims of criminal assault and rape. *Journal of Traumatic Stress, 9*, 253–267.

Davidson, J., & Foa, E. B. (1991). Diagnostic issues in posttraumatic stress disorder: Considerations for DSM–IV. *Journal of Abnormal Psychology, 100*, 346–355.

Davidson, J., Kudler, H., Saunders, W. B., & Smith, R. D. (1989). Symptom and comorbidity patterns in World War II and Vietnam veterans with PTSD. *Comprehensive Psychiatry, 31,* 162–170.

Davidson, J. R. T., Book, S. W., Colket, J. T., Tupler, L. A., Roth, S., David, D., Hertzberg, M., Mellman, T., Beckham, J. C., Smith, R. D., Davison, R. M., Katz, R., & Feldman, M. E. (1997). Assessment of a new self-rating scale of post-traumatic disorder. *Psychological Medicine, 27,* 153–160.

Davidson, J. R. T., & Fairbank, J. A. (1993). The epidemiology of posttraumatic stress disorder. In J. R. T. Davidson & E. B. Foa (Eds.), *Posttraumatic stress disorder: DSM–IV and beyond* (pp. 147–169). Washington, DC: American Psychiatric Press.

Davidson, J. R. T., Hughes, D., & Blazer, D. (1991). Posttraumatic stress disorder in the community: An epidemiological study. *Psychological Medicine, 21,* 1–9.

Davidson, J. R. T., Smith, R. D., & Kudler, H. S. (1989). Validity and reliability of the *DSM–III* criteria for posttraumatic stress disorder: An epidemiological study. *Psychological Medicine, 21,* 1–9.

Deahl, M. P., Gilham, A. B., Thomas, J., Searle, M. M., & Srinivasan, M. (1994). Psychological sequelae following the Gulf War: Factors associated with subsequent morbidity and the effectiveness of psychological debriefing. *British Journal of Psychiatry, 165,* 60–65.

DeBellis, M. D. (1997). Posttraumatic stress disorder and acute stress disorder. In R. T. Ammerman & M. Hersen (Eds.), *Handbook of prevention and treatment with children and adolescents: Interventions in the real world context* (pp. 455–494). New York: Wiley.

Deblinger, E. (1994, August). *Update on treatment outcome studies.* Paper presented at the 102nd Annual Convention of the American Psychological Association, Los Angeles.

Deblinger, E., McLeer, S. V., & Henry, D. (1990). Cognitive behavioral treatment for sexually abused children suffering post-traumatic stress: Preliminary findings. *Journal of the American Academy of Child and Adolescent Psychiatry, 29,* 747–752.

Delahanty, D. L., Herberman, H. B., Craig, K. J., Hayward, M. C., Fullerton, C. S., Ursano, R. J., & Baum, A. (1997). Acute and chronic distress and posttraumatic stress disorder as a function of responsibility for serious motor vehicle accidents. *Journal of Consulting and Clinical Psychology, 65,* 560–567.

Devilly, G. J., & Spence, S. H. (1999). The relative efficacy and treatment distress of EMDR and a cognitive behavioral treatment protocol in the amelioration of posttraumatic stress disorder. *Journal of Anxiety Disorders, 13,* 131–157.

Devilly, G. J., Spence, S. H., & Rapee, R. M. (1998). Statistical and reliable change with eye movement desensitization and reprocessing: Treating trauma within a veteran population. *Behavior Therapy, 29,* 435–455.

Dunmore, E., Clark, D. M., & Ehlers, A. (1997). Cognitive factors in persistent versus recovered post-traumatic stress disorder after physical or sexual assault: A pilot study. *Behavioural and Cognitive Psychotherapy, 25,* 147–159.

Dunn, T. M., Schwartz, M., Hatfield, R. W., & Wiegele, M. (1996). Measuring effectiveness of eye movement desensitization and reprocessing (EMDR) in non-clinical anxiety: A multi-subject, yoked control design. *Journal of Behavior Therapy and Experimental Psychiatry, 27*, 231–239.

Dyregrov, A. (1989). Caring for helpers in disaster situations: Psychological debriefing. *Disaster Management, 2*, 25–30.

Earls, F., Smith, E., Reich, W., & Jung, K. G. (1988). Investigating psychopathological consequences of a disaster in children: A pilot study incorporating a structured diagnostic interview. *Journal of the American Academy of Child Psychiatry, 27*, 90–95.

Ehlers, A., Clark, D., Winton, E., Jaycox, L., Meadows, E., & Foa, E. B. (1998). Predicting response to exposure treatment in PTSD: The role of mental defeat and alienation. *Journal of Traumatic Stress, 11*, 457–471.

Ehlers, A., Mayou, R. A., & Bryant, B. (1997). *Psychological predictors of chronic PTSD after motor vehicle accidents.* Manuscript submitted for publication.

Ehlers, A., Mayou, R. A., & Bryant, B. (1998). Psychological predictors of chronic posttraumatic stress disorder after motor vehicle accidents. *Journal of Abnormal Psychology, 107*, 508–519.

Ehlers, A., & Steil, R. (1995). Maintenance of intrusive memories in posttraumatic stress disorder: A cognitive approach. *Behavioural and Cognitive Psychotherapy, 23*, 217–249.

Epstein, S. (1991). Impulse control and self-destructive behavior. In L. P. Lipsitt & L. L. Mitick (Eds.), *Self-regulatory behavior and risk-taking: Causes and consequences* (pp. 273–284). Norwood, NJ: Ablex.

Erdelyi, M. H. (1994). Hypnotic hypermnesia: The empty set of hypermnesia. *International Journal of Clinical and Experimental Hypnosis, 42*, 379–390.

Ersland, S., Weisaeth, L., & Sund, A. (1989). The stress upon rescuers involved in an oil rig disaster: "Alexander L. Kielland" 1980. *Acta Psychiatrica Scandinavica, 80*(Suppl. 355), 38–49.

Eth, S., & Pynoos, R. S. (1985). *Posttraumatic stress in children.* Washington, DC: American Psychiatric Association.

Eysenck, M. W. (1989). Trait anxiety and stress. In S. Fisher & J. Reason (Eds.), *Handbook of life stress cognition and health.* New York: Wiley.

Fairbank, J. A., McCaffrey, R. J., & Keane, T. M. (1985). Psychometric detection of fabricated symptoms of posttraumatic stress disorder. *American Journal of Psychiatry, 142*, 501–503.

Feinstein, A. (1989). Posttraumatic stress disorder: A descriptive study supporting *DSM–III–R* criteria. *American Journal of Psychiatry, 146*, 665–666.

Finkelhor, D., & Berliner, L. (1995). Research on the treatment of sexually abused children: A review and recommendations. *Journal of the American Academy of Child and Adolescent Psychiatry, 34*, 1408–1423.

Finkelhor, D., & Hotaling, G. T. (1984). Sexual abuse in national incidence study of child abuse and neglect: An appraisal. *Child Abuse and Neglect, 8*, 23–32.

Fletcher, K. E. (1996). Childhood posttraumatic stress disorder. In E. J. Mash &

R. A. Barkley (Eds.), *Child psychopathology* (pp. 242–276). New York: Guilford Press.

Foa, E. B., Cashman, L., Jaycox, L., & Perry, K. (1997). The validation of a self-report measure of posttraumatic stress disorder: The posttraumatic diagnostic scale. *Psychological Assessment, 9,* 445–451.

Foa, E. B., Dancu, C. V., Hembree, E. A., Jaycox, L. H., Meadows, E. A., & Street, G. P. (1999). A comparison of exposure therapy, stress inoculation training, and their combination for reducing posttraumatic stress disorder in female assault victims. *Journal of Consulting and Clinical Psychology, 67,* 194–200.

Foa, E. B., Ehlers, A., Clark, D. M., Tolin, D. F., & Orsillo, S. M. (1998). *The Post-Traumatic Cognitions Inventory (PTCI): Development and validation.* Manuscript submitted for publication.

Foa, E. B., Feeny, N. C., Zoellner, L. A., Fitzgibbons, L. A., & Hembree, E. A. (1998, November). *Treatment of chronic PTSD: Prolonged exposure with and without cognitive restructuring.* Paper presented at the 14th Annual Meeting of the International Society of Traumatic Stress Studies, Washington, DC.

Foa, E. B., Feske, U., Murdock, T. B., Kozak, M. J., & McCarthy, P. R. (1991). Processing of threat-related information in rape victims. *Journal of Abnormal Psychology, 100,* 156–162.

Foa, E. B., Franklin, M. E., Perry, K. J., & Herbert, J. D. (1996). Cognitive bias in generalized social phobia. *Journal of Abnormal Psychology, 15,* 433–439.

Foa, E. B., & Hearst-Ikeda, D. (1996). Emotional dissociation in response to trauma: An information-processing approach. In L. K. Michelson & W. J. Ray (Eds.), *Handbook of dissociation: Theoretical and clinical perspectives* (pp. 207–222). New York: Plenum.

Foa, E. B., Hearst-Ikeda, D., & Perry, K. J. (1995). Evaluation of a brief cognitive–behavioral program for the prevention of chronic PTSD in recent assault victims. *Journal of Consulting and Clinical Psychology, 63,* 948–955.

Foa, E. B., & Kozak, M. J. (1986). Emotional processing of fear: Exposure to corrective information. *Psychological Bulletin, 99,* 20–35.

Foa, E. B., & Meadows, E. A. (1997). Psychosocial treatments for posttraumatic stress disorder: A critical review. *Annual Review of Psychology, 48,* 449–480.

Foa, E. B., Molnar, C., & Cashman, L. (1995). Change in rape narratives during exposure therapy for posttraumatic stress disorder. *Journal of Traumatic Stress, 8,* 675–690.

Foa, E. B., & Riggs, D. S. (1993). Posttraumatic stress disorder in rape victims. In J. Oldham, M. B. Riba, & A. Tasman (Eds.), *American Psychiatric Press review of psychiatry* (Vol. 12, pp. 273–303). Washington, DC: American Psychiatric Press.

Foa, E. B., Riggs, D., Dancu, C. V., & Rothbaum, B. O. (1993). Reliability and validity of a brief instrument for assessing post-traumatic stress disorder. *Journal of Traumatic Stress, 6,* 459–473.

Foa, E. B., Riggs, D. S., & Gershung, B. (1995). Arousal, numbing and intrusion:

Symptom structure of posttraumatic stress disorder. *American Journal of Psychiatry, 152,* 116–120.

Foa, E. B., & Rothbaum, B. O. (1989). Behavioral psychotherapy for posttraumatic stress disorder. *International Review of Psychiatry, 1,* 219–226.

Foa, E. B., & Rothbaum, B. O. (1997). *Treating the trauma of rape: Cognitive–behavioral therapy for PTSD.* New York: Guilford Press.

Foa, E. B., Rothbaum, B. O., Riggs, D. S., & Murdock, T. B. (1991). Treatment of posttraumatic stress disorder in rape victims: A comparison between cognitive–behavioral procedures and counseling. *Journal of Consulting and Clinical Psychology, 59,* 715–723.

Foa, E. B., Steketee, G., & Rothbaum, B. O. (1989). Behavioral/cognitive conceptualizations of post-traumatic stress disorder. *Behavior Therapy, 20,* 155–176.

Foley, T., & Spates, C. R. (1995). Eye movement desensitization and reprocessing of public speaking anxiety: A partial dismantling. *Journal of Behavior Therapy and Experimental Psychiatry, 26,* 321–329.

Folkman, S., & Lazarus, R. S. (1980). An analysis of coping in a middle-aged community sample. *Journal of Health and Social Behavior, 21,* 219–239.

Fontana, A., & Rosenheck, R. (1994). A short form of the Mississippi Scale for Measuring Change in Combat-Related PTSD. *Journal of Traumatic Stress, 7,* 407–414.

Frank, E., Anderson, B., Stewart, B. D., Dancu, C., Hughes, C., & West, D. (1988). Efficacy of cognitive behavior therapy and systematic desensitization in the treatment of rape trauma. *Behavior Therapy, 19,* 403–420.

Frank, E., & Stewart, B. D. (1983). Physical aggression: Treating the victim. In E. A. Bleckman (Ed.), *Behavior modification with women* (pp. 245–272). New York: Guilford Press.

Frank, E., & Stewart, B. D. (1984). Depressive symptoms in rape victims. *Journal of Affective Disorders, 1,* 269–277.

Frankel, F. H. (1994). The concept of flashbacks in historical perspective. *International Journal of Clinical and Experimental Hypnosis, 42,* 321–336.

Freinkel, A., Koopman, C., & Spiegel, D. (1994). Dissociative symptoms in media witnesses of an execution. *American Journal of Psychiatry, 151,* 1335–1339.

Friedman, M. J. (1991). Biological approaches to the diagnosis and treatment of posttraumatic stress disorder. *Journal of Traumatic Stress, 4,* 67–91.

Frischholz, E. J., Braun, B. G., Sachs, R. G., Schwartz, D. R., Lewis, J., Shaeffer, D., Westergaard, C., & Pasquotto, M. A. (1992). Construct validity of the Dissociative Experiences Scale: II. Its relationship to hypnotizability. *American Journal of Clinical Hypnosis, 35,* 145–152.

Frueh, B. C., Smith, D. W., & Barker, S. E. (in press). Compensation seeking status and psychometric assessment of combat veterans seeking treatment for PTSD. *Journal of Traumatic Stress.*

Frueh, B. C., Turner, S. M., & Beidel, D. C. (1995). Exposure therapy for combat-related PTSD: A critical review. *Clinical Psychology Review, 15,* 799–815.

Fullerton, C. S., McCarroll, J. E., Ursano, R. J., & Wright, K. M. (1992). Psychological responses of rescue workers: Fire fighters and trauma. *American Journal of Orthopsychiatry, 62,* 371–378.

Galente, R., & Foa, D. (1986). An epidemiological study of psychic trauma and treatment effectiveness for children after a natural disaster. *Journal of the American Academy of Child and Adolescent Psychiatry, 25,* 3357–3363.

Ganaway, G. K. (1994). Transference and countertransference shaping influences on dissociative syndromes. In S. J. Lynn & J. W. Rhue (Eds.), *Dissociation clinical and theoretical perspectives* (pp. 317–337). New York: Guilford Press.

Garmezy, N. (1986). Children under severe stress: Critique and comments. *Journal of the American Academy of Child Psychiatry, 25,* 384–392.

Garmezy, N., & Rutter, M. (1985). Acute reactions to stress. In M. Rutter & L. Hersov (Eds.), *Child and adolescent psychiatry: Modern approaches* (2nd ed., pp. 152–176). Oxford, England: Blackwell.

Gerardi, R. J., Blanchard, E. B., & Kolb, L. C. (1989). Ability of Vietnam veterans to dissimulate a psychophysiological assessment for post-traumatic stress disorder. *Behavior Therapy, 20,* 229–243.

Glass, A. J. (1959). Psychological aspects of disaster. *Journal of the American Medical Association, 171,* 222–225.

Goenjian, A., Pynoos, R. S., Steinberg, A. M., Najarian, L. M., Asarnow, J. R., Karayan, I., Ghurabi, M., & Fairbanks, L. A. (1995). Psychiatric co-morbidity in children after the 1988 earthquake in Armenia. *Journal of the American Academy of Child and Adolescent Psychiatry, 34,* 1174–1184.

Goldberg, D. P., & Hillier, V. F. (1979). A scaled version of the General Health Questionnaire. *Psychological Medicine, 9,* 139–145.

Gomes-Schwartz, B., Horowitz, J. M., Cardarelli, A. P., & Sauzier, M. (1990). The aftermath of child sexual abuse: 18 months later. In B. Gomes-Schwartz, J. M. Horowitz, & A. P. Cardarelli (Eds.), *Child sexual abuse: The initial effects* (pp. 132–152). Newbury Park, CA: Sage.

Goodwin, J. (1988). Posttraumatic stress symptoms in abused children. *Journal of the American Academy of Child and Adolescent Psychiatry, 23,* 231–237.

Gordon, R., & Wraith, R. (1993). Responses of children and adolescents to disasters. In J. P. Wilson & B. Raphael (Eds.), *International handbook of traumatic stress syndromes* (pp. 561–575). New York: Plenum.

Gosselin, P., & Matthews, W. J. (1995). Eye movement desensitization and reprocessing in the treatment of test anxiety: A study of the effects of expectancy and eye movement. *Journal of Behavior Therapy and Experimental Psychiatry, 26,* 331–337.

Grant, B. L., & Coons, D. J. (1983). Guilty verdict in a murder committed by a veteran with post-traumatic stress disorder. *Bulletin of the American Academy of Psychiatry and the Law, 11,* 355–358.

Green, M. M., McFarlane, A. C., Hunter, C. E., & Griggs, W. M. (1993). Undiagnosed post-traumatic stress disorder following motor vehicle accidents. *Medical Journal of Australia, 159,* 529–534.

Greene, R. L. (1991). *The MMPI–2/MMPI: An interpretative manual.* Boston: Allyn & Bacon.

Griffin, M. G., Resick, P. A., & Mechanic, M. B. (1997). Objective assessment of peritraumatic dissociation: Psychophysiological indicators. *American Journal of Psychiatry, 154,* 1081–1088.

Griffiths, J., & Watts, R. (1992). *The Kempsey and Grafton bus crashes: The aftermath.* East Lismore, Australia: Instructional Design Solutions.

Grigsby, J. (1986). Depersonalization following minor closed head injury. *International Journal of Clinical Neuropsychology, 8,* 65–69.

Grigsby, J., & Kaye, K. (1993). Incidence and correlates of depersonalization following head trauma. *Brain Injury, 7,* 507–513.

Grinker, K. P. (1945). Psychiatric disorders in combat crews overseas and in returnees. *Medical Clinics of North America, 29,* 729–739.

Grinker, R. R., & Spiegel, J. J. (1945). *Men under stress.* Philadelphia: Blakiston.

Gronwall, D., & Wrightson, P. (1980). Duration of post-traumatic amnesia after mild head injury. *Journal of Clinical Neuropsychology, 2,* 51–60.

Guthrie, R. M., & Bryant, R. A. (in press). Attempting suppression of traumatic memories in acute stress disorder. *Behavior Research and Therapy.*

Hartsough, D. M., & Myers, D. G. (1985). *Disaster work and mental health: Prevention and control of stress among workers.* Rockville, MD: National Institute of Mental Health.

Harvey, A. G., & Bryant, R. A. (1998a). Acute stress disorder following mild traumatic brain injury. *Journal of Nervous and Mental Disease, 186,* 333–337.

Harvey, A. G., & Bryant, R. A. (1998b). The effect of attempted thought suppression in acute stress disorder. *Behaviour Research and Therapy, 36,* 583–590.

Harvey, A. G., & Bryant, R. A. (1998c). Predictors of acute stress disorder following mild traumatic brain injury. *Brain Injury, 12,* 147–154.

Harvey, A. G., & Bryant, R. A. (1998d). The relationship between acute stress disorder and posttraumatic stress disorder: A prospective evaluation of motor vehicle accident survivors. *Journal of Consulting and Clinical Psychology, 66,* 507–512.

Harvey, A. G., & Bryant, R. A. (1999a). *Distortions in memory for posttraumatic symptoms.* Manuscript submitted for publication.

Harvey, A. G., & Bryant, R. A. (1999b). *An integrative model of acute stress disorder.* Manuscript submitted for publication.

Harvey, A. G., & Bryant, R. A. (1999c). Acute stress disorder across trauma populations. *Journal of Nervous and Mental Disease, 187,* 443–446.

Harvey, A. G., & Bryant, R. A. (1999d). Predictors of acute stress following motor vehicle accidents. *Journal of Traumatic Stress, 12,* 519–525.

Harvey, A. G., & Bryant, R. A. (in press-a). Dissociative symptoms in acute stress disorder. *Journal of Traumatic Stress.*

Harvey, A. G., & Bryant, R. A. (in press-b). A qualitative investigation of traumatic memories. *British Journal of Clinical Psychology.*

Harvey, A. G., & Bryant, R. A. (in press-c). A two-year prospective evaluation of the relationship between acute stress disorder and posttraumatic stress disorder. *Journal of Consulting and Clinical Psychology.*

Harvey, A. G., & Bryant, R. A. (in press-d). A two-year prospective evaluation of the relationship between acute stress disorder and posttraumatic stress disorder following mild traumatic brain injury. *American Journal of Psychiatry.*

Harvey, A. G., Bryant, R. A., & Dang, S. (1998). Autobiographical memory in acute stress disorder and posttraumatic stress disorder. *Journal of Consulting and Clinical Psychology, 66,* 500–506.

Harvey, A. G., Bryant, R. A., & Rapee, R. M. (1996). Preconscious processing of threat in post-traumatic stress disorder. *Cognitive Research and Therapy, 20,* 613–623.

Hathoway, S. R., & McKinley, J. C. (1991). *MMPI–2: Minnesota Multiphasic Personality Inventory.* Minnesota: University of Minnesota Press.

Helzer, J. E., Robins, L. N., & McEvoy, L. (1987). Post-traumatic stress disorder in the general population: Findings of the Epidemiological Catchment Area survey. *New England Journal of Medicine, 317,* 1630–1634.

Herman, J. L., Perry, J. C., & van der Kolk, B. A. (1989). Childhood trauma in borderline personality disorder. *American Journal of Psychiatry, 146,* 490–495.

Hickling, E. J., & Blanchard, E. B. (1997). The private practice psychologist and manual-based treatments: Post-traumatic stress disorder secondary to motor vehicle accidents. *Behaviour Research and Therapy, 35,* 191–203.

Hickling, E. J., Gillen, E. B., Blanchard, E. B., Buckley, T., & Taylor, A. (1998). Traumatic brain injury and posttraumatic stress disorder: A preliminary investigation of neuropsychological test results in PTSD secondary to motor vehicle accidents. *Brain Injury, 12,* 265–274.

Hilgard, E. R. (1977). *Divided consciousness: Multiple controls in human thought and action.* New York: Wiley Interscience.

Holen, A. (1993). The North Sea oil rig disaster. In J. P. Wilson & B. Raphael (Eds.), *International handbook of traumatic stress syndromes* (pp. 471–478). New York: Plenum.

Horowitz, M. J. (1976). *Stress response syndromes.* Northvale, NJ: Jason Aronson.

Horowitz, M. J. (1986). *Stress response syndromes* (2nd ed.). New York: Jason Aronson.

Horowitz, M. J., Weiss, D. S., & Marmar, C. (1987). Diagnosis of posttraumatic stress disorder. *Journal of Nervous and Mental Disease, 175,* 267–268.

Horowitz, M. J., Wilner, N., & Alvarez, W. (1979). The Impact of Event Scale: A measure of subjective stress. *Psychosomatic Medicine, 41,* 209–218.

Howarth, I., & Dussuyer, I. D. (1988). Helping people cope with the long-term effects of stress. In S. Fisher & J. Reason (Eds.), *Handbook of life stress, cognition and health* (pp. 653–667). New York: Wiley.

Hyer, L., O'Leary, W. C., Saucer, R. T., Blount, J., Harrison, W. R., & Boudewyns,

P. A. (1986). Inpatient diagnosis of posttraumatic stress disorder. *Journal of Consulting and Clinical Psychology, 54*, 698–702.

Hytten, K. (1989). Helicopter crash in water: Effects of simulator escape training. *Acta Psychiatrica Scandinavica, 80*(Suppl. 355), 73–78.

Hytten, L., & Hasle, A. (1989). Firefighters: A study of stress and coping. *Acta Psychiatrica Scandinavica, 80*(Suppl. 355), 50–55.

Illinitch, R. C., & Titus, M. P. (1977). Caretakers as victims: The Big Thompson flood, 1976. *Smith College Studies in Social Work, 48*, 67–68.

Janet, P. (1907). *The major symptoms of hysteria.* New York: Mcmillan.

Janis, J. L. (1971). *Stress and frustration.* New York: Harcourt Brace Jovanovich.

Janoff-Bulman, R. (1992). *Shattered assumptions: Towards a new psychology of trauma.* New York: Free Press

Jaycox, L. H., & Foa, E. B. (1996). Obstacles in implementing exposure therapy for PTSD: Case discussions and practical solutions. *Clinical Psychology and Psychotherapy, 3*, 176–184.

Jaycox, L. H., Perry, K., Freshman, M., Stafford, J., & Foa, E. B. (1995, November). *Factors related to improvement in assault victims treated for PTSD.* Paper presented at the annual meeting of the International Society of Traumatic Stress Studies, Boston.

Jennett, B., & Teasdale, G. (1981). *Management of head injuries.* Philadelphia: Davis.

Jones, F. D., & Johnson, A. W. (1975). Medical and psychiatric treatment policy and practice in Vietnam. *Journal of Social Issues, 31*, 49–65.

Jones, J. C., & Barlow, D. H. (1990). The etiology of post-traumatic stress disorder. *Clinical Psychology Review, 10*, 299–328.

Kardiner, A. (1941). *The traumatic neuroses of war.* New York: Hoeber.

Kardiner, A., & Spiegel, H. (1947). *War stress and neurotic illness.* New York: Hoeber.

Keane, T. M., Caddell, J. M., & Taylor, K. L. (1988). Mississippi Scale for Combat-Related Posttraumatic Stress Disorder: Three studies in reliability and validity. *Journal of Consulting and Clinical Psychology, 56*, 85–90.

Keane, T. M., Fairbank, J. A., Caddell, J. M., & Zimering, R. T. (1989). Implosive flooding therapy reduces symptoms of PTSD in Vietnam combat veterans. *Behavior Therapy, 20*, 245–260.

Keane, T. M., Gerardi, R. J., Lyons, J. A., & Wolfe, J. (1988). The interrelationship of substance abuse and posttraumatic stress disorder: Epidemiological and clinical considerations. In M. Galanter (Ed.), *Recent developments in alcoholism* (Vol. 6, pp. 27–48). New York: Plenum.

Keane, T. M., & Penk, W. (1988). The prevalence of post-traumatic stress disorder [Letter to the editor]. *New England Journal of Medicine, 318*, 1690–1691.

Keane, T. M., & Wolfe, J. (1990). Comorbidity in post-traumatic stress disorder: An analysis of community and clinical studies. *Journal of Applied Social Psychology, 20*, 1776–1788.

Keane, T. M., Wolfe, J., & Taylor, K. L. (1987). Post-traumatic stress disorder: Evidence for diagnostic validity and methods of psychological assessment. *Journal of Clinical Psychology, 43*, 32–43.

Keane, T. M., Zimering, R. T., & Caddell, R. T. (1985). A behavioral formulation of PTSD in Vietnam veterans. *The Behavior Therapist, 8*, 9–12.

Kenardy, J. A., Webster, R. A., Lewin, T. J., Carr, V. J., Hazell, P. L., & Carter, G. L. (1996). Stress debriefing and patterns of recovery following a natural disaster. *Journal of Traumatic Stress, 9*, 37–49.

Kendall-Tackett, K. A., Williams, L., & Finkelhor, D. (1993). Impact of sexual abuse on children: A review and synthesis of recent empirical studies. *Psychological Bulletin, 113*, 164–180.

Kihlstrom, J. F. (1997). Suffering from reminiscences: Exhumed memory, implicit memory, and the return of the repressed. In M. Conway (Ed.), *Recovered memories and false memories* (pp. 100–117) Oxford, England: Oxford University Press.

Kihlstrom, J. F., Glisky, M. L., & Angiulo, M. J. (1994). Dissociative tendencies and dissociative disorders. *Journal of Abnormal Psychology, 103*, 117–124.

Kilpatrick, D. G., & Calhoun, K. S. (1988). Early behavioral treatment for rape trauma: Efficacy or artifact? *Behavior Therapy, 19*, 421–427.

Kilpatrick, D. G., & Veronen, L. J. (1983). Treatment for rape-related problems: Crisis intervention is not enough. In L. H. Cohen, W. L. Claiborn, & C. A. Spector (Eds.), *Crisis intervention* (pp. 165–185). New York: Human Sciences Press.

Kilpatrick, D. G., Veronen, L. J., & Best, C. L. (1985). Factors predicting psychological distress among rape victims. In C. R. Figley (Ed.), *Trauma and its wake* (pp. 113–141). New York: Brunner/Mazel.

Kilpatrick, D. G., Veronen, L. J., & Resick, P. A. (1982). Psychological sequelae to rape: Assessment and treatment strategies. In D. M. Dolays & R. L. Meredith (Eds.), *Behavioral medicine: Assessment and treatment strategies* (pp. 473–497). New York: Plenum.

King, L. A., King, D. W., Fairbank, J. A., & Keane, T. M. (1998). Resilience–recovery factors in posttraumatic stress disorder among female and male Vietnam veterans: Hardiness, postwar social support, and additional stressful life events. *Journal of Personality and Social Psychology, 74*, 420–434.

Kinzie, D., Sack, W. H., Angell, R. H., Manson, S., & Rath, B. (1986). The psychiatric effects of massive trauma on Cambodian children: I. The children. *Journal of the American Academy of Child Psychiatry, 25*, 370–376.

Kluft, R. P. (1987). An update on multiple personality disorder. *Hospital and Community Psychiatry, 38*, 363–373.

Kolb, L. C. (1987). A neuropsychological hypothesis explaining post-traumatic stress disorder. *American Journal of Psychiatry, 144*, 989–995.

Koopman, C., Classen, C., Cardeña, E., & Spiegel, D. (1995). When disaster strikes, acute stress disorder may follow. *Journal of Traumatic Stress, 8*, 29–46.

Koopman, C., Classen, C., & Spiegel, D. (1994). Predictors of posttraumatic stress symptoms among survivors of the Oakland/Berkeley, Calif., firestorm. *American Journal of Psychiatry, 151,* 888–894.

Koopman, C., Classen, C., & Spiegel, D. (1996). Dissociative responses in the immediate aftermath of the Oakland/Berkeley firestorm. *Journal of Traumatic Stress, 9,* 521–540.

Koren, D., Arnon, I., & Klein, E. (1999). Acute stress response and posttraumatic stress disorder in traffic accident victims: A one-year prospective, follow-up study. *American Journal of Psychiatry, 156,* 374–378.

Kramer, T., Buckhout, R., & Eugenio, P. (1990). Weapon focus, arousal, and eyewitness memory: Attention must be paid. *Law and Human Behavior, 14,* 167–184.

Krystal, H. (1968). *Massive psychic trauma.* New York: International Universities Press.

Krystal, H. (1991). Integration and self-healing in post-traumatic stress: A ten-year retrospective. *American Imago, 48,* 93–118.

Krystal, J. H., Kosten, T. R., Southwick, S., Mason, J. W., Perry, B. D., & Giller, E. L. (1989). Neurobiological aspects of PTSD: Review of clinical and preclinical studies. *Behavior Therapy, 20,* 177–198.

Krystal, J. H., Southwick, S. M., & Charney, D. S. (1995). Post traumatic stress disorder: Psychobiological mechanisms of traumatic remembrance. In D. L. Schacter (Ed.), *Memory distortion: How minds, brains and societies construct the past* (pp. 150–172). Cambridge, MA: Harvard University Press.

Kulka, R. A., Schlenger, W. E., Fairbank, J. A., Hough, R. L., Jordan, B. K., Marmar, C. R., & Weiss, D. S. (1990). *Trauma and the Vietnam War generation: Report of findings from the National Vietnam Veterans Readjustment Study.* New York: Brunner/Mazel.

Lahz, S., & Bryant, R. A. (1996). Incidence of chronic pain following traumatic brain injury. *Archives of Physical Medicine and Rehabilitation, 77,* 889–891.

Lang, P. J. (1977). Imagery in therapy: An information processing analysis of fear. *Behavior Therapy, 8,* 862–886.

Lang, P. J. (1979). A bioinformational theory of emotional imagery. *Psychophysiology, 16,* 495–512.

Lee, C., Slade, P., & Lygo, V. (1996). The influence of psychological debriefing on emotional adaptation in females following early miscarriage. *British Journal of Medical Psychology, 69,* 47–58.

Lee, E., & Lu, F. (1989). Assessment and treatment of Asian-American survivors of mass violence. *Journal of Traumatic Stress, 2,* 93–120.

Levin, H. S., Gary, H. E., High, W. M., Mattis, S., Ruff, R. M., Eisenberg, H. M., Marshall, L. F., & Tabaddor, K. (1987). Minor head injury and the postconcussive syndrome: Methodological issues in outcome studies. In H. S. Levin, J. Grafman, & H. M. Eisenberg (Eds.), *Neurobehavioral recovery from head injury* (pp. 262–275). New York: Oxford University Press.

Lewis, K. (1978). On reducing the child snatching syndrome. *Children Today, 7,* 19–35.

Lieberman, M. A. (1982). The effects of social support on responses to stress. In L. Goldberger & L. Brenitz (Eds.), *Handbook of stress* (pp. 764–783). New York: Free Press.

Lindemann, E. (1944). Symptomatology and management of acute grief. *American Journal of Psychiatry, 101,* 141–148.

Lishman, W. A. (1988). Physiogenesis and psychogenesis in the "post concussional syndrome." *British Journal of Psychiatry, 153,* 460–469.

Litz, B. T., & Keane, T. M. (1989). Information processing in anxiety disorders: Application to the understanding of post-traumatic stress disorder. *Clinical Psychology Review, 9,* 243–257.

Lohr, J. M., Kleinknecht, R. A., Tolin, D. F., & Barrett, R. H. (1996). The clinical status of the clinical application of eye movement desensitization and reprocessing (EMDR). *Journal of Behavior Therapy and Experimental Psychiatry, 26,* 285–302.

Lohr, J. M., Lilienfeld, S. O., Tolin, D. F., & Herbert, J. D. (1999). Eye movement desensitization and reprocessing: An analysis of specific versus nonspecific treatment factors. *Journal of Anxiety Disorders, 13,* 185–207.

Ludwig, A. M. (1983). The psychobiological functions of dissociation. *American Journal of Clinical Hypnosis, 26,* 93–99.

Lynn, S. J., Lock, T. G., Myers, B., & Payne, D. G. (1997). Recalling the unrecallable: Should hypnosis be used to recover memories in psychotherapy? *Current Directions in Psychological Science, 6,* 79–83.

Lynn, S. J., & McConkey, K. M. (1997). *Truth in memory.* New York: Guilford Press.

Maas, A., & Kohnken, G. (1989). Eyewitness identification. *Law and Human Behaviour, 11,* 397–408.

Manson, S. M. (1997). Cross-cultural and multiethnic assessment of trauma. In J. P. Wilson & T. M. Keane (Eds.), *Assessing psychological trauma and PTSD* (pp. 239–266). New York: Guilford Press.

March, J. S. (1993). The stressor criterion in DSM–IV posttraumatic stress disorder. In J. R. Davidson & E. B. Foa (Eds.), *Posttraumatic stress disorder in review: Recent research and future developments* (pp. 37–54). Washington, DC: American Psychiatric Press.

Marks, I. M. (1987). *Fears, phobias, and rituals: Panic, anxiety, and their disorders.* Oxford, England: Oxford University Press.

Marks, I. M., Lovell, K., Norshirvani, H., Livanou, M., & Thrasher, S. (1998). Treatment of posttraumatic stress disorder by exposure and/or cognitive restructuring: A controlled study. *Archives of General Psychiatry, 55,* 317–325.

Marmor, C. R. (1997). Trauma and dissociation. *PTSD Research Quarterly, 8,* 1–8.

Marmor, C. R., Weiss, D. S., Metzler, T. J., & Delucchi, K. (1996). Characteristics of emergency services personnel related to peritraumatic dissociation during critical incident exposure. *American Journal of Psychiatry, 153* (Festschrift supplement), 94–102.

Marmor, C. R., Weiss, D. S., Schlenger, W. E., Fairbank, J. A., Jordan, K., Kulka, R. A., & Hough, R. L. (1994). Peritraumatic dissociation and posttraumatic stress in male Vietnam theater veterans. *American Journal of Psychiatry, 151,* 902–907.

Mayor, R., Bryant, B., & Duthie, R. (1993). Psychiatric consequences of road accidents. *British Medical Journal, 307,* 647–651.

McCann, I. L., & Pearlman, L. A. (1990). *Psychological trauma and the adult survivor: Theory, therapy, and transformation.* New York: Brunner/Mazel.

McCarroll, J. E., Ursano, R. J., Fullerton, C. S., & Lundy, A. C. (1995). Anticipatory stress of handling human remains from the Persian Gulf War: Predictors of intrusion and avoidance. *Journal of Nervous and Mental Disease, 183,* 700–705.

McCarroll, J. E., Ursano, R. J., Ventis, W. L., Fullerton, C. S., Oates, G. L., Friedman, H., Shean, G. L., & Wright, K. M. (1993). Anticipation of handling the dead: Effects of gender and experience. *British Journal of Clinical Psychology, 32,* 466–468.

McConkey, K. M., & Sheehan, P. W. (1995). *Hypnosis, memory, and behavior in criminal investigation.* New York: Guilford Press.

McFarlane, A. C. (1986). Posttraumatic morbidity of a disaster. *Journal of Nervous and Mental Disease, 174,* 4–14.

McFarlane, A. C. (1987). Posttraumatic phenomena in a longitudinal study of children following a natural disaster. *Journal of the American Academy of Child and Adolescent Psychiatry, 26,* 794–796.

McFarlane, A. C. (1988a). The longitudinal course of posttraumatic morbidity: The range of outcomes and predictors. *Journal of Nervous and Mental Disease, 176,* 30–39.

McFarlane, A. C. (1988b). Relationship between psychiatric impairment and a natural disaster: The role of distress. *Psychological Medicine, 18,* 129–139.

McFarlane, A. C. (1992a). Avoidance and intrusion in posttraumatic stress disorder. *Journal of Nervous and Mental Disease, 180,* 439–445.

McFarlane, A. C. (1992b). Commentary: Posttraumatic stress disorder among injured survivors of a terrorist attack. Predictive value of early intrusive and avoidance symptoms. *Journal of Nervous and Mental Disease, 180,* 599–560.

McFarlane, A. C. (in press). Attitudes to victims: Issues for medicine, the law, and society. In C. Sumner, M. Israel, M. O'Connor, & R. Snare (Eds.), *International victimology: Selected papers from the 8th International Symposium on Victimology.* Canberra: Australian Institute of Criminology.

McFarlane, A. C., Atchison, M., & Yehuda, R. (1997). The acute stress response following motor vehicle accidents and its relation to PTSD. In R. Yehuda & A. C. McFarlane (Eds.), *Psychobiology of posttraumatic stress disorder* (pp. 433–436). New York: New York Academy of Sciences.

McMillan, T. M. (1991). Posttraumatic stress disorder and severe head injury. *British Journal of Psychiatry, 159,* 431–433.

McNally, R. J. (1999). Research on eye movement desensitization and reprocessing (EMDR) as a treatment for PTSD? *PTSD Research Quarterly, 10,* 1–7.

McNally, R. J., Amir, N., & Lipke, H. J. (1996). Subliminal processing of threat cues in posttraumatic stress disorder? *Journal of Anxiety Disorders, 10,* 115–128.

McNally, R. J., English, G. E., & Lipke, H. J. (1993). Assessment of intrusive cognition in PTSD: Use of the modified Stroop paradigm. *Journal of Traumatic Stress, 6,* 33–41.

McNally, R. J., & Foa, E. B. (1987). Cognition and agoraphobia: Bias in the interpretation of threat. *Cognitive Therapy and Research, 11,* 567–581.

McNally, R. J., Kaspi, S. P., Riemann, B. C., & Zeitlin, S. B. (1990). Selective processing of threat cues in posttraumatic stress disorder. *Journal of Abnormal Psychology, 99,* 396–402.

Meichenbaum, D. (1974). *Cognitive behavior modification.* Morristown, NJ: General Learning Press.

Meichenbaum, D. (1975). Self-instructional methods. In F. H. Kanfer & A. P. Goldstein (Eds.), *Helping people change* (pp. 357–391). New York: Pergamon Press.

Middelboe, T., Anderson, H. S., Birket-Smith, M., & Friis, M. L. (1992). Minor head injury: Impact on general health after 1 year. A prospective follow-up study. *Acta Neurologica Scandinavica, 85,* 5–9.

Mikulincer, M., & Solomon, Z. (1988). Attributional style and combat-related posttraumatic stress disorder. *Journal of Abnormal Psychology, 97,* 308–313.

Milgram, N. A. (1998). Children under stress. In T. H. Ollendick & M. Hersen (Eds.), *Handbook of child psychopathology* (3rd ed., pp. 505–533). New York: Plenum.

Milgram, N. A., Toubania, Y. H., Klingman, A., Raviv, A., & Goldstein, I. (1988). Situational exposure and personal loss in children's acute and chronic stress reactions to a school bus disaster. *Journal of Traumatic Stress, 1,* 339–352.

Mitchell, J. (1982). The psychological impact of the Air Florida 90 disaster on fire rescue, paramedic, and police officer personnel. In R. A. Cowley (Ed.), *Mass casualties: A lesson learned approach, accidents, civil disorders, natural disasters, terrorism* (DOT Publication No. HS806302, pp. 239–244). Washington, DC: U.S. Department of Transportation.

Mitchell, J. (1983). When disaster strikes . . . The critical incident stress debriefing process. *Journal of Emergency Medical Services, 8,* 36–39.

Mitchell, J., & Bray, G. (1990). *Emergency services stress.* Englewood Cliffs, NJ: Prentice-Hall.

Mitchell, J. T., & Dyregrov, A. (1993). Traumatic stress in disaster workers and emergency personnel. In J. P. Wilson & B. Raphael (Eds.), *International handbook of traumatic stress syndromes* (pp. 905–914). New York: Plenum.

Morgan, A. H., & Hilgard, J. R. (1978–1979). The Stanford Hypnotic Clinical Scale for adults. *American Journal of Clinical Hypnosis, 21*(Suppl. 3), 1134–147.

Morgan, I. A., Matthews, G., & Winton, M. (1995). Coping and personality as predictors of post-traumatic intrusions, numbing, avoidance and general distress: A study of victims of the Perth flood. *Behavioural and Cognitive Psychotherapy, 23*, 251–264.

Mott, F. W. (1919). *War neuroses and shell shock*. London: Oxford Medical Publications.

Mulder, R. T., Beautrais, A. L., Joyce, P. R., & Fergusson, D. M. (1998). Relationship between dissociation, childhood sexual abuse, childhood physical abuse, and mental illness in a general population sample. *American Journal of Psychiatry, 155*, 806–811.

Myers, D. G. (1989). Mental health and disaster, preventive approaches to intervention. In R. Gist & B. Lubin (Eds.), *Psychological aspects of disaster* (pp. 190–228). New York: Wiley.

Nader, K. O. (1997). Assessing traumatic experiences in children. In J. P. Wilson & T. M. Keane (Eds.), *Assessing psychological trauma and PTSD* (pp. 291–348). New York: Guilford Press.

Nader, K., Pynoos, R.S., Fairbanks, L., & Frederick, C. (1990). Childhood PTSD reactions one year after a sniper attack. *American Journal of Psychiatry, 147*, 1526–1530.

Nash, M. R., Hulsey, T. L., Sexton, M. C., Harralson, T. I., & Lambert, W. (1993). Long-term sequelae of childhood sexual abuse: Perceived family environment, psychopathology, and dissociation. *Journal of Consulting and Clinical Psychology, 61*, 276–283.

Nemiah, J. C. (1989). Janet redivivus [Editorial]. *American Journal of Psychiatry, 146*, 1527–1529.

Newman, E., Kaloupek, D. G., & Keane, T. M. (1996). Assessment of posttraumatic stress disorder in clinical and research settings. In B. A. van der Kolk, A. C. McFarlane, & L. Weisaeth (Eds.), *Traumatic stress: The effects of overwhelming experience on mind, body, and society* (pp. 242–275). New York: Guilford Press.

Nezu, A. M., & Carnevale, G. J. (1987). Interpersonal problem solving and coping reactions of Vietnam veterans with posttraumatic stress disorder. *Journal of Abnormal Psychology, 96*, 155–157.

Nishith, P., Hearst, D. E., Mueser, K. T., & Foa, E. B. (1995). PTSD and major depression: Methodological and treatment considerations in a single case design. *Behavior Therapy, 26*, 319–335.

Norris, F. H., & Murrell, S. A. (1988). Prior experience as a moderator of disaster impact on anxiety symptoms in older adults. *American Journal of Community Psychology, 16*, 665–683.

Norris, F. H., & Perilla, N. (1996). Reliability, validity, and cross-language stability of the Revised Civilian Mississippi Scale for PTSD. *Journal of Traumatic Stress, 9*, 285–298.

North, C. S., Smith, E. M., & Spitznagel, E. L. (1994). Post-traumatic stress disorder in survivors of a mass shooting. *American Journal of Psychiatry, 151,* 82–88.

Norton, G. R., Ross, C. A., & Novotny, M. F. (1990). Factors that predict scores on the Dissociative Experiences Scale. *Journal of Clinical Psychology, 46,* 273–277.

O'Brien, L. S., & Hughes, S. J. (1991). Symptoms of post-traumatic stress disorder in Falklands veterans five years after the conflict. *British Journal of Psychiatry, 159,* 135–141.

Ohry, A., Solomon, Z., & Rattock, J. (1996). Post traumatic stress disorder in traumatic brain injury. *Brain Injury, 10,* 687–695.

Ollendick, T. H., Yule, W., & Ollier, K. (1991). Fears in British children and their relationship to manifest anxiety and depression. *Journal of Child Psychology and Psychiatry, 32,* 321–331.

Oppenheim, H. (1889). *Die traumatische Neurosen* [The traumatic neuroses]. Berlin: Hirschwald.

Orr, S. P., Claiborn, J. M., Altman, B., Forgue, D. F., de Jong, J. B., Pitman, R. K., & Herz, L. R. (1990). Psychometric profile of posttraumatic stress disorder, anxiety, and healthy Vietnam veterans: Correlations with psychophysiologic responses. *Journal of Consulting and Clinical Psychology, 58,* 329–335.

Orr, S. P., & Kaloupek, D. G. (1997). Psychophysiological assessment of posttraumatic stress disorder. In J. P. Wilson & T. M. Keane (Eds.), *Assessing psychological trauma and PTSD* (pp. 69–97). New York: Guilford Press.

Orr, S. P., & Pitman, R. K. (1993). Psychophysiologic assessment of attempts to simulate posttraumatic stress disorder. *Biological Psychiatry, 33,* 127–129.

Öst, L. G. (1987). Applied relaxation: Description of a coping technique and review of controlled studies. *Behaviour Research and Therapy, 25,* 397–409.

Page, H. (1895). Injuries of the spine and spinal cord without apparent mechanical lesion. In M. R. Trimble (Ed.), *Posttraumatic neurosis: From railroad spine to whiplash* (p. 29). London: J. Churchill.

Pallak, M. S., Pittman, T. S., Heller, J. F., & Munson, P. (1975). The effect of arousal on Stroop color–word task. *Bulletin of the Psychonomic Society, 6,* 248–250.

Parkinson, L., & Rachman, S. J. (1981). The nature of intrusive thoughts. *Advances in Behavior Research and Therapy, 3,* 101–110.

Patterson, D. R., Carrigan, L., Questad, K. A., & Robinson, R. (1990). Posttraumatic stress disorder in hospitalized patients with burn injuries. *Journal of Burn Care and Rehabilitation, 11,* 181–184.

Peniston, E. G. (1986). EMG biofeedback-assisted desensitization treatment for Vietnam combat veterans with post-traumatic stress disorder. *Clinical Biofeedback and Health, 9,* 35–41.

Perconte, S. T., & Goreczeny, A. J. (1990). Failure to detect fabricated posttraumatic stress disorder with the use of the MMPI in a clinical population. *American Journal of Psychiatry, 147,* 1057–1060.

Perry, S., Difede, J., Musngi, G., Frances, A. J., & Jacobsberg, L. (1992). Predictors of posttraumatic stress disorder after burn injury. *American Journal of Psychiatry, 149*, 931–935.

Piccione, C., Hilgard, E. R., & Zimbardo, P. G. (1989). On the degree of stability of measured hypnotizability over a 25-year period. *Journal of Personality and Social Psychology, 56*, 289–295.

Pincus, H. A., Frances, A., Davis, W. W., First, M. B., & Widiger, T. A. (1992). DSM–IV and new diagnostic categories: Holding the line on proliferation. *American Journal of Psychiatry, 149*, 112–117.

Pitman, R. K. (1993). Biological findings in posttraumatic stress disorder: Implications for *DSM–IV* classification. In J. R. T. Davidson & E. B. Foa (Eds.), *Posttraumatic stress disorder: DSM–IV and beyond* (pp. 173–190). Washington, DC: American Psychiatric Press.

Pitman, R. K., Altman, B., Greenwald, E., Longpre, R. E., Macklin, M. L., Poiré, R. E., & Steketee, G. S. (1991). Psychiatric complications during flooding therapy for posttraumatic stress disorder. *Journal of Clinical Psychiatry, 52*, 17–20.

Pitman, R. K., & Orr, S. P. (1993). Psychophysiologic testing for post-traumatic stress disorder: Forensic psychiatric application. *Bulletin of the American Academy of Psychiatry and the Law, 21*, 37–52.

Pitman, R. K., Orr, S. P., Altman, B., Longpre, R. E., Poiré, R. E., & Macklin, M. I. (1996). Emotional processing during eye movement desensitization and reprocessing therapy of Vietnam veterans with chronic posttraumatic stress disorder. *Comprehensive Psychiatry, 37*, 419–429.

Pitman, R. K., Orr, S. P., Forgue, D. F., de Jong, J. B., & Claiborn, J. M. (1987). Psychophysiologic assessment of post-traumatic stress disorder imagery in Vietnam combat veterans. *Archives of General Psychiatry, 44*, 970–975.

Pitman, R. K., Sparr, L. F., Saunders, L. S., & McFarlane, A. C. (1996). Legal issues in posttraumatic stress disorder. In B. A. van der Kolk, A. C. McFarlane, & L. Weisaeth (Eds.), *Traumatic stress: The effects of overwhelming experience on mind, body, and society* (pp. 378–397). New York: Guilford Press.

Plutchik, R. (1989). Measuring emotions and their derivatives. In R. Plutchik & H. Kellerman (Eds.), *The measurement of emotions* (pp. 1–35). New York: Academic Press.

Poole, D. A., Lindsay, D. S., Memon, A., & Bull, R. (1995). Psychotherapy and the recovery of memories of childhood sexual abuse: U.S. and British practitioners' opinions, practices, and experiences. *Journal of Consulting and Clinical Psychology, 63*, 426–437.

Pope, H. G., Jr., Oliva, P. S., & Hudson, J. I. (in press). Repressed memories: The scientific status. In D. L. Faigman, D. H. Kaye, M. J. Saks, & J. Sanders (Eds.), *Modern scientific evidence: The law and science of expert testimony* (Rev. ed.). St. Paul, MN: West.

Prince, M. (1978). *The dissociation of a personality.* New York: Oxford University Press. (Original work published 1905)

Putnam, F. W. (1989). Pierre Janet and modern views of dissociation. *Journal of Traumatic Stress, 2*, 413–429.

Putnam, F. W., Guroff, J. J., Silberman, E. K., Baraban, L., & Post, R. M. (1986). The clinical phenomenology of multiple personality disorder: A review of 100 recent cases. *Journal of Clinical Psychiatry, 47*, 285–293.

Pynoos, R. S., & Eth, S. (1986). Witness to violence: The child interview. *Journal of the American Academy of Child and Adolescent Psychiatry, 25*, 306–319.

Pynoos, R. S., Frederick, C., Nader, K., Arroyo, W., Steinberg, A., Eth, S., Nunez, F., & Fairbanks, L. (1987). Life threat and posttraumatic stress in school-age children. *Archives of General Psychiatry, 44*, 1057–1063.

Pynoos, R. S., & Nader, K. (1993). Issues in the treatment of posttraumatic stress disorder in children and adolescents. In S. Goldston, J. Yager, C. Heinicke, & R. S. Pynoos (Eds.), *Preventing mental health disturbances in children* (pp. 211–233). Washington, DC: American Psychiatric Press.

Quarantelli, E. L. (1985). An assessment of conflicting views on mental health: The consequences of traumatic events. In C. R. Figley (Ed.), *Trauma and its wake* (pp. 173–215). New York: Brunner/Mazel.

Rachman, S. J., & de Silva, P. (1978). Abnormal and normal obsessions. *Behaviour Research and Therapy, 16*, 101–110.

Raphael, B. (1986). *When disaster strikes: How individuals and communities cope with catastrophe*. New York: Basic Books.

Raphael, B., & Martinek, N. (1997). Assessing traumatic bereavement and post-traumatic stress disorder. In J. P. Wilson & T. M. Keane (Eds.), *Assessing psychological trauma and PTSD* (pp. 373–395). New York: Guilford Press.

Raphael, B., Meldrum, L., & McFarlane, A. C. (1995). Does debriefing after psychological trauma work? Time for randomised controlled trials. *British Medical Journal, 310*, 1479–1480.

Raphael, B., Wilson, J., Meldrum, L., & McFarlane, A. C. (1996). Acute preventive interventions. In B. A. van der Kolk, A. C. McFarlane, & L. Weisaeth (Eds.), *Traumatic stress: The effects of overwhelming experience on mind, body, and society* (pp. 463–479). New York: Guilford Press.

Renfrey, G., & Spates, C. R. (1994). Eye movement desensitization: A partial dismantling study. *Journal of Behavior Therapy and Experimental Psychiatry, 25*, 231–239.

Resick, P. A. (1988). *Reactions of female and male victims of rape or robbery* (Final report, NIJ Grant No. 85-IJ-CV-0042). Washington, DC: National Institute of Justice.

Resick, P. A., Jordan, C. G., Girelli, S. A., Hutter, C. K., & Marhoefer-Dvorak, S. (1988). A comparative outcome study of behavioral group therapy for sexual assault victims. *Behavior Therapy, 19*, 385–401.

Resick, P. A., Nishith, P., Weaver, T., & Astin, M. (1998, November). *Preliminary findings of a controlled trial comparing cognitive processing therapy and prolonged exposure*. Paper presented at the 14th Annual Meeting of the International Society of Traumatic Stress Studies, Washington DC.

Resick, P. A., & Schnicke, M. K. (1992a). Cognitive processing therapy for sexual assault victims. *Journal of Consulting and Clinical Psychology, 60,* 748–756.

Resick, P. A., & Schnicke, M. K. (1992b, November). *Cognitive processing therapy for sexual assault victims.* Paper presented at the 8th Annual Meeting of the International Society of Traumatic Stress Studies, Los Angeles.

Resick, P. A., & Schnicke, M. K. (1993). *Cognitive processing therapy for rape victims: A treatment manual.* London: Sage.

Resick, P. A., Schnicke, M. K., & Markway, B. G. (1991, November). *The relationship between cognitive content and posttraumatic stress disorder.* Paper presented at the Annual Meeting of the Association for Advancement of Behavior Therapy, New York.

Resnick, H., Yehuda, R., Pitman, R. K., & Foy, D. W. (1995). Effect of previous trauma on acute plasma cortisol level following rape. *American Journal of Psychiatry, 152,* 1675–1677.

Resnick, P. J. (1994). Malingering. In R. Rosner (Ed.), *Principles and practice of forensic psychiatry* (pp. 417–426). New York: Chapman & Hall.

Richards, D. A., Lovell, K., & Marks, I. M. (1994). Post-traumatic stress disorder: Evaluation of a behavioral treatment program. *Journal of Traumatic Stress, 7,* 669–680.

Riggs, D. S., Dancu, C. V., Gershuny, B. S., Greenberg, D., & Foa, E. B. (1992). Anger and post-traumatic stress disorder in female crime victims. *Journal of Traumatic Stress, 5,* 613–625.

Riggs, D. S., Rothbaum, B. O., & Foa, E. B. (1995). A prospective examination of symptoms of posttraumatic stress disorder in victims of nonsexual assault. *Journal of Interpersonal Violence, 10,* 201–213.

Rind, B., Tromovitch, P., & Bauserman, R. (1998). A meta-analytic examination of assumed properties of child sexual abuse using college samples. *Psychological Bulletin, 124,* 22–53.

Robins, E., & Guze, S. B. (1970). Establishment of diagnostic validity in psychiatric illness: Its application to schizophrenia. *American Journal of Psychiatry, 126,* 983–987.

Robins, L. N., & Helzer, J. E. (1985). *Diagnostic Interview Schedule* (Version III-A). St. Louis, MO: Washington University, Department of Psychiatry.

Robins, L. N., Helzer, J. E., Croughan, J. L., & Ratliff, K. S. (1981). National Institute of Mental Health Diagnostic Interview Schedule: Its history, characteristics, and validity. *Archives of General Psychiatry, 38,* 381–389.

Robins, L. N., & Smith, E. M. (1983). *Diagnostic Interview Schedule/Disaster Supplement.* St. Louis: Washington School of Medicine, Department of Psychiatry.

Robinson, R. C., & Mitchell, J. T. (1993). Evaluation of psychological debriefings. *Journal of Traumatic Stress, 6,* 367–382.

Rogers, R. (1997). *Clinical assessment of malingering and deception* (2nd ed.). New York: Guilford Press.

Rosen, G. M. (1999). Treatment fidelity and research on eye movement desensitization and reprocessing (EMDR). *Journal of Anxiety Disorders, 13,* 173–184.

Ross, C. A., Joshi, S., & Currie, R. (1991). Dissociative experiences in the general population: A factor analysis. *Hospital and Community Psychiatry, 42,* 297–301.

Rothbaum, B. O. (1997). A controlled study of eye movement desensitization and reprocessing in the treatment of posttraumatic stress disordered sexual assault victims. *Bulletin of the Menninger Clinic, 61,* 1–18.

Rothbaum, B. O., Foa, E. B., Riggs, D. S., Murdock, T., & Walsh, W. (1992). A prospective examination of post-traumatic stress disorder in rape victims. *Journal of Traumatic Stress, 5,* 455–475.

Rutherford, W. H. (1989). Postconcussive symptoms: Relationship to acute neurological indices, individual differences, and circumstances of injury. In H. S. Levin, J. Grafman, & H. M. Eisenberg (Eds.), *Neurobehavioral recovery from head injury* (pp. 217–228). New York: Oxford University Press.

Rychtarik, R. G., Silverman, W. K., Van Landingham, W. P., & Prue, D. M. (1984). Treatment of an incest victim with implosive therapy: A case study. *Behavior Therapy, 15,* 410–420.

Sack, W. H., Clarke, G., Him, G., Dickason, D., Goff, B., Lanham, K., & Kinzie, J. D. (1993). A six year follow-up of Cambodian adolescents. *Journal of American Academy of Child and Adolescent Psychiatry, 32,* 3–15.

Saigh, P. A. (1986). In vitro flooding in the treatment of a 6-year-old boy's post traumatic stress disorder. *Behavioral Research Therapy, 24,* 685–688.

Saigh, P. A. (1989). The development and validation of the Children's Posttraumatic Stress Disorder Inventory. *International Journal of Special Education, 4,* 75–84.

Salkovskis, P. M. (1991). The importance of behaviour in the maintenance of anxiety and panic: A cognitive account. *Cognitive and Behavioural Psychotherapy, 19,* 6–19.

Sandberg, D. A., & Lynn, S. J. (1992). Dissociative experiences, psychopathology and adjustment, and child and adolescent maltreatment in female college students. *Journal of Abnormal Psychology, 101,* 717–723.

Sanderson, A., & Carpenter, R. (1992). Eye movement desensitization versus image confrontation: A single-session crossover study of 58 phobic subjects. *Journal of Behavior Therapy and Experimental Psychiatry, 23,* 269–275.

Sarason, I. G., Johnson, J. H., Berberich, J. P., & Siegel, J. M. (1979). Helping police officers to cope with stress: A cognitive–behavioral approach. *American Journal of Community Psychiatry, 7,* 593–603.

Sbordone, R. J., & Liter, J. C. (1995). Mild traumatic brain injury does not produce post-traumatic stress disorder. *Brain Injury, 9,* 405–412.

Scheck, M. M., Schaeffer, J. A., & Gillette, C. (1998). Brief psychological intervention with traumatized young women: The efficacy of eye movement desensitization and reprocessing. *Journal of Traumatic Stress, 11,* 25–44.

Schwarz, E. D., & Kowalski, J. M. (1991a). Malignant memories: PTSD in children and adults after a school shooting. *Journal of the American Academy of Child and Adolescent Psychiatry, 30,* 936–944.

Schwarz, E. D., & Kowalski, J. M. (1991b). Posttraumatic stress disorder after a school shooting: Effects of symptom threshold selection and diagnosis by *DSM–III, DSM–III–R*, or proposed *DSM–IV. American Journal of Psychiatry, 148*, 592–597.

Schwarz, E. D., & Kowalski, J. M. (1992). Malignant memories: Reluctance to utilize health services after a disaster. *Journal of Nervous and Mental Disease, 180*, 767–772.

Sedgwick, R. (1975). Psychological responses to stress. *Journal of Psychiatric Nursing and Mental Health Services, 74*, 12–17.

Shalev, A. Y. (1992). Posttraumatic stress disorder among injured survivors of a terrorist attack: Predictive value of early intrusion and avoidance symptoms. *Journal of Nervous and Mental Disease, 180*, 505–509.

Shalev, A. Y. (in press). Historical concepts and present patterns: Stress management and debriefing. In J. P. Wilson & B. Raphael (Eds.), *Stress debriefing: Theory, practice and challenge*. Cambridge, England: Cambridge University Press.

Shalev, A. Y., Freedman, S., Peri, T., Brandes, D., Sahar, T., Orr, S. P., & Pitman, R. K. (1998). Prospective study of posttraumatic stress disorder and depression following trauma. *American Journal of Psychiatry, 155*, 630–637.

Shalev, A. Y., Orr, S. P., & Pitman, R. K. (1993). Psychophysiologic assessment of traumatic imagery in Israeli civilian patients with posttraumatic stress disorder. *American Journal of Psychiatry, 150*, 620–624.

Shalev, A. Y., Peri, T., Canetti, L., & Schreiber, S. (1996). Predictors of PTSD in injured trauma survivors: A prospective study. *American Journal of Psychiatry, 153*, 219–225.

Shalev, A. Y., Sahar, T., Freedman, S., Peri, T., Glick, N., Brandes, D., Orr, S. P., & Pitman, R. K. (1998). A prospective study of heart rate responses following trauma and the subsequent development of PTSD. *Archives of General Psychiatry, 55*, 553–559.

Shalev, A. Y., Schreiber, S., & Galai, T. (1993). Early psychological responses to traumatic injury. *Journal of Traumatic Stress, 6*, 441–450.

Shapiro, F. (1995). *Eye movement desensitization and reprocessing: Basic principles, protocols, and procedures*. New York: Guilford Press.

Shore, J. H., Vollmer, W. M., & Tatum, E. L. (1989). Community patterns of posttraumatic stress disorders. *Journal of Nervous and Mental Disease, 177*, 681–685.

Silva, C. E., & Kirsch, I. (1992). Interpretative sets, expectancy, fantasy proneness, and dissociation as predictors of hypnotic response. *Journal of Personality and Social Psychology, 63*, 847–856.

Singer, M. T., & Lalich, J. (1996). *"Crazy" therapies: What are they? Do they work?* San Francisco: Jossey-Bass.

Sivec, H. J., & Lynn, S. J. (1995). Dissociative and neuropsychological symptoms: The question of differential diagnosis. *Clinical Psychology Review, 15*, 297–316.

Sloan, P. (1988). Post-traumatic stress in survivors of an airplane crash-landing: A clinical and exploratory research intervention. *Journal of Traumatic Stress, 1*, 211–229.

Smith, K., & Bryant, R. A. (in press). The generality of cognitive bias in acute stress disorder. *Behaviour Research and Therapy*.

Snow, B. R., Stellman, J. M., Stellman, S. D., & Sommer, J. F. (1988). Post-traumatic stress disorder among American Legionnaires in relation to combat experience in Vietnam: Associated and contributing factors. *Environmental Research, 47*, 175–192.

Solomon, S. D., & Canino, G. J. (1990). Appropriateness of *DSM–III–R* criteria for posttraumatic stress disorder. *Comprehensive Psychiatry, 31*, 227–237.

Solomon, S. D., Gerrity, E. T., & Muff, A. M. (1992). Efficacy of treatments for posttraumatic stress disorder: An empirical review. *Journal of the American Medical Association, 268*, 633–638.

Solomon, Z. (1989). Untreated combat related PTSD—Why some Israeli veterans do not seek help. *Israeli Journal of Psychiatry and Related Sciences, 26*, 111–123.

Solomon, Z. (1993a). *Combat stress reaction: The enduring toll of war*. New York: Plenum.

Solomon, Z. (1993b). Immediate and long-term effects of traumatic combat stress among Israeli veterans of the Lebanon War. In J. P. Wilson & B. Raphael (Eds.), *International handbook of traumatic stress syndromes* (pp. 321–332). New York: Plenum.

Solomon, Z., & Benbenishty, R. (1986). The role of proximity, immediacy, and expectancy in frontline treatment of combat stress reaction among Israelis in the Lebanon War. *American Journal of Psychiatry, 143*, 613–617.

Solomon, Z., Laor, N., & McFarlane, A. C. (1996). Acute posttraumatic reactions in soldiers and civilians. In B. A. van der Kolk, A. C. McFarlane, & L. Weisaeth (Eds.), *Traumatic stress: The effects of overwhelming experience on mind, body, and society* (pp. 102–114). New York: Guilford Press.

Solomon, Z., Laor, N., Weiler, D., Muller, U. F., Hadar, O., Waysman, M., Koslowsky, M., Yakar, M. B., & Bleich, A. (1993). The psychological impact of the Gulf War: A study of acute stress in Israeli evacuees [Letter to the editor]. *Archives of General Psychiatry, 50*, 320–321.

Solomon, Z., & Mikulincer, M. (1992). Aftermaths of combat stress reactions: A three-year study. *British Journal of Clinical Psychology, 31*, 21–32.

Solomon, Z., Mikulincer, M., & Benbenishty, R. (1989). Combat stress reactions: Clinical manifestations and correlates. *Military Psychology, 1*, 35–47.

Solomon, Z., Mikulincer, M., & Flum, H. (1988). Negative life events, coping responses, and combat-related psychopathology: A prospective study. *Journal of Abnormal Psychology, 97*, 302–307.

Solomon, Z., Mikulincer, M., & Jakob, B. R. (1987). Exposure to recurrent combat stress: Combat stress reactions among Israeli soldiers in the Lebanon War. *Psychological Medicine, 17*, 433–440.

Solomon, Z., Shalev, A., Spiro, S. E., Dolev, A., Bleich, A., Waysman, M., & Cooper, S. (1992). Negative psychometric outcomes: Self-report measures and a follow-up telephone survey. *Journal of Traumatic Stress, 5*, 225–246.

Southwick, S. M., Morgan, C. A., Nicolaou, A. L., & Charney, D. S. (1997). Consistency of memory for combat-related traumatic events in veterans of Operation Desert Storm. *American Journal of Psychiatry, 154*, 173–177.

Southwick, S. M., Yehuda, R., & Giller, E. L. (1993). Personality disorders in treatment-seeking combat veterans with post-traumatic stress disorder. *American Journal of Psychiatry, 150*, 1020–1023.

Sparr, L. F., Reaves, M. E., & Atkinson, R. M. (1987). Military combat, posttraumatic stress disorder, and criminal behavior in Vietnam veterans. *Bulletin of the American Academy of Psychiatry and the Law, 15*, 141–162.

Speed, N., Engdahl, B., Schwartz, J., & Eberly, R. (1989). Posttraumatic stress disorder as a consequence of the POW experience. *Journal of Nervous and Mental Disease, 177*, 147–153.

Speir, D. E. (1989, June). Application and use of post-traumatic stress disorder as a defense to criminal conduct. *Army Lawyer*, pp. 17–22.

Spiegel, D. (1991). Dissociation and trauma. In A. Tasman & S. M. Goldfinger (Eds.), *American Psychiatric Press review of psychiatry* (Vol. 10, pp. 261–275). Washington, DC: American Psychiatric Press.

Spiegel, D. (1996). Dissociative disorders. In R. E. Hales & S. C. Yudofsky (Eds.), *Synopsis of psychiatry* (pp. 583–604). Washington, DC: American Psychiatric Press.

Spiegel, D., & Classen, C. (1995). Acute stress disorder. In G. O. Gabbard (Ed.), *Treatments of psychiatric disorders* (Vol. 2, pp. 1521–1535). Washington, DC: American Psychiatric Press.

Spiegel, D., Hunt, T., & Dondershine, H. E. (1988). Dissociation and hypnotizability in posttraumatic stress disorder. *American Journal of Psychiatry, 145*, 301–314.

Spiegel, D., Koopman, C., Cardeña, E., & Classen, C. (1996). Dissociative symptoms in the diagnosis of acute stress disorder. In L. K. Michelson & W. J. Ray (Eds.), *Handbook of dissociation: Theoretical, empirical, and clinical perspectives* (pp. 367–380). New York: Plenum.

Spiegel, D., Koopman, C., & Classen, C. (1994). Acute stress disorder and dissociation. *Australian Journal of Clinical and Experimental Hypnosis, 22*, 11–23.

Spiegel, H., & Spiegel, D. (1987). *Trance and treatment*. New York: Basic Books.

Spielberger, C. D., Gorsuch, R. L., Lushene, R., Vagg, P. R., & Jacobs, G. A. (1983). *Manual for the State–Trait Anxiety Inventory*. Palo Alto, CA: Consulting Psychologists Press.

Spitzer, R. L., Gibbon, M., & Williams, J. B. W. (1996). *Structured Clinical Interview for DSM–IV Axis I disorders*. New York: New York State Psychiatric Institute, Biometrics Research Department.

Stabb, J. P., Grieger, T. A., Fullerton, C. S., & Ursano, R. J. (1996). Acute stress disorder, subsequent posttraumatic stress disorder and depression after a series of typhoons. *Anxiety*, *2*, 219–225.

Stam, H. (1996). *Measurement of stress, trauma, and adaptation*. Lutherville, MD: Sidran Press.

Steinberg, M. (1993). *Structured clinical interview for DSM–IV dissociative disorders (SCID–D)*. Washington, DC: American Psychiatric Press.

Steinberg, M. (1995). *Handbook for the assessment of dissociation: A clinical guide*. Washington, DC: American Psychiatric Press.

Steinberg, M., Cicchetti, D. V., Buchanan, J., Hall, P. E., & Rounsaville, B. J. (1989–1992). *NIMH field trials of the Structured Clinical Interview for DSM–IV Dissociative Disorders (SCID–D)*. New Haven, CT: Yale University School of Medicine.

Stone, A. A. (1993). Post-traumatic stress disorder and the law: Critical review of the new frontier. *Bulletin of the American Academy of Psychiatry and the Law*, *21*, 23–36.

Stutman, R. K., & Bliss, E. L. (1985). Posttraumatic stress disorder, hypnotizability, and imagery. *American Journal of Psychiatry*, *142*, 741–743.

Tarrier, N., Pilgrim, H., Sommerfield, C., Faragher, B., Reynolds, M., Graham, E., & Barrowclough, C. (1999). A randomized trial of cognitive therapy and imaginal exposure in the treatment of chronic posttraumatic stress disorder. *Journal of Consulting and Clinical Psychology*, *67*, 13–18

Terr, L. C. (1979). Children of Chowchilla: A study of psychic trauma. *Psychoanalytic Study of the Child*, *34*, 547–621.

Terr, L. C. (1983). Chowchilla revisited: The effects of psychic trauma four years after a school bus kidnapping. *American Journal of Psychiatry*, *140*, 1543–1550.

Thrasher, S. M., Dalgleish, T., & Yule, W. (1994). Information processing in posttraumatic stress disorder. *Behaviour Research and Therapy*, *32*, 247–254.

Tillman, J. G., Nash, M. R., & Lerner, P. M. (1994). Does trauma cause dissociative pathology? In S. J. Lynn & J. W. Rhue (Eds.), *Dissociation: Clinical and theoretical perspectives* (pp. 395–413). New York: Guilford Press.

Titchener, J. T., & Kapp, F. T. (1976). Family and character change at Buffalo Creek. *American Journal of Psychiatry*, *133*, 295–299.

Tolin, D. F., Montgomery, M. S., Kleinknecht, R. A., & Lohr, J. M. (1996). An evaluation of eye movement desensitization and reprocessing (EMDR). *Innovations in Clinical Practice*, *14*, 423–437.

True, W. R., Rice, J., Eisen, S. A., Heath, A. C., Goldberg, J., Lyons, M. G., & Nowak, J. (1993). A twin study of genetic and environmental contributions to liability for posttraumatic stress symptoms. *Archives of General Psychiatry*, *50*, 257–264.

Turner, S. W., Thompson, J., & Rosser, R. M. (1993). The King's Cross fire: Early psychological response and implications for organizing a "phase-two" response. In J. P. Wilson & B. Raphael (Eds.), *International handbook of traumatic stress syndromes* (pp. 451–459). New York: Plenum.

Tyrer, P. (1989). Community psychiatry: Are we coping? [Letter]. *British Journal of Hospital Medicine, 42,* 426.

Ursano, R. J., Grieger, T. A., & McCarroll, J. E. (1996). Prevention of posttraumatic stress: Consultation, training, and early treatment. In B. A. van der Kolk, A. C. McFarlane, & L. Weisaeth (Eds.), *Traumatic stress: The effects of overwhelming experience on mind, body, and society* (pp. 441–462). New York: Guilford Press.

van der Kolk, B. A. (1996a). The psychobiology of PTSD. In B. A. van der Kolk, A. C. McFarlane, & L. Weisaeth (Eds.), *Traumatic stress: The effects of overwhelming experience on mind, body, and society* (pp. 214–241). New York: Guilford Press.

van der Kolk, B. A. (1996b). Trauma and memory. In B. A. van der Kolk, A. C. McFarlane, & L. Weisaeth (Eds.), *Traumatic stress: The effects of overwhelming experience on mind, body, and society* (pp. 279–301). New York: Guilford Press.

van der Kolk, B. A., Greenberg, M. S., Boyd, H., & Krystal, J. H. (1985). Inescapable shock, neurotransmitters and addiction to trauma: Towards a psychobiology of posttraumatic stress. *Biological Psychiatry, 20,* 314–325.

van der Kolk, B. A., Greenberg, M. S., Orr, S. P., & Pitman, R. K. (1989). Endogenous opioids and stress induced analgesia in posttraumatic stress disorder. *Psychopharmacology Bulletin, 25,* 108–112.

van der Kolk, B. A., & Saporta, J. (1993). Biological response to psychic trauma. In J. P. Wilson & B. Raphael (Eds.), *International handbook of traumatic stress syndromes* (pp. 25–33). New York: Plenum.

van der Kolk, B. A., & van der Hart, O. (1989). Pierre Janet and the breakdown of adaptation in psychological trauma. *American Journal of Psychiatry, 146,* 1530–1540.

van der Kolk, B. A., & van der Hart, O. (1991). The intrusive past: The flexibility of memory and the engraving of trauma. *American Imago, 48,* 425–454.

van der Kolk, B. A., Weisaeth, L., & van der Hart, O. (1996). History of trauma in psychiatry. In B. A. van der Kolk, A. C. McFarlane, & L. Weisaeth (Eds.), *Traumatic stress: The effects of overwhelming experience on mind, body, and society* (pp. 47–74). New York: Guilford Press.

Vaughan, K., & Tarrier, N. (1992). The use of image habituation training with posttraumatic stress disorders. *British Journal of Psychiatry, 161,* 658–664.

Veronen, L. J., & Kilpatrick, D. G. (1982, August). *A brief behavioral intervention procedure for rape victims.* Paper presented at the 90th Annual Convention of the American Psychological Association, Washington, DC.

Veronen, L. J., & Kilpatrick, D. G. (1983). Stress management for rape victims. In D. Meichenbaum & M. E. Jaremko (Eds.), *Stress reduction and prevention* (pp. 341–374). New York: Plenum.

Vrana, S., & Lauterbach, D. (1994). Prevalence of traumatic events and posttraumatic psychological symptoms in a nonclinical sample of college students. *Journal of Traumatic Stress, 7,* 289–302.

Vreven, D., Gudanowski, D., King, L., & King, D. (1995). The Civilian Version of the Mississippi PTSD Scale: A psychometric evaluation. *Journal of Traumatic Stress, 8,* 91–110.

Wagenaar, W. A., & Groeneweg, J. (1990). The memory of concentration camp survivors. *Applied Cognitive Psychology, 4,* 77–87.

Wakefield, J. C. (1996). DSM–IV: Are we making diagnostic progress? *Contemporary Psychology, 41,* 646–652.

Waller, N. G., Putnam, F. W., & Carlson, E. B. (1996). Types of dissociation and dissociative types: A taxometric analysis of dissociative experiences. *Psychological Methods, 1,* 300–321.

Warda, G., & Bryant, R. A. (1998a). Cognitive bias in acute stress disorder. *Behaviour Research and Therapy, 36,* 1177–1183.

Warda, G., & Bryant, R. A. (1998b). Thought control strategies in acute stress disorder. *Behaviour Research and Therapy, 36,* 1171–1175.

Waterman, J. (1993). Mediators of effects on children: What enhances optimal functioning and promotes healing? In J. Waterman, R. J. Kelly, J. McCord, & M. K. Oliveri (Eds.), *Behind the playground walls: Sexual abuse in preschools* (pp. 222–239). New York: Guilford Press.

Watson, C. G., Juba, M. P., Manifold, V., Kucala, T., & Anderson, P. E. D. (1991). The PTSD interview: Rationale, description, reliability, and concurrent validity of a DSM–III–based technique. *Journal of Clinical Psychology, 47,* 179–188.

Weathers, F. W. (1993). *Empirically derived scoring rules for the Clinician-Administered PTSD Scale.* Unpublished manuscript.

Weathers, F. W., Blake, D. D., Krinsley, K. E., Haddad, W., Huska, J. A., & Keane, T. M. (1992, November). *The Clinician Administered PTSD Scale: Reliability and construct validity.* Paper presented at the 26th Annual Meeting of Association for Advancement of Behavior Therapy, Boston.

Weisaeth, L. (1989a). The stressors and the post-traumatic stress syndrome after an industrial disaster. *Acta Psychiatrica Scandinavica, 80*(Suppl. 355), 25–37.

Weisaeth, L. (1989b). A study of behavioral responses to an industrial disaster. *Acta Psychiatrica Scandinavica, 80*(Suppl. 355), 13–24.

Weisaeth, L. (1995). Risk and preventive intervention. In B. Raphael & E. Burrows (Eds.), *Handbook of preventive psychiatry* (pp. 301–322). Amsterdam: Elsevier.

Weisenberg, M., Schwarzwald, J., Waysman, M., Solomon, Z., & Klingman, A. (1993). Coping of school-age children in the sealed room during Scud missile bombardment and postwar stress reactions. *Journal of Consulting and Clinical Psychology, 61,* 462–467.

Weiss, D. S., & Marmar, C. R. (1997). The Impact of Event Scale—Revised. In J. P. Wilson & T. M. Keane (Eds.), *Assessing psychological trauma and PTSD* (pp. 399–411). New York: Guilford Press.

Weiss, D. S., Marmar, C. R., Metzler, T. J., & Ronfeldt, H. M. (1995). Predicting symptomatic distress in emergency services personnel. *Journal of Consulting and Clinical Psychology, 63,* 361–368.

Wells, A., & Davies, M. (1994). The Thought Control Questionnaire: A measure of individual differences in the control of unwanted thoughts. *Behaviour Research and Therapy, 32,* 871–878.

Wessely, S., Rose, S., & Bisson, J. (1997). A systematic review of brief psychological interventions ('debriefing') for treatment of immediate trauma-related symptoms and the prevention of posttraumatic stress disorder. [CD ROM] *The Cochrane Library.* Oxford, England: Update Software Inc.

Wilkinson, C. B., & Vera, E. (1985). The management and treatment of disaster victims. *Psychiatric Annals, 15,* 174–184.

Williams, J. M. G. (1996). Depression and the specificity of autobiographical memory. In D. C. Rubin (Ed.), *Remembering our past: Studies in autobiographical memory* (pp. 244–267). Cambridge, England: Cambridge University Press.

Wilson, D. L., Silver, S. M., Covi, W. G., & Foster, S. (1996). Eye movement desensitization and reprocessing: Effectiveness and autonomic correlates. *Journal of Behavior Therapy and Experimental Psychiatry, 27,* 219–229.

Wilson, J. P. (1989). *Trauma, transformation, and healing: An integrative approach to theory, research, and post-traumatic therapy.* New York: Brunner/Mazel.

Wilson, P. H. (1992). *Principles and practice of relapse prevention.* New York: Guilford Press.

Wilson, S. A., Becker, L. A., & Tinker, R. H. (1995). Eye movement desensitization and reprocessing (EMDR) treatment for psychologically traumatized individuals. *Journal of Consulting and Clinical Psychology, 63,* 928–937.

Wilson, S. A., Becker, L. A., & Tinker, R. H. (1997). Fifteen-month follow-up of eye movement desensitization and reprocessing (EMDR) treatment of posttraumatic stress disorder and psychological trauma. *Journal of Consulting and Clinical Psychology, 65,* 1047–1056.

Wolfe, V. V., Gentile, C., & Wolfe, D. A. (1989). The impact of sexual abuse on children: A PTSD formulation. *Behavior Therapy, 20,* 215–228.

Wolpe, J. (1958). *Psychotherapy by reciprocal inhibition.* Stanford, CA: Stanford University Press.

World Health Organization. (1948). *International statistical classification of diseases, injuries, and causes of death* (6th ed., rev.). Geneva, Switzerland: Author.

World Health Organization. (1969). *Manual of the international statistical classification of diseases, injuries, and causes of death.* (8th ed., rev.). Geneva, Switzerland: Author.

World Health Organization. (1977). *International statistical classification of diseases, injuries, and causes of death.* (9th ed., rev.). Geneva, Switzerland: Author.

World Health Organization. (1992). *International classification of diseases and related health problems* (10th ed., rev.). Geneva, Switzerland: Author.

Yassen, J., & Glass, L. (1984). Sexual assault survivors groups: A feminist practice perspective. *Social Work, 3,* 252–257.

Yehuda, R. (1997). Sensitization of the hypothalamic–pituitary–adrenal axis in posttraumatic stress disorder. In R. Yehuda & A. C. McFarlane (Eds.), *Psy-*

chobiology of posttraumatic stress disorder (pp. 57–75). New York: New York Academy of Sciences.

Yule, W. (1992). Post-traumatic stress disorder in child survivors of shipping disasters: The sinking of the 'Jupiter.' *Psychotherapy and Psychosomatics, 57,* 200–205.

Yule, W., & Udwin, O. (1991). Screening child survivors for post traumatic stress disorders: Experiences from the 'Jupiter' sinking. *British Journal of Clinical Psychology, 30,* 131–138.

Zatzick, D. F., Marmar, C. R., Weiss, D. S., & Metzler, T. (1994). Does trauma-linked dissociation vary across ethnic groups? *Journal of Nervous Mental Disease, 182,* 576–582.

Zilberg, N. J., Weiss, D. S., & Horowitz, M. J. (1982). The Impact of Event Scale: A cross-validation study and some empirical evidence supporting a conceptual model of stress response syndromes. *Journal of Consulting and Clinical Psychology, 50,* 407–414.

Zuckerman, M., & Spielberger, C. D. (1976). *Emotions and anxiety.* New York: Wiley.

AUTHOR INDEX

233

Pynoos, R. S., 158, 159, 160

Quarantelli, E. L., 168
Questad, K. A., 21

Rachman, S. J., 46, 47
Rapee, R. M., 16, 81
Raphael, B., 57, 138, 154, 155, 163, 164, 165, 170
Rath, B., 157–58
Ratliff, K. S., 65
Rattock, J., 150
Raviv, A., 159
Reaves, M. E., 177
Reich, W., 159
Renfrey, G., 81
Resick, P. A., 37, 46, 70, 79, 80, 82, 141, 145
Resnick, H., 37
Resnick, P. J., 176
Richards, D. A., 78
Riemann, B. C., 16
Riggs, D., 23
Riggs, D. S., 20, 21, 24, 28, 30, 40, 78, 79, 85, 137, 138, 149
Rind, B., 12
Robins, E., 49, 50
Robins, L. N., 21, 44, 65
Robinson, R., 21
Robinson, R. C., 168
Rogers, R., 183
Roitblat, H. L., 15
Ronfeldt, H. M., 45
Rose, S., 23, 29, 36, 170
Rosen, G. M., 80
Rosenheck, R., 66
Ross, C. A., 25, 45
Rosser, R. M., 168
Rosser-Hogan, R., 12
Rothbaum, B. O., 11, 20, 21, 23, 26, 28, 40, 48, 75, 78, 79, 80, 81, 82, 85, 110, 141, 149, 166
Rounsaville, B. J., 61
Rush, A. J., 101
Rusnak, K., 80
Rutherford, W. H., 153
Rutter, M., 157
Ryan, J. J., 154

Rychtarik, R. G., 145

Sack, W. H., 157–58, 159
Sackville, T., 23, 24, 40, 59, 84, 85, 141, 169, 171, 176
Sahar, T., 36, 70, 82, 93
Saigh, P. A., 159, 160
Salkovskis, P. M., 55
Sandberg, D. A., 25, 67
Sanderson, A., 81
Saporta, J., 11
Sarason, I. G., 167
Saunders, L. S., 175
Saunders, W. B., 25
Sauzier, M., 161
Sbordone, R. J., 150
Schaeffer, J. A., 80
Scheck, M. M., 80
Schlenger, W. E., 141
Schneider, P., 12
Schnicke, M. K., 70, 79
Schreiber, S., 22, 24, 45, 46
Schuerman, J., 161
Schwartz, J., 44
Schwartz, M., 81
Schwarz, E. D., 27, 47, 51, 158, 159
Schwarzwald, J., 158
Searle, M. M., 170
Sedgwick, R., 164
Sexton, M. C., 13
Shalev, A. Y., 15, 22, 24, 26, 27, 31, 36, 45, 46, 54, 67, 68, 70, 82, 85, 93, 141, 170, 171, 173
Shapiro, F., 80
Shaw, B. F., 101
Sheehan, P. W., 179
Shore, J. H., 54
Shoyer, B. G., 24
Siegel, J. M., 167
Silberman, E. K., 13
Silva, C. E., 67
Silver, S. M., 81
Silverman, W. K., 145
Singer, M. T., 80
Sivec, H. J., 151
Slade, P., 170
Sloan, P., 22, 23, 48
Smith, D. W., 176
Smith, E., 159

SUBJECT INDEX

Anxiety-management skills or techniques
    (*continued*)
  problems in, 100–101
Arousal, 7, 47–48
  acute, 15, 27, 93
  and CIS, 164
  explanation of to client, 91, 92
  reduction of, 170–71
ASD. *See* Acute stress disorder
ASDI (Acute Stress Disorder Interview),
    23, 24, 59–61, 62–63, 189–93
ASDS (Acute Stress Disorder Scale),
    62–64, 195–96
Assessment
  clinical considerations in, 51–58
  and comorbidity or previous psychopa-
    thology, 53–54, 68–69
  and coping style, 69
  for malingering, 184–86
  measures of
      for ASD, 59–64, 71
      for PTSD, 59, 64–68
  psychophysiological, 70, 185
  timing of, 55–56
  traumatic cognition scales, 69–70
Attentional bias, 16
Attributions, 36
Automatic maladaptive thoughts, 101
Autonomic arousal, 23
Avoidance, 7, 22, 47
  acute, 26–27, 47
  predictive power of, 31
  as treatment obstacle, 55, 75, 135–36
      appropriate vs. inappropriate, 143–
      44

Bart (accident victim), 7–9
Beck Anxiety Inventory (BAI), 62, 63
Beck Depression Inventory (BDI), 32, 62,
    63
Beck Depression Inventory-2 (BDI-2), 68
Behavioral theories on trauma response,
    11
Beliefs
  catastrophic, 139
  irrational, 110–13
  negative, 105, 107–10
  pervasive, 101
Bias
  attentional, 16
  cognitive, 35–36
Biological indicators, of ASD symptoms,
    181–82

Biological processes, 36–37
Biological theories on trauma response,
    11, 14–15, 152
Borderline personality disorder, and expo-
    sure, 140, 145
Brain injury, traumatic, 49, 149–54
Breathing control, 97–98

CADSS (Clinician-Administered Dissoci-
    ative States Scale), 67–68
CAPS (Clinician Administered PTSD
    Scale), 65
  and ASDS, 63–64
Case example (Martin), 116–20
  analysis of, 120–22
Catastrophic beliefs, as treatment obsta-
    cle, 139
Charcot, Jean-Martin, 4
Childhood abuse
  and family environment, 161
  scarcity of studies on, 161
  sexual, 12–13, 57, 157
Childhood trauma, 57, 157
  memory of, 178, 180–81
Children, as special population, 157–61
CIS (critical incident stress), 164
CISD (critical incident stress debriefing),
    165–66, 170
Civilian Mississippi Scale, 66–67
Clinical considerations in assessment,
    51–58
Clinical interviews, and genuine vs.
    feigned ASD, 182–83
Clinician-administered assessment mea-
    sures
  for ASD, 59–61
  for PTSD, 64–66
Clinician-Administered Dissociative
    States Scale (CADSS), 67–68
Clinician Administered PTSD Scale
    (CAPS), 65
  and ASDS, 63–64
Coconut Grove fire, Boston (1942), 4
Cognitive-behavioral therapy (CBT)
  and anger, 138
  and ASD, 85, 161
  and children, 161
  for PTSD, 76–82
  rationale for, 75–76
Cognitive bias, 35–36
Cognitive processes, in ASD, 33–36

Treatment (*continued*)
  inappropriate cases of, 56
  for motor-vehicle-accident group, 83
Earthquakes, children as victims of, 160
Emergency workers, 154–57
  assessment problems with, 52
  and debriefing, 169
  and prior trauma, 140, 156–57
  training for, 167
Environment, and assessment, 52–53
Environmental demands, on emergency
    workers, 154–55
Excessive avoidance, 135–36
Exclusion of medical condition or sub-
    stance abuse, 49
Exposure therapies, 76, 77–78, 85
  and brain injury, 152–53
  for children, 160
  and cognitive restructuring, 79
  contraindications or obstacles to, 145–
    46
    anger, 137–38, 145
    anxiety, 139, 145
    avoidance, 55, 136
    comorbidity, 140, 146
    depression or suicide risk, 141, 145
    grief, 138
    numbing, 55
    ongoing stressors, 142, 146
    substance abuse, 141, 146
    unfavorable cultural interpretations,
      143
  imaginal (flooding), 77, 78, 116–20,
    160
  in vivo, 77, 78, 122, 124–31
  and memory reconstruction, 178
  prolonged (PE), 78, 79, 80, 82, 83, 84,
    113–16, 171
Extreme anxiety, 138–39
Eye movement desensitization and re-
    processing (EMDR), 80–81

Feedback, at commencement of treat-
    ment, 90–91
Firefighters. *See also* Emergency workers
  and assessment, 52, 56
  in debriefing example, 171–72
  and pretrauma training, 167
Flooding (imaginal exposure), 77, 78,
    116–20, 160

Grief, as treatment obstacle, 138

Gulf War (Operation Desert Storm)
  and body handling by soldiers, 167–68,
    170
  civilians involved in, 48
  Israeli children involved in, 158

Hierarchy of feared or avoided situations,
    125–28
Holocaust survivors, 13
Home invasion traumas, and avoidance,
    143–44
Hyperventilation, 98
Hypervigilance, 9, 23, 31
Hypnosis
  and dissociation, 137
  and memory reconstruction, 179, 180
Hypnotizability
  and dissociation, 12, 32
  and PTSD, 13

ICD (*International Statistical Classification
    of Diseases, Injuries, and Causes of
    Death*), 5, 9–10
Identification, of emergency workers with
    victims, 155
IES (Impact of Event Scale), 26, 62, 63,
    68
IES-R (Impact of Event Scale-Revised),
    68
Imaginal exposure (flooding), 77, 78, 160
  transcript on, 116–20
Impact of Event Scale (IES), 26, 62, 63,
    68
Impact of Event Scale-Revised (IES-R),
    68
Impairment, 7
Information-processing theories, 34, 79
Insomnia, 22
Integrative model of ASD, 37–40
Integrative theories on trauma response,
    17
*International Statistical Classification of Dis-
    eases, Injuries, and Causes of
    Death* (ICD), 5, 9–10
Interviews
  Acute Stress Disorder Interview, 23,
    24, 59–61, 62–63, 189–93
  clinical interviews on malingering,
    182–83

and Diagnostic Interview Schedule (DIS), 65–66
Posttraumatic Stress Disorder Interview (PTSD-I), 65
PTSD Symptom Scale Interview (PSS-I), 65
Structured Clinical Interview for *DSM-IV* (SCID-IV), 64, 68
Structured Clinical Interview for *DSM-IV* Dissociative Disorders (SCID-D), 61
Intrusive phenomena, 16, 22, 46, 152
and avoidance, 26–27
and ASD assessment, 184
as PTSD predictors, 26
In vivo exposure, 77, 78, 122, 124–31
In Vivo Exposure Form, 129
Irrational beliefs, 110–13
Irritability, 23, 31
Isometric relaxation, 99–100

Janet, P., 4
Jupiter ship disaster, child survivors of, 160

Legal issues, 175, 188
ASD and compensation, 176–77
in criminal law, 177
genuine vs. feigned ASD, 181–84
and guidelines for assessing ASD, 184–86
impact of legal procedures, 186–88
memory contamination, 177–81

Maggie (case example), 179–80
Maladaptive thoughts, automatic, 101
Malingering
and clinical presentation, 182–83
guidelines for detecting, 183–86
Martin (case example), 116–20
analysis of, 120–22
Meaning, of trauma, 56
Memories, traumatic, 25, 33–34, 57, 76
Memory contamination, 177–81
Military personnel. *See* Emergency workers
Mississippi Scale for Combat-Related PTSD, 65, 66

Mississippi Scale for Posttraumatic Stress Disorder, 28
Morphine, and symptoms of altered awareness, 49
Motivation
in assessment, 51–52
and treatment, 142
Motor vehicle acident victims
in autobiographical memory experiment, 34
cognitive responses of, 35
and course of PTSD, 28
in early intervention study, 83
and traumatic memories, 33
Multiple survivors of traumatic event, 144–45
Multiple traumas, and PTSD severity, 168
Muscle-relaxation training, 94–97

Negative thoughts or beliefs, and cognitive therapy, 105, 107–10
Network theories of trauma, 15–17, 37–38, 45, 75, 79, 140
Neuronal functions, 14–15
Neurosis, traumatic, 3, 15
Nightmares, 8, 22, 31
Norepinephrine, 14
Numbing, 8, 22, 30
in case example, 121
and exposure therapies, 55
and malingering, 184
predictive power of, 31

Obstacles to treatment. *See* Treatment obstacles
Operation Desert Storm. *See* Gulf War
Organizational issues, in assessment, 52
Organizational structures, for emergency workers, 156

Panic attacks, 139, 145
Paramedics. *See* Emergency workers
Peritraumatic Dissociative Experiences Questionnnaire (PDEQ), 67
Personal Beliefs and Reactions Scale (PBRS), 70
Pervasive beliefs, 101

ABOUT THE AUTHORS

Richard A. Bryant, PhD, is associate professor of psychology, University of New South Wales, Sydney, Australia. He is director of the Clinical Psychology Program at the university. He is also director of the posttraumatic stress disorder (PTSD) unit at Westmead Hospital in Sydney. He has published over 80 peer-reviewed journal articles on trauma, dissociation, and hypnosis. He has received multiple research grants, including grants from the National Health Medical Research Council and Australian Research Council. He has received numerous awards, including the Australian Psychological Society's (APS's) 1996 Early Career Award and the APS Ian Campbell Award for Clinical Psychology Excellence. He has served as a consultant to many disaster agencies, including government agencies controlling bushfires, criminal assault, naval disasters, and transport disasters. He has conducted pioneering research in acute stress disorder and developed the initial assessment and treatment.

Allison G. Harvey, PhD, is a university lecturer in the department of experimental psychology, University of Oxford, United Kingdom and a fellow of St. Anne's College. Her doctorate, completed in 1997 at the University of New South Wales, Australia, involved an extensive analysis of acute stress disorder. In addition, she has collaborated with Dr. Bryant in the development of assessment and treatment protocols for victims of trauma. Her research interests include acute stress disorder, posttraumatic stress disorder, and sleep disorders, particularly insomnia. She has over 30 published articles in peer reviewed journals. Awards for her research achievements include the Sir Robert Menzies Memorial Research Scholarship in 1995, the Queens Trust Award for Young Australians in 1997, and the Chaim Danielle Early Career Award, presented in 1998 by the International Society for Traumatic Stress Studies for outstanding and fundamental contributions to the field of traumatic stress.